The Mental Anatomies of William Godwin and Mary Shelley

The Mental Anatomies of William Godwin and Mary Shelley

William D. Brewer

Madison • Teaneck
Fairleigh Dickinson University Press
London: Associated University Presses

Associated University Presses
440 Forsgate Drive
Cranbury, NJ 08512

Associated University Presses
16 Barter Street
London WC1A 2AH, England

Associated University Presses
P.O. Box 338, Port Credit
Mississauga, Ontario
Canada L5G 4L8

The paper used in this publication meets the requirements of the American National Standard for Permanence of Paper for Printed Library Materials Z39.48-1984.

Library of Congress Cataloging-in-Publication Data

Brewer, William D. (William Dean)
The mental anatomies of William Godwin and Mary Shelley / William D. Brewer.
p. cm.
Includes bibliographical references and index.
ISBN 0-8386-3870-8 (alk. paper)
1. Shelley, Mary Wollstonecraft, 1797–1851—Knowledge—Psychology. 2. Godwin, William, 1756–1836—Knowledge—Psychology. 3. Psychological fiction, English—History and criticism. 4. Godwin, William, 1756–1836—Influence. 5. Fathers and daughters in literature. 6. Psychology in literature. I. Title.

PR5398 .B74 2001
823′.609353—dc21 00-057303

PRINTED IN THE UNITED STATES OF AMERICA

To Tracy, Meaghan, Kirsten, Rori, and Aidan

Contents

Acknowledgments

AN OFF-CAMPUS SCHOLARLY ASSIGNMENT ALLOWED ME TO WRITE A major portion of this book. I am grateful to my colleagues in the Department of English at Appalachian State University, my chair Daniel F. Hurley, and Dean Sink of the College of Arts and Sciences for providing me with the opportunity to dedicate a semester to scholarship. I would also like to thank the anonymous reader who evaluated this study for Fairleigh Dickinson University Press and who provided me with some excellent suggestions for revision. Harry Keyishian, the Director of Fairleigh Dickinson Press, Christine A. Retz, Managing Editor of Associated University Presses, and Julien Yoseloff, Director of Associated University Presses, have been supportive and helpful throughout the publication process. Parts of chapters 2 and 5 were previously published in *European Romantic Review* and *Southern Humanities Review* (respectively). I am grateful to Grant Scott, co-editor of *European Romantic Review,* and Dan R. Latimer, co-editor of *Southern Humanities Review,* for their permission to reprint revised versions of these essays. A section of chapter 4 appeared in *Papers on Language and Literature,* vol. 30, No. 4, Fall 1994, copyright © 1994 by The Board of Trustees, Southern Illinois University Edwardsville and is reproduced by permission.

I also owe a profound debt to my family for their love and support. This book is dedicated to them.

A Note on Texts

For the most part, I have relied on the recently published Pickering & Chatto editions of William Godwin's and Mary Shelley's works. These volumes are, however, expensive to obtain and are absent from many libraries. I have, therefore, cited from more widely disseminated (and less expensive) paperback editions when well-edited editions are available. Here is a list of the basic texts I cite throughout this book:

William Godwin:

Caleb Williams, ed. David McCracken (New York: Norton, 1977).

Cloudesley, ed. Maurice Hindle, *Collected Novels and Memoirs of William Godwin*, 8 vols. (London: Pickering & Chatto, 1992), vol. 7.

Deloraine, ed. Maurice Hindle, *Collected Novels and Memoirs of William Godwin*, vol. 8.

Fleetwood, ed. Pamela Clemit, *Collected Novels and Memoirs of William Godwin*, vol. 5.

Mandeville, ed. Pamela Clemit, *Collected Novels and Memoirs of William Godwin*, vol. 6.

Political and Philosophical Writings of William Godwin, general ed. Mark Philp, 7 vols. (London: Pickering & Chatto, 1993).

St. Leon, ed. Pamela Clemit (Oxford: Oxford Univ. Press, 1994).

Mary Shelley:

Collected Tales and Stories, with Original Engravings, ed. Charles E. Robinson (Baltimore: Johns Hopkins Univ. Press, 1976).

Falkner, a Novel, ed. Pamela Clemit, *The Novels and Selected Works of Mary Shelley*, 8 vols. (London: Pickering & Chatto, 1996), vol. 7.

The Fortunes of Perkin Warbeck: A Romance, ed. Doucet Devin Fischer, *The Novels and Selected Works of Mary Shelley*, vol. 5.

Frankenstein (1818 ed.), *The Mary Shelley Reader*, ed. Betty T. Bennett and Charles E. Robinson (New York: Oxford Univ. Press, 1990), 11–165.

The Journals of Mary Shelley: 1814–1844, ed. Paula R. Feldman and Diana Scott-Kilvert (Baltimore: Johns Hopkins University Press, 1987).

The Last Man, ed. Hugh J. Luke, Jr. (Lincoln: Univ. of Nebraska Press, 1965).

The Letters of Mary Wollstonecraft Shelley, ed. Betty T. Bennett, 3 vols. (Baltimore: Johns Hopkins Univ. Press, 1980–88).

Lodore, ed. Fiona Stafford, *The Novels and Selected Works of Mary Shelley*, vol. 6.

Mathilda, *The Mary Shelley Reader*, 175–246.

Rambles in Germany and Italy, in 1840, 1842, and 1843, in *Travel Writing*, ed. Jeanne Moskal, *The Novels and Selected Works of Mary Shelley*, vol. 8.

Valperga: or, the Life and Adventures of Castruccio, Prince of Lucca, ed. Nora Crook, *The Novels and Selected Works of Mary Shelley*, vol. 3.

Percy Bysshe Shelley:

Shelley's Poetry and Prose, ed. Donald H. Reiman and Sharon B. Powers (New York: Norton, 1977).

Lord Byron:

Byron, ed. Jerome J. McGann, The Oxford Authors (Oxford: Oxford Univ. Press, 1986).

The Mental Anatomies of William Godwin and Mary Shelley

Introduction: The Mental Anatomies of William Godwin and Mary Shelley

IN HIS GROUNDBREAKING TREATISE *AN INQUIRY INTO THE HUMAN Mind* (1764), the philosopher Thomas Reid argues that the mind, like the body, may be analyzed through dissection: "All that we know of the body, is owing to anatomical dissection and observation, and it must be by an anatomy of the mind that we can discover its powers and principles."[1] During the Romantic period, a number of authors embraced this eighteenth-century project of dissecting the psyche's "powers and principles" and performed mental anatomies in their novels, dramas, and poems. For example, in his account of the composition of *Things as They Are; or, The Adventures of Caleb Williams* (1794), William Godwin writes that his novel provided him with an exceptional opportunity for psychological exploration:

> [First-person narration] was infinitely the best adapted, . . . to my vein of delineation, where the thing in which my imagination revelled the most freely, was the analysis of the private and internal operations of the mind, employing my metaphysical dissecting knife in tracing and laying bare the involutions of motive, and recording the gradually accumulating impulses, which led the personages I had to describe primarily to adopt the particular way of proceeding in which they afterwards embarked.[2]

Mary Hays, a disciple of Godwin and Mary Wollstonecraft, asserts in the Preface to her novel *Memoirs of Emma Courtney* (1796) that "[t]he most interesting, and the most useful, fictions, are . . . such, as delineating the progress, and tracing the consequences, of one strong, indulged, passion, or prejudice, afford materials, by which the philosopher may calculate the powers of the human mind, and learn the springs which set it in motion." In the "Introductory Discourse" to her *A Series of Plays: in which It Is Attempted to Delineate the Stronger Passions of the Mind* (1798), the dramatist Joanna Baillie contends that the most important role of a tragedy is to unveil "the human mind under the dominion of . . . strong and fixed passions [and] communicate . . . those feelings, whose irregular bursts, abrupt transitions, sudden pauses, and half-uttered suggestions, scorn all harmony of measured verse, all method and order of relation."[3] Along with many of their contemporaries, these writers believed that the workings of the human mind could be dissected, analyzed, and ultimately understood.

This volume focuses primarily on the fictional mental anatomies of William Godwin and Mary Shelley.[4] Several of their earliest critics commented on their fascination with human motivation and abnormal mental states. In a review of *Mandeville*, John Gibson Lockhart contends that Godwin's novels reflect the "modern" belief "that the world of thought is the proper theatre of man." According to Lockhart, Godwin's protagonists each exemplify a different mental illness:

> Caleb Williams . . . seems to view the whole field of human existence through the damp vapours and cold bars of a solitary dungeon. The sufferings, through which he tells us he has passed, are depicted indeed with all the distinctness and clearness of realities; but this we silently attribute, while we listen, to an imagination invigorated with the supernatural acuteness of disease. . . . St Leon, too, is a maniac, but his madness is instructive as well as terrible. . . . The madness which has seized upon him is calm and tearless; we feel that, on that very account, it is the most dreadful of inflictions . . . [Mandeville] is more essentially and entirely a madman than either of his brethren. The raving of Caleb is produced by extreme tyrannies, that of St Leon by super-human gifts; the misery of Mandeville is the growth of the fertile but unassisted soil of his own gloomy thoughts.[5]

Whereas Lockhart appears to view Godwin's fictional "maniacs" in a positive light, another reviewer, John Wilson Croker, finds himself obliged "to pronounce [*Mandeville*] intolerably tedious and disgusting, though its author has proved himself intimately skilled in the perversity of the human mind, and in all the blackest and most horrible passions of the human heart."[6] In her 1830 review of *Cloudesley*, however, Mary Shelley praises her father's ability to project himself into his novels' characters in order to anatomize "their secret hearts": "By dint of mastery of thought, he transfuses himself into the very souls of his personages; he dives into their secret hearts, and lays bare, even to their anatomy, their workings; not a pulsation escapes him,—while yet all is blended into one whole, which forms the pervading impulse of the individual he brings before us."[7] For these commentators, Godwin's great strength as a novelist is his ability to portray characters, motives, ruling passions, types of insanity, and "the perversity of the human mind" in convincing and affecting ways.

Some early responses to Mary Shelley's *Frankenstein; or, The Modern Prometheus* (published anonymously in 1818) also focus on its presentations of mental states and passions. In a hostile review reminiscent of his earlier condemnation of *Mandeville*, Croker writes:

> [*Frankenstein*] is piously dedicated to Mr. Godwin, and is written in the spirit of his school. The dreams of insanity are embodied in the strong and striking language of the insane, and the author, notwithstanding the rationality of the preface, often leaves us in doubt whether he [*sic*] is not as mad as his hero. Mr. Godwin is the patriarch of a literary family, whose chief skill is in delineating the wanderings of the intellect, and which strangely delights in the most afflicting and humiliating of human miseries. His disciples are a kind of *out-pensioners of Bedlam*, and, like "Mad Bess" or "Mad Tom," are occasionally visited with paroxysms of genius and fits of expression, which makes sober-minded people wonder and shudder.[8]

According to an anonymous reviewer of *The Edinburgh Magazine, and Literary Miscellany*, *Frankenstein* "is formed on the Godwinian manner" and possesses "something of the same mastery in harsh and savage delineations of passion."[9] Percy Bysshe Shelley also regarded *Frankenstein* as a psychological novel, maintaining, in his preface to the 1818 edition, that the work's main importance is that it "affords a point of view to the imagination for the delineating of human passions more comprehensive and commanding than any which the ordinary relations of existing events can yield."[10] He reaffirms this judgment in his review of *Frankenstein*: "This Novel . . . rests its claim on being a source of powerful and profound emotion. The elementary feelings of the human mind are exposed to view."[11] Thus the early assessments of Mary Shelley's first and most famous novel identified it as the production of a new member of Godwin's "school" of psychological writers, a view that Shelley, by dedicating her work to Godwin, and Percy Shelley, by writing a preface emphasizing the work's delineation of human passion, did much to encourage.

Recent critical assessments of the Godwin-Shelley relationship have, however, focused on their shared political concerns and the ways in which Godwin influenced his daughter's "choice of profession and her subsequent literary career."[12] Although Pamela

Clemit takes note of the psychological elements in the fiction of Godwin, Shelley, and the American writer Charles Brockden Brown, she is primarily interested in their politics. In *The Godwinian Novel*, she considers Godwin, Shelley, and Brown as members of a school of writers who adhered "to the narrative model pioneered in *Caleb Williams*" and whose novels were influenced, in various ways, by Godwin's political philosophy.[13] Clemit argues, for example, that "In *Frankenstein*, [Shelley] expands Godwin's characteristic blend of philosophy and fiction to present an uncompromising critique of optimistic myths of revolutionary change."[14] In another recent study of Godwin and Shelley, Katherine C. Hill-Miller focuses on their father-daughter relationship and on how Shelley "portrays the figure of the father in the pages of her novels."[15] Hill-Miller's psychoanalytic approach to Godwin's and Shelley's fiction examines the "incestuous patterns of emotion [which] are certainly at work in the relationship between Mary Shelley and William Godwin."[16]

In contrast, this study of Godwin and Shelley explores the influence of Enlightenment and Romantic-era theories of the mind on their writings and how these writers use their fiction to explore such psychological phenomena as ruling passions, madness, the therapeutic value of confessions (both spoken and written), and the significance of dreams. They were enthusiastic students of Jean-Jacques Rousseau's *Confessions* (1782), which, according to Mary Shelley, is "written in a . . . liberal and even prodigal spirit of intellectual candour [and] is to be ranked as an inestimable acquisition" to the body of literature devoted to investigating the mind.[17] Justifying the confessional nature of his essay "Of Diffidence" (1831), which he compares to "the Confessions of St Augustine or of Jean Jacques Rousseau," Godwin argues: "we are all of us framed in a great measure on the same model, and the analysis of the individual may often stand for the analysis of a species. While I describe myself therefore, I shall probably at the same time be describing no inconsiderable number of my fellow-beings."[18] For the most part, however, Godwin and Shelley chose not to write autobiographically, preferring, instead, to create a multitude of fictional characters, including Caleb Williams, Fleetwood, St. Leon, Frankenstein, Frankenstein's monster, Mandeville, Mathilda, Beatrice of Ferrara, Lionel Verney, Lord Danvers, Deloraine, and Falkner, who feel compelled to unburden themselves either through written or spoken narratives.

In Godwin's unpublished "Essay of History and Romance"

(1797), he contends that the "romance or novel" is more emotive, more illuminating, and less limited than historical texts:

> The historian is confined to individual incident and individual man, and must hang upon that his invention or conjecture as he can. The writer of romance collects his materials from all sources, experience, report, and the records of human affairs; then generalises them; and finally selects, . . . those instances which he is best qualified to pourtray [*sic*], and which he judges most calculated to impress the heart and improve the faculties of his reader. In this point of view we should be apt to pronounce that romance was a nobler species of composition than history.[19]

He writes even more enthusiastically about the contributions that imaginative works can make to "the science of man" in his Preface to *Cloudesley: A Tale* (1830):[20]

> man is a more complex machine, than is "dreamed of in our philosophy": and it is probable that the skill of no moral anatomist has yet been consummate enough fully to solve the obscurities of any one of the great worthies of ancient or modern times. . . . Analysis is . . . a science more commensurate to human faculties than synthesis. When the creator of the world of imagination, the poet, or the writer of fiction, introduces his ideal personage to the public, he enters upon the task with a preconception of the qualities that belong to this being, the principle of his actions, and its necessary concomitants. He has thus two advantages: in the first place, his express office is to draw just conclusions from assigned premises, a task of no extraordinary difficulty: and secondly, while he endeavours to aid those conclusions by consulting . . . the suggestions of his own heart, instructed as he is besides by converse with the world, and a careful survey of the encounters that present themselves to his observation, he is much less liable to be cribbed and cabined in by those unlooked-for phenomena, which, in the history of an individual, seem to have a malicious pleasure in thrusting themselves forward to subvert our best digested theories. In this sense then it is infallibly true, that fictitious history, when it is the work of a competent hand, is more to be depended upon, and comprises more of the science of man, than whatever can be exhibited by the historian. (*Cloudesley*, 7–8).

Thus, in Godwin's view, literary works can serve as thought-experiments in the "science" of mental anatomy. They are imaginary laboratories in which writers can conduct psychological experiments on their characters, laboratories in which they can control the variables of environment, education, and situation, and attempt to determine their effects on a given personality.[21] Like David Hume, Godwin recognizes that in order to understand "the essence of mind" a mental anatomist must rely on "careful and exact experiments, and the observation of those particular effects, which result from [the mind's] different circumstances and situations," but unlike Hume, Godwin performs his experiments in literary as well as philosophical texts.[22] According to Godwin, whereas historians must deal with a bewildering array of factors in their analyses of human motivation, a writer of fiction can eliminate many of these variables by isolating a character's "qualities," "the principle of his [or her] actions, and their necessary concomitants."

This process of reducing the human mind to its basic elements in order to study it can be compared to the method outlined by William Wordsworth in an 1802 letter: "where are we to find the best measure of [human nature]? I answer, [from with]in; by stripping our own hearts naked, and by looking out of ourselves to[wards me]n who lead the simplest lives most according to nature[,] men who [ha]ve never known false refinements, wayward and artificial desires, false criti[ci]sms, effeminate habits of thinking or feeling."[23] Like Wordsworth, who begins his analysis of human nature by looking within himself, Godwin identifies "the oracle in his bosom, the suggestions of his own heart," as the ultimate source of his psychological insights. However, as Reid observes, "the anatomist of the mind cannot have the same advantage" as anatomists of the body: "It is his own mind only that he can examine, with any degree of accuracy and distinctness. . . . He may, from outward signs, collect the operations of other minds; but these signs are for the most part ambiguous, and must be interpreted by what he perceives in himself."[24] In particular, historical figures, caught in a complex web of personal, religious, social, ideological, economic, and political factors, tend to resist psychological exploration. Godwin, like Wordsworth, is perfectly aware of the difficulties inherent in the analysis of complex individuals. Thus he typically chooses to anatomize fictional characters who possess a limited range of qualities and principles of action, just as Wordsworth bases many of his portraits of human nature on rural people "who lead the simplest lives."

Like Godwin and Wordsworth, Shelley believes that self-examination is the key to mental anatomy. In a journal entry dated 25, February 1822, she vows to study herself: "let me fearlessly descend into the remotest caverns of my own mind—carry the torch of self knowledge into its dimmest recesses—but too happy if I dislodge any evil spirit or ensh[r]ine a new deity in some hitherto uninhabited nook.''[25] She maintains in her review-essay "Giovanni Villani" that self-analysis provides the basis for virtually any exploration of the psyche, whether it takes the form of an autobiography, biography, work of fiction, or philosophical essay:

> [The] habit of self-analysation and display has also caused many men of genius to undertake works where the individual feeling of the author embues the whole subject with a peculiar hue. . . . Such persons turn to the human heart as the undiscovered country. They visit and revisit their own; endeavour to understand its workings, to fathom its depths, and to leave no lurking thought or disguised feeling in the hiding places where so many thoughts and feelings, for fear of shocking the tender consciences of those inexpert in the task of self-examination, delight to seclude themselves. As a help to the science of self-knowledge, and also as a continuance of it, they wish to study the minds of others, and particularly of those of the greatest merit. . . . Sometimes, [however,] despairing to attain the knowledge of the secrets of the best and wisest, they are pleased to trace human feeling wherever it is artlessly and truly pourtrayed [*sic*].[26]

Along the same lines, Percy Bysshe Shelley points out in his review of Thomas Jefferson Hogg's *Memoirs of Prince Alexy Haimatoff* (1814) that "The science of mind to which history, poetry, [and] biography serve as the materials, consists in the discernment of shades and distinctions where the unenlightened discover nothing but a shapeless and unmeaning mass."[27] Although neither Mary Shelley nor her husband privileges imaginative writing as Godwin does in his Preface to *Cloudesley*, Mary Shelley agrees with her father that analyses of historical figures "of the greatest merit" are much more difficult than studies of "human feeling wherever it is artlessly and truly pourtrayed."

In *Enquiry Concerning Political Justice* (1798 ed.), Godwin explains his usage of the word "mind," asserting that "if there be any one thing that we know more certainly than another, it is the existence of our own thoughts, ideas, perceptions or sensations . . ., and that they are ordinarily linked together so as to produce the complex notion of unity or personal identity. Now it is this series of thoughts thus linked together, without considering whether they reside in any or what substratum, that is most aptly expressed by the term mind."[28] This definition recalls Hume's conception of "the human mind . . . as a system of different perceptions or different existences, which are link'd together by the relation of cause and effect, and mutually produce, destroy, influence, and modify each other."[29] Like Hume, Godwin equates the mind with "personal identity" or self, and many of his and Shelley's confessional narratives display the main character's inner self by recounting the "series of thoughts . . . linked together" that form the protagonist's "personal identity."[30]

Godwin refuses, however, to hazard a guess regarding the mind's location. He confesses his ignorance in his essay "On Body and Mind" (1831): "By the mind we understand that within us which feels and thinks, the seat of sensation and reason. Where it resides we cannot tell, nor can authoritatively pronounce, as the apostle says, . . . 'whether it is in the body, or out of the body.' "[31] In his study of insanity during "the age of reason," Michel Foucault claims that

> In the classical period, it is futile to try to distinguish physical therapeutics from psychological medications, for the simple reason that psychology did not exist . . . [W]hen the simple life of a labourer was prescribed for a melancholic, when the comedy of his delirium was acted out before him, this was not a psychological intervention, since the movement of the spirits in the nerves, the density of the humors were principally involved.[32]

During the eighteenth and early nineteenth centuries, moreover, mad-doctors or "Antimaniac Physicians" commonly relied on "bleeding, blisters, caustics, rough cathartics, the gumms and fætid anti-hysterics, opium, mineral waters, cold bathing, and vomits" in their efforts to treat mental illness.[33] Because of the primitive state of late eighteenth- and early nineteenth-century psychiatry, Godwin and Shelley had little reliable medical data on which to base their explorations of the psyche. Thus for the most part they derived their psychological conceptions and theories from personal observations, philosophical treatises, and literary works.

Both Godwin and Shelley held mental anatomists in high regard. In Shelley's biographical essay on Michel de Montaigne (published 1838–39), she praises him for "his skilful anatomy of his own mind and passions."[34] For Godwin, the most profound mental anatomist is Shakespeare, "the great master of the human soul" (*Mandeville*, 59) whom he celebrates in his essay "Of the Durability of Human Achievements and Productions" (1831) for "those exquisite delineations of character, those transcendent bursts of passion, and that perfect anatomy of the human heart, which render [his] master-pieces . . . a property for all nations and all times."[35] Shelley greatly admires Robert Burton's *The Anatomy of Melancholy* (1621), which seeks to "anatomize [the] humour of melancholy, through all his parts and species . . . that it may be the better avoided."[36] She writes that "the zest with which it is read [is] heightened by the proof the author gave in his death of his entire initiation into the arcana of his science."[37] According to Shelley, Burton, Rousseau, Montaigne, James Boswell, Reverend Joseph Spence, Lady Mary Wortley Montagu, and her mother Mary Wollstonecraft were great explorers of "the noblest of terræ incognitæ, the soul of man."[38]

As Godwin indicates in the first edition of *Enquiry Concerning Political Justice* (1793), he considers John Locke as one of the great authorities on the mind and its operations. Godwin writes that "Literature has unfolded the nature of the human mind, and Locke and others have established certain maxims respecting man, as Newton has done respecting matter, that are generally admitted for unquestionable."[39] In Locke's *An Essay Concerning Human Understanding* (1690), he describes how ideas are associated in the mind:

> Ideas that in themselves are not all of kin, come to be so united in some men's minds, that it is very hard to separate them; they always keep in company, and the one no sooner at any time comes into the understanding, but its associate appears with it; and if they are more than two which are thus united, the whole gang, always inseparable, show themselves together. This strong combination of ideas, not allied by nature, the mind makes in itself either voluntarily or by chance; and hence it comes in different men to be very different, according to their different inclinations, educations, interests, &c. *Custom* settles habits of thinking in the understanding, as well as of determining the will, and of motions in the body: all which seems to be but trains of motions in the animal spirits, which, once set a going, continue in the same steps they have been used to; which, by often treading, are worn into a smooth path, and the motion in it becomes easy, and as it were natural.[40]

In *Observations on Man, His Frame, His Duty, and His Expectations* (1749), David Hartley extends and refines Locke's theory of associations, arguing that the basic principles of the human mind can be determined and subjected to scientific analysis: "The science of mind is not less demonstrative, and far more important, than the science of Newton; but we must proceed on similar principles."[41] According to Hartley, "the Doctrine of Association explains . . . the Rise and Progress of those voluntary and semi-voluntary Powers, which we exert over our Ideas, Affections, and bodily Motions . . .; and, by doing this, teaches us how to regulate and improve these powers."[42] He maintains that the key to controlling the mind is understanding its evolution, or how it has been formed by associations of ideas.

In accordance with Lockean and Hartleian psychology, Godwin and Shelley often have the narrators of their works describe, in painstaking detail, the series of associations that motivate their actions and determine their fates.[43] For example, in Caleb Williams's account of the climactic scene in which he impulsively pries open Falkland's trunk, he explains how "One sentiment flows by necessity of nature into another sentiment of the same general character" (*Caleb Williams*, 133), and Frankenstein speculates that "the train of [his] ideas [might] never have received that fatal impulse that led to [his] ruin" if his father had explained his objection to Cornelius Agrippa (*The Mary Shelley Reader*, 30). At the end of his last novel, *Deloraine* (1833), Godwin has the title character emphasize that thoughts must always be carefully monitored and controlled, or tragedy can result: "There is scarcely an instant that passes over our heads, that may not have its freight of infamy. How ought we to watch over our thoughts, that we may not so much as imagine any enormity! How exactly regulated and nicely balanced ought to be our meditations, that no provocation may take from us the mastery of ourselves, and hurry us headlong ten thousand fathoms beyond the level of a sound discretion!" (285). Part of the reason that Godwin and Shelley choose to employ so many confessional narratives in their fictions is that such detailed accounts allow readers to analyze the associations of ideas that shape the characters' worldviews and proclivities. Like Rousseau's *Confessions*, these narratives can be considered as mental histories that attempt to make their protagonist's "soul transparent to the reader's eye" ("ame [*sic*] transparente aux yeux du lecteur").[44]

In most cases, however, the significances of Godwin's and Shelley's mental anatomies are far from clear. Like several of Godwin's other protagonists, Caleb Williams often fails to grasp the psychological motivations for his actions. The forces that impel him to lift up the lid of Falkland's trunk and uncover his master's secret seem to defy rational explanation: "Was it possible I could have forgotten for a moment the awe creating manners of Falkland, and the inexorable fury I should awake in his soul? . . . I have always been at a loss to account for my having plunged thus headlong into an act so monstrous. There is something in it of unexplained and involuntary sympathy'' (133). Shelley's novel *The Last Man* (1826) also considers the power of human perversity. The narrator, Lionel Verney, reflects on his sister's inability to find inner peace after having discovered her husband's infidelity: ''man is a strange animal. We cannot calculate on his forces like that of an engine; and, though an impulse draw with a forty-horse power at what appears willing to yield to one, yet in contempt of calculation the movement is not effected'' (114). Even a minor character like Sir Richard Gray in Shelley's short story ''The Elder Son'' (1834) proves capable of ''one of those inconceivable changes which sometimes occur in the history of human nature'' (*Collected Tales and Stories*, 264), and in her response to the scientific theories of Sir Richard Phillips (author of *The Proximate Causes of Material Phenomena* [1821 and 1824]), Shelley indicates that the mind's complexity would most likely baffle any would-be Frankenstein: ''I own I have great respect for that faculty we carry about us called *Mind*—and I fear that no Frankenstein can so arrange the gases as to be able to make any combination of them produce thought.''[45]

As Godwin writes in *The Enquirer. Reflections on Education, Manners, and Literature. In a Series of Essays* (1797), ''The world, instead of being, as the vanity of some men has taught them to assert, a labyrinth of which they hold the clue, is in reality full of enigmas which no penetration of man has hitherto been able to solve.''[46] For both Godwin and Shelley, the mind can be observed, anatomized, and experimented with, but many of its ''enigmas'' cannot be explained by late eighteenth- and early nineteenth-century philosophy and science. In a work of fiction, however, in which the author controls all of the factors that go into the formation of a character's personality, the mind can be more easily dissected than it can be in real life. But even fictional characters, inasmuch as they are modeled on actual human beings, occasionally find themselves under the control of perverse impulses that seem to defy rational explanation.

In his introduction to Foucault's *Madness and Civilization*, José Barchelon complains that ''Too many historical books about psychic disorders look at the past in the light of the present; they single out only what has positive and direct relevance to present-day psychiatry.'' Although *The Mental Anatomies of William Godwin and Mary Shelley* is more literary than historical in its emphasis, like *Madness and Civilization* it attempts to re-create psychological concepts ''as they must have existed in their time."[47] Godwin and Shelley obviously lacked the psychological terminology we take for granted now. In fact, the term "psychology" was not in general use during the Romantic period: in Godwin's "Letter of Advice to a Young American," he writes that "*metaphysics* is the theoretical science of the human mind."[48] Moreover, while Shelley and her circle employed hypnotism (which they called magnetism), they used it to treat physical rather than psychological conditions. In Pisa, Percy Shelley suffered from nephritis, or inflammation of the kidneys. Thomas Medwin, well-versed in the teachings of Friedrich Anton Mesmer, magnetized him twice to relieve the symptoms, and "a lady" magnetized him again following Medwin's departure. According to Medwin, "he was magnetised by a lady, . . . and during [the] operation, he made the same reply to an inquiry as to his disease, and its cure, as he had done to me,—'What would cure me would kill me,'—meaning lithotomy [the surgical removal of stones from the bladder]."[49] The late eighteenth- and early nineteenth-century belief that a magnetized patient could diagnose and prescribe for "their own [physical] ailments, and quite often for the ailments of others," is a far cry from the twentieth-century use of hypnotism to reveal and treat psychological traumas.[50]

I do not, however, want to suggest that Freudian, post-Freudian, or cognitive readings of Romantic writings are invalid. Clearly, certain passages in Godwin's and Shelley's works, like St. Leon's homoerotic dream of being rescued from Bethlem Gabor's prison and Frankenstein's oedipal nightmare about his dead mother, lend themselves to Freudian interpretations. One could also argue that Godwin's vision of human perfectibility in *Enquiry Concerning Political Justice* is a precursor of B. F. Skinner's *Walden Two* and that his and Shelley's Hartleian conception of dreams as associationist reshufflings of waking thoughts anticipates the findings of neurobiologists.[51] However, by restricting ourselves to twentieth-century psychological approaches, we risk losing sight of the important seventeenth-, eighteenth-, and early nineteenth-century influences on Godwin's and Shelley's explorations of the human mind. As Peter Melville Logan observes in his fascinating study of hysteria in *Caleb Williams*,

> in confronting the physiological premises for pre-Freudian ideas about hysteria, the cultural logic they embody, and the boundaries for the fluid implications that can follow from them, strange bodies come into view, and the association of hysteria with a compulsion to speak is one of the most foreign, since it is the point on which hysteria

in 1800 differs most dramatically from hysteria today in psychoanalytic discourse.[52]

In *Mandeville*, Godwin's portrait of obsessional hatred reflects Joanna Baillie's anatomy of hatred in her tragedy *De Monfort* (see *Mandeville*, 8) and Hume's analysis of passion in *Treatise of Human Nature*. Godwin's and Shelley's conceptions of verbal and written word therapy owe a great deal to the Catholic sacrament of auricular confession and Adam Smith's discussion of the salutary effects of conversation in *The Theory of Moral Sentiments* (1759), and Shelley's fictional explorations of dreams should be considered in light of Hartley's and Erasmus Darwin's discussions of oneiric phenomena as well as the ancient belief that dreams are prophetic.

Thus to appreciate the complexity, diversity, and originality of Godwin's and Shelley's mental anatomies, one needs to examine their works within the contexts of the terms, texts, and scientific/philosophical theories available to them. In many cases, associationist psychology and the theory of the ruling passions enable them to provide fascinating and sophisticated insights into their characters' mental processes and behaviors. As Jerome McGann has observed, it is necessary to be "in touch with worlds, people, and experiences from the past, . . . in the full range of their pastness and differentials[,] . . . to gain a measure by which our own present interests and ideologies may be critically observed. . . . Indeed, the past is the *only* fixed measure we can turn to and use in a critical and self-correcting way."[53] In my analysis of Godwin's and Shelley's writings I have tried to recognize and respect their "pastness" and provide a historically contextualized understanding of their mental anatomies that can be compared to the productions of later "voyagers in the noblest of terræ incognitæ, the soul of man." Paul Youngquist warns in his study of William Blake that "The danger of applying psychoanalytic hypotheses and methods to a highly psychological poetry like Blake's is that the results simply compare one interpretation of the mind with another."[54] In order to keep the focus on Godwin's and Shelley's interpretations of the mind, I avoid twentieth-century psychological terminology and ideas in this book.

This study contends that Godwin's and Shelley's literary mental anatomies should be regarded as exploratory and often inconclusive thought-experiments. I have organized it by themes rather than by chronology or works. Although this method entails some duplication as I refer back to texts discussed in earlier chapters, it orders the evidence so that the reader can see how ideas regarding the mind and its operations are developed, complicated, and reassessed throughout the writings of these two authors. Unlike most studies of Godwin and Shelley, this book does not privilege their masterworks (*Caleb Williams* and *Frankenstein*, respectively). For the most part, it focuses on their lesser-known writings. In an effort to contextualize their fictional treatments of psychological phenomena, I also consider the works of other Romantic-era writers, including Mary Wollstonecraft, Joanna Baillie, Mary Hays, Percy Bysshe Shelley, Lord Byron, and Charles Brockden Brown, as well as the seventeenth- and eighteenth-century philosophical and medical theories that informed Godwin's and Shelley's presentations of mental states and types of behavior.

Although Godwin provided much of Shelley's education before she eloped with Percy Shelley at the age of sixteen and became his daughter's intellectual and literary collaborator after she returned to England following her husband's death, it would be a mistake to conclude that their outlooks and interests were identical. Godwin raised his daughter to be "a philosopher, even . . . a Cynic," not an uncritical disciple.[55] While Godwin asserts that "man" is perfectible in *Enquiry Concerning Political Justice* and declares his admiration for the intellectual achievements of his species in his preface to *Thoughts on Man, His Nature, Productions, and Discoveries* (1831), Shelley's works, especially *The Last Man*, suggest a much more pessimistic appraisal of humankind's prospects and capabilities.[56] More important, the protagonists of Godwin's novels are all male, whereas many of Shelley's major characters, such as Mathilda, Euthanasia, Beatrice, Perdita, Evadne, and Cornelia Santerre, are female. In a sense, Shelley's fictional explorations of the mental development of women complement Godwin's anatomies of self-conscious male narrators.

Chapter 1 of *The Mental Anatomies of William Godwin and Mary Shelley* discusses the confessional narratives produced by Godwin and Shelley. Modeled, to an extent, on Rousseau's *Confessions*, these works first show how a protagonist's mind is formed and then describe how he or she responds to a given set of circumstances and situations. Godwin and Shelley essentially provide the reader with a case study of a certain kind of individual from which he or she can gain moral and psychological insights. In many cases, however, the unreliability of the narrators who relate these confessional tales complicates the reader's task.

Chapter 2 deals with obsessional or "ruling" passions in Godwin's and Shelley's works. In Chapter 3, I focus on their presentations of madness. Unlike several of their reviewers, Godwin and Shelley blur the distinction between madness and sanity; anyone is, under certain conditions, capable of pathological behavior. Godwin's Enlightenment horror of mental alienation contrasts, however, with Shelley's association of madness with poetry, genius, and altruism. In Chapter 4, I turn to language therapy, which is an extremely important theme in Godwin's and Shelley's works. Their novels suggest that linguistic self-expression, whether it takes oral or written form, can provide, at least temporarily, emotional ventilation and increased self-knowledge. Finally, in Chapter 5, I discuss their fictional presentations of reveries and dreams and contrast Godwin's skepticism regarding dreams with Shelley's suspicion, after her husband's death by drowning, that they can be prophetic.

While examining Godwin's and Shelley's mental anatomies, we should remember Frankenstein's tentative remarks to Walton before he narrates his story: "I do not know that the relation of my misfortunes will be useful to you, yet, if you are inclined, listen to my tale. I believe that the strange incidents connected with it will afford a view of nature, which may enlarge your faculties and understanding" (*The Mary Shelley Reader*, 25). It is Godwin's and Shelley's hope that through reading their fictional explorations of the human mind we, like Walton, will "enlarge [our] faculties and understanding," gaining insights into our own psyches and those of others.

1
The Transparent Mind

WHILE MARY SHELLEY'S USE OF ROUSSEAU'S AUTOBIOGRAPHICAL writings in *Frankenstein* has been discussed in some detail, the influence of his *Confessions* on Godwin's novels and Shelley's works other than *Frankenstein* has not been thoroughly examined.[1] Of particular importance to Godwin and Shelley is Rousseau's theory that an individual's inner self can be honestly and comprehensively revealed in a text and that this uncovering of the self will enhance the reader's understanding of the human mind. In his unfinished essay "Analysis of Own Character" (manuscript dated 1798), Godwin asks, "Why does a man feel any degree of eagerness to expose his character to the world?" He answers his own question: "Such a disclosure is . . . of high value; it adds to the science of the human mind, and, by the operation of comparison, enables each reader to make an estimate of himself."[2] Although neither Godwin nor Shelley ever wrote full-scale autobiographies, they did produce fictional narratives in which their protagonists recount their lives in psychologically revealing ways. As Marilyn Butler and Mark Philp observe, one of the features of a "Godwin novel" is the adoption of "an introspective, first-person narrator, whose analyses of character and passions, especially his own, turn each novel into a psychological fictional autobiography in the self-probing, self-exposing style inaugurated by Rousseau."[3] In this chapter I will explore the influence of Rousseau's *Confessions* and his conceptions of mental transparency, sincerity, and environmental conditioning on Godwin's and Shelley's mental anatomies.

Godwin's fascination with Rousseau pervades his works. In *Enquiry Concerning Political Justice*, Rousseau is quoted frequently, and Godwin declares that *Émile* (1762), Rousseau's book on education, "is upon the whole to be regarded as the principal reservoir of philosophical truth as yet existing in the world, but with a perpetual mixture of absurdity and mistake."[4] Rousseau's

Confessions inspired Godwin to commence an autobiography, "with the intention of being nearly as explicit as Rousseau in the composition of his Confessions," but for some reason he never completed the project.[5] His autobiographical fragment, most of which was probably written in the late 1790s, reflects his interest in analyzing and understanding the peculiarities of his mental development.[6] Toward the end of the fragment, which breaks off in his fifteenth year, he describes his habit of "stealing down" to the library of his instructor, the Reverend Samuel Newton, to read "the Ancient History of Rollin":

> I seated myself on these occasions in a chair close to the shelf to which the book belonged, that I might restore it to its place in a moment. Why did I do this? Why did I not ask for the loan of the book, which would probably not have been refused?—This was an essential part of my character. It might have been refused; and what then? What should I have done then? Beside, I never asked for a thing then, if I could help it, where there was a chance of being refused. I was under the control of a despot [i.e., Newton]; and I resolved he should not be a despot to me, where I could avoid it. Never mortal felt more energetically the sentiment, "My mind, my mind, shall be the master of me!"[7]

Few writers before Rousseau would have regarded Godwin's habit of surreptitiously reading his tutor's book as an expression of "an essential part of [his] character." His childhood behavior offers, however, an important insight into the growth of his mind and foreshadows his later career as a Jacobin philosopher, iconoclast, and novelist. In fact, Peter Marshall points out that "the situation of Caleb and his master Falkland neatly parallels the relationship between Godwin and Newton."[8] Godwin's account of his youthful act of defiance also recalls a number of sections in *Confessions* in which Rousseau describes how the principles and sentiments of his adulthood stem from the experiences of his childhood and adolescence. From Rousseau, Godwin learned that even mundane experiences and apparently inconsequential behavior can reveal much about a person's character and subsequent destiny.

Like his unfinished autobiography, Godwin's novels are heavily influenced by *Confessions*, particularly by Rousseau's claim of complete self-transparency. For example, in *St. Leon* the title character declares that he will present his life honestly, revealing everything but his alchemical secrets: "I have laid it down to myself in this narrative as a sacred principle, to relate the simple, unaltered truth'' (30). He pledges to tell the truth even if it reflects negatively on him: "it is not my intention in this history to pass myself for better than I am. I have laid down to myself the sacred maxim of absolute truth and impartiality'' (42). Similarly, in *Fleetwood: or, The New Man of Feeling* (1805), Godwin has his protagonist assert that "The proper topic of the narrative [he is] writing is the record of [his] errors'' (21). *Fleetwood* also contains a sympathetic description of Rousseau by Fleetwood's friend Macneil, who claims to have known him:

> When [Rousseau] was induced to dwell for a time upon the universal combination which he believed to be formed against him, he then undoubtedly suffered. But he had such resources in his own mind! He could so wholly abstract himself from this painful contemplation; his vein of enthusiasm was so sublime; there was such a childlike simplicity often uppermost in his carriage; his gaiety upon certain occasions was so good-humoured, sportive, and unbroken! It was difficult for me to persuade myself that the person I saw at such times, was the same as at others was beset with such horrible visions. (159)

As Edward Duffy points out, "Godwin's representation of Rousseau in *Fleetwood* is anything but simple. . . . While it is conceded that Rousseau suffered from 'horrible visions,' it is likewise insisted that in *La Nouvelle Héloïse* he had developed a 'vein of [sublime] enthusiasm.' ''[9] For Godwin, Rousseau was not only a brilliant (if flawed) philosopher: he was also a fascinating psychological case study, an unstable mixture of idealism and madness.

Shelley would have noted references to Rousseau in the works of her parents and husband. He is referred to as "the true Prometheus of sentiment'' in Wollstonecraft's *The Wrongs of Woman* and is taken to task for his attitudes toward women in her *A Vindication of the Rights of Woman* (1792).[10] A fervent admirer of Rousseau, Percy Shelley regarded his *La Nouvelle Héloïse* as "an overflowing . . . of sublimest genius, and more than human sensibility.''[11] In her journals, Mary Shelley records that she read *Les confessions: Suivies des rêveries du promeneur solitaire* on 31 July and 1 August 1816, and again in early November 1817.[12] Rousseau clearly is an important influence on *Frankenstein*, begun in June 1816 and completed in May 1817, which contains two long confessional narratives. Paul Cantor argues that *Frankenstein* "undertakes an imaginative recreation of the *Second Discourse*,'' and David Marshall links Shelley's masterwork to *La Nouvelle Héloïse*, *Rêveries du promeneur solitaire* (1782), *L'Essai sur l'origine des langues* (1781), and *Confessions*.[13] Shelley refers to Rousseau as "one of the most interesting personages of modern times" in an essay she wrote about Madame D'Houtetôt for Byron's and Leigh Hunt's journal *The Liberal* (1823),[14] praises the "intellectual candour" of the *Confessions* in her review of Giovanni Villani,[15] and wrote a biographical essay on Rousseau for *Eminent Literary and Scientific Men of France* in *The Cabinet Cyclopaedia* (1838–39). Although her *Rambles in Germany and Italy, in 1840, 1842, and 1843* (1844) is primarily a record of the "daily occurrences" (65) of her travels, it is also, like Rousseau's *Confessions* and Wollstonecraft's *A Short Residence in Sweden, Norway and Denmark* (1796), an account of the author's "recollections and associations" (*Rambles*, 148).

Most important, Rousseau provided Shelley with two confessional narratives (*Confessions* and *Rêveries*) on which she could model her fictional explorations of the human psyche. Her 1839 essay on Rousseau in *The Cabinet Cyclopaedia* reflects Shelley's fascination with *Confessions* and her ambivalent feelings toward Rousseau. Like Godwin, she pays tribute to Rousseau's abilities as a mental anatomist: "he penetrated deeply into the secret springs of human action. Man's nature was often exposed as a map before him—and he knew its various bearings and powers—although he was ill able . . . to control its impulses as they existed within himself."[16] She writes that his *Confessions*, if read in their entirety, can provide readers with many psychological insights: "To any one who loves to make a study of human nature, the 'Confessions' are an invaluable book, and disclose the secret of many hearts to those who have courage to penetrate into the recesses of their own. But, to be useful, they must be read as they are, with the author's observations and minute anatomy of motive."[17] According to Shelley, moreover, "No author knows better than Rousseau how to spread a charm over the internal movements of the mind, over the struggles of passion, over romantic reveries that absorb the soul, abstracting it from real life and our fellow-creatures, and causing it to find its joys in itself."[18] However, although she is convinced of the sincerity of Rousseau's *Confessions*, Shelley finds that this work fails to reveal him completely. While she believes that "Every word we read stamps the 'Confessions' with truth, and animates them with a living image," she concludes that "though sincere in an unexampled degree, it is difficult to appreciate [Rousseau's] character from the 'Confessions.' "[19] Rousseau is simply too complex to be fully represented in a single autobiographical text, no matter how sincere.

Shelley's *Frankenstein*, *Mathilda* (written 1819), Beatrice's story in *Valperga: or, The Life and Adventures of Castruccio, Prince of Lucca* (1823) (251–61), *The Last Man*, "The Parvenue" (1836), and the "Falkner's Narrative" section of *Falkner. A Novel* (1837) (154–93) can all be considered as responses to Rousseau's autobiographical writings. Like Godwin's confessional narratives, these works are presented as sincere first-person accounts of the protagonists' life stories: "The truth, the pure and sacred truth, will alone find expression in these pages" (*Falkner*, 154) writes Falkner near the beginning of his confession. However, the significances of the tales they tell are often far from clear. The questions posed at the beginning of Shelley's short story, "The Parvenue," reflect the uncertainties inherent in these kinds of narratives:

> Why do I write my melancholy story? Is it as a lesson, to prevent any other from wishing to rise to rank superior to that in which they are born? No! miserable as I am, others might have been happy, I doubt not, in my position: the chalice has been poisoned for me alone! Am I evil-minded—am I wicked? What have been my errors, that I am now an outcast and a wretch? I will tell my story—let others judge me; my mind is bewildered, I cannot judge myself. (*Collected Tales and Stories*, 266)

Shelley's characters are often motivated by impulses or feelings for which they cannot account: the unnamed "parvenue" does not know why she writes her tale, and "a feeling that [she] cannot define" (*The Mary Shelley Reader*, 175) impels the eponymous narrator of *Mathilda* to recount her history. As moral exempla, these confessions are seldom straightforward, and their readers must arrive at their own conclusions.

Of course, the work on which Shelley models these first-person narratives, Rousseau's *Confessions*, is also a perplexing text that presents complicated mental states and examples of strange, even perverse behavior. In fact, in his description of one episode Rousseau claims that his actions were caused by "a kind of delirium":

> I was walking . . . with M. de Francueil in the Palais-Royal when he took out his watch, looked at it, and said, "Let us go [to] the Opera." I agreed, and we went. He bought two tickets for the amphitheatre, gave me one and went on ahead with the other. I followed him in, but on reaching the doorway found it congested. When I looked in, I saw that everyone was standing. So, thinking I might easily be lost in the crowd, . . . I went out again, presented my ticket, asked for my money

back, and walked away. But what I had not suspected was that the moment I got to the door everyone sat down and M. de Francueil clearly perceived that I was no longer there. Nothing could have been so far from my natural disposition as this act. But I note it as a proof that there are moments of a kind of delirium in which men cannot be judged by what they do.

[Je me promenois avec M. de Francueil au Palais royal. . . . Il tire sa montre, la regarde, et me dit : allons à l'Opera : Je le veux bien; Nous allons. Il prend deux billets d'Amphitheatre, m'en donne un, et passe le premier avec l'autre; je le suis, il entre. En entrant après lui, je trouve la porte embarrassée. Je regarde; je vois tout le monde debout. Je juge que je pourrai bien me perdre dans cette foule. . . . Je sors, je reprends ma contremarque, puis mon argent, et je m'en vais, sans songer qu'à peine avois-jue atteint la porte que tout le monde étoit assis, et qu'alors M. de Franceuil voyoit clairement que je n'y étois plus. Comme jamais rien ne fut plus éloigné de mon humeur que ce trait-là, je le note, pour montrer qu'il y a des momens d'une espéce de délire, où il ne faut point juger des hommes par leurs actions.][20]

Elsewhere in *Confessions* he asserts: "there are times when I am so unlike myself that I might be taken for someone else of an entirely opposite character" [il y a des tems où je suis si peu semblable à moi-même qu'on me prendroit pour un autre homme de caractére tout opposé].[21] According to him, the selves of most individuals are unstable and shifting: "It has been observed that the majority of men are often in the course of their lives quite unlike themselves" [L'on a remarqué que la plus part des hommes sont dans le cours de leur vie souvent dissemblables à eux-mêmes et semblent se transformer en des hommes tout différens].[22] Insofar as Rousseau, like many other people, is vulnerable to "certain moments of incomprehensible delirium in which" he is not himself [des momens de délire inconcevables où je n'étois plus moi-même], the task of understanding him and his actions becomes incredibly difficult, if not impossible.[23]

But this is precisely the task that Rousseau and several of Godwin's protagonists set for the readers of their narratives. Rousseau makes the following contract with the reader of his *Confessions*:

by relating [to the reader] in simple detail all that has happened to me, all that I have done, all that I have felt, I cannot lead him into error, unless wilfully [*sic*]; and even if I wish to, I shall not easily succeed by this method. His task is to assemble these elements and to assess the being who is made up of them. The summing-up will be of his own making. But, with this in view, it is not enough for my story to be truthful, it must be detailed as well. It is not for me to judge of the relative importance of events; I must relate them all, and leave the selection to him . . . I have only one thing to fear in this enterprise; not that I may say too much or tell untruths, but that I may not tell everything and may conceal the truth.

[en lui détaillant avec simplicité tout ce qui m'est arrivé, tout ce que je fait, tout ce que j'ai pensé, tout ce que j'ai senti, je ne puis l'induire en erreur à moins que je ne le veuille, encore même en le voulant n'y parviendrois-je pas aisément de cette façon. C'est à lui d'assembler ces élémens et de déterminer l'être qu'ils composent; le résultat doit être son ouvrage, et s'il se trompe alors, toute l'erreur sera de son fait. Or il ne suffit pas pour cette fin que mes recits soient fidelles il faut aussi qu'ils soient exacts. Ce n'est pas à moi de juger de l'importance des faits, je les dois tous dire, et lui laisser le soin de choisir. . . . Je n'ai qu'une chose à craindre dans cette entreprise; ce n'est pas de trop dire ou de dire des mensonges; mais c'est de ne pas tout dire, et de taire des vérités.][24]

Rousseau puts a tremendous burden on his readers, who must "judge of the relative importance of events" and make their assessments based on the many details he supplies. As Jean Starobinski observes, in *Confessions* "Rousseau . . . ascribes to his readers the task of making a unity of multiplicity."[25]

Like Rousseau, Godwin envisions reading as an intellectually demanding process: "True reading is investigation, not a passive reception of what our author has given us, but an active enquiry, appreciation and digestion of his subject."[26] Godwin's Rousseauistic novel *Mandeville* features a narrator who self-consciously relates every factor, no matter how mundane, that may have had a formative effect. Mandeville explains his methodology to his readers:

Many readers will consider the detail I have here given as frivolous and commonplace. . . . It is the express purpose of the narrative in which I am engaged, to show how the concurrence of a variety of causes operate to form a character: and if I were to omit any circumstance that possessed a very strong influence on my mind, the person into whose hands this story may happen to fall, would have an imperfect picture of the man who is set before him, and would want some of the particulars necessary to the development of the tale. (79)[27]

Both Godwin's protagonist and Rousseau claim to have faith in the ability of a discerning reader to sift through the innumerable details they recount and determine which ones are crucial.

Rousseau, Godwin, and Shelley all recognize the power of environmental conditioning and believe that in order to understand an individual one must take into account his or her upbringing and subsequent experiences. In *The Confessions*, Rousseau describes how he outlined a book, to be entitled *la morale sensitive, ou le matérialisme du Sage*, in which he planned to show how individuals can avoid negative changes in personality through controlling "previous impressions from external objects" ("l'impression antérieure des objets exterieurs"):

> Climates, seasons, sounds, colours, darkness, light, the elements, food, noise, silence, movement, repose: they all act on our machines, and consequently upon our souls, and they all offer us innumerable and almost certain opportunities for controlling those feelings which we allow to dominate us at their very onset.
>
> [Les climats, les saisons, les sons, les couleurs, l'obscurité, la lumiére, les élemens, les alimens, le bruit, le silence, le mouvement, le repos, tout agit sur notre machine et sur notre ame [*sic*] par consequent; tout nous offre mille prises presque assurées pour gouverner dans leur origine les sentimens dont nous nous laissons dominer.][28]

Similarly, in *Enquiry Concerning Political Justice*, Godwin boldly declares that the "mind is a topic of science," and that "The character of any man is the result of a long series of impressions communicated to his mind, and modifying it in a certain manner, so as to enable us, from a number of these modifications and impressions being given, to predict his conduct."[29] Thus Mr. Collins, in *Caleb Williams*, does not regard "vicious" individuals like the title character "as proper objects of indignation and scorn." He pompously informs Caleb that he considers him "as a machine": "you did not make yourself; you are just what circumstances irresistibly compelled you to be" (*Caleb Williams*, 310). If everything we perceive acts "on our machines, and consequently upon our souls," virtually nothing we experience is irrelevant to the formation of our minds, and a comprehensive narrative of our life histories must take into account a bewildering array of factors. One reason that Frankenstein's monster must describe "the original æra of [his] being" (*The Mary Shelley Reader*, 76) in such detail to his hostile and impatient creator is that according to Lockean (and Hartleian) psychology, Frankenstein cannot make informed judgments regarding his character and behavior without knowing how the monster's mind has been shaped by sense impressions and other environmental factors.

Historical and social factors also play an important role in the mental development of Godwin's and Shelley's protagonists. Both writers carefully present their characters as the products of specific historical periods and social milieux. As Godwin writes in "Analysis of Own Character," "If it is curious to observe the propensities of the mind which appear so early that philosophers dispute whether they date from before or after the period of birth, it is no less curious to remark how much is indisputably to be attributed to the empire of circumstances."[30] He also stresses the importance of social conditioning in *The Enquirer*: "Man in society is variously influenced by the characters of his fellow men; he is an imitative animal, and, like the camelion [*sic*], owes the colour he assumes, to the colour of the surrounding objects."[31] Moreover, in his massive four-volume *Life of Geoffrey Chaucer* (1803–4), Godwin asserts that "The full and complete life of a poet would include an extensive survey of the manners, the opinions, the arts and the literature, of the age in which the poet lived. That is the only way in which we can become truly acquainted with the history of his mind, and the causes which made him what he was."[32] Godwin applied these insights to his fiction, and *St. Leon*, *Fleetwood*, *Mandeville*, *Cloudesley*, and *Deloraine* are all packed with historical, cultural, and geographical information.

Like her father, Mary Shelley was a meticulous researcher, and both *Valperga* and *The Fortunes of Perkin Warbeck, A Romance* (1830) reflect her desire to portray her protagonists within the contexts of the historical and social factors that formed their psyches.[33] As Betty T. Bennett writes, "Underlying both novels . . . is an exploration of the historical forces which shape the lives of individuals."[34] *Valperga* is set at the beginning of the fourteenth century, "when Italy . . . began to emerge from the darkness of the ruin of the Western Empire, and to catch from the East the returning rays of literature and science." In it, Shelley shows how the minds of her major characters are shaped by this time of transition, during which "Lombardy and Tuscany, the most civilized districts of Italy, exhibited astonishing specimens of human genius; but . . . were torn to pieces by domestic faction, and almost destroyed by the fury of civil wars" (7). Here, as elsewhere in her fiction, she portrays individuals as the products of such factors as family legacies, social situations, national identities, and educational opportunities.[35]

Like Rousseau's persona in *Confessions*, the narrators of Godwin's and Shelley's fictional confessions tend to be self-conscious: they advance a number of different theories regarding who, if anyone, will read their stories and the contexts within which they will be interpreted. Even Shelley's Lionel Verney, the last man, imagines the existence of a new race that will, at some future time, provide an audience for his manuscript. The motivations of Godwin's and Shelley's protagonists for recounting their life histories also vary: some confessions reflect a sense of guilt, some are vindications, some are presented as cautionary tales, and others appear to be driven by a need for emotional ventilation. While a number of Godwin's and Shelley's confessional narratives are entirely fictional, several contain autobiographical elements.[36] In nearly all of these fictional confessions the narrator has a need to tell his or her tale, even in cases in which there is no one to read it, or in which the recital of the narrator's story proves more confusing than illuminating. These narratives resemble *Confessions* in their tendency to focus on feelings and mental states rather than events: "I may omit or transpose facts," Rousseau writes,

> but I cannot go wrong about what I have felt, or about what my feelings have led me to do; and these are the chief subjects of my story. The true object of my confessions is to reveal my inner thoughts exactly in all the situations of my life. It is the history of my soul that I have promised to recount.
>
> [Je puis faire des omissions dans les faits, des transpositions, des erreurs de dates; mais je ne puis me tromper sur ce que j'ai senti, ni sur ce que mes sentimens m'ont fait faire; et voila dequoi principalement il s'agit. L'objet propre de mes confessions est de faire connoitre exactement mon interieur dans toutes les situations de ma vie. C'est l'histoire de mon ame [*sic*] que j'ai promise.][37]

In *Confessions*, Rousseau pledges to hide nothing from the reader: "Since I have undertaken to reveal myself absolutely to the public, nothing about me must remain hidden or obscure" [Dans l'entreprise que j'ai faite de me montrer tout entier au public, il faut que rien de moi ne lui reste obscur ou caché].[38] This belief in the importance of self-revelation through sincere discourse is reflected throughout Godwin's writings. For him, sincerity is perhaps the most important virtue a person can possess: "The powerful recommendations attendant upon sincerity are obvious. It is intimately connected with the general dissemination of innocence, energy, intellectual improvement, and philanthropy."[39] Moreover, he contends that sincere communication enables people to realize their potential: "We . . . best fulfil the scope of our nature, when we sincerely and unreservedly communicate to each other our feelings and apprehensions. Speech should be to man in the nature of a fair complexion, the transparent medium through which the workings of the mind should be made legible."[40]

Rousseau's doctrine of sincerity serves as a moral yardstick in Godwin's and Shelley's fictional works against which many of their characters are measured and found wanting. As Gary Kelly has observed, the "theme of failed sincerity in [*Caleb Williams*] probably owes a great deal to . . . Jean-Jacques Rousseau."[41] Failures in sincerity also haunt Godwin's St. Leon and Shelley's Frankenstein, whose secret experiments result in tragedy. In Godwin's and Shelley's confessional narratives, characters are often too reticent, duplicitous, or deranged to provide each other or the reader with a "transparent medium through which the workings of the mind [are] made legible."

Like Rousseau in the *Confessions*, the title character of *Caleb Williams* presents his sensations in a sometimes painstakingly detailed manner. He describes his obsessional curiosity regarding whether or not his master, Falkland, has committed murder. When Falkland, in his capacity as justice of the peace, is compelled to hear a case involving murder and cannot bear to hear the accused man "describe the depth of his compunction for [his] involuntary fault," Caleb becomes convinced of his guilt. After Falkland leaves the room "with every mark of horror and despair," Caleb retires to the garden in order to vent his emotions:

> My mind was full almost to bursting. . . . I felt as if my animal system had undergone a total revolution. My blood boiled within me. I was conscious to [*sic*] a kind of rapture for which I could not account. I was solemn, yet full of rapid emotion, burning with indignation and energy. In the very tempest and hurricane of the passions, I seemed to enjoy the most soul-ravishing calm. I cannot better express the then state of my mind, than by saying, I was never so perfectly alive as at that moment. (129–30)

An amateur mental anatomist, Caleb is obsessed with both his master's states of mind and his own. But for him, as for a number of Godwin's other narrators, many of the operations of the mind remain inexplicable. A "tempest and hurricane of the passions" can coexist with "the most soul-ravishing calm," rapture with indignation. Moreover, the perversity of human nature frequently triumphs over reason. After Falkland warns Caleb not to attempt to leave his service, Caleb decides to do the very thing his master has forbidden: "I seemed to be in a state in which reason had no power. I felt as if I could cooly survey the several arguments of the case, perceive that they had prudence, truth and common sense on their side; and then answer, I am under the guidance of a director more energetic than you" (154). Caleb, like Rousseau in the *Confessions*, is prone to "des momens de délire inconcevables" in which his feelings and actions seem to defy rational explanation.

After having spent some time observing and interpreting Falkland's behavior, Caleb begins to consider himself "a competent adept in the different modes in which the human intellect displays its secret workings" (123). At the end of the novel, however, he realizes that his refusal to communicate frankly with Falkland contributed to their bitter estrangement: "I now see [my] mistake in all its enormity. I am sure that, if I had opened my heart to Mr. Falkland, if I had told to him privately the tale that I have now been telling, he could not have resisted my reasonable demand" (323). Caleb over-estimates his abilities as a mental anatomist: he recognizes Falkland's vindictiveness but overlooks his master's capacity to respond compassionately to his "frank and fervent expostulation" (323). Similarly, St. Leon believes that he once possessed "a more than common insight into the characters of mankind" (*St. Leon*, 144) but later realizes that despite his knowledge of "the leading secrets of natural magic, [he is] a mere tyro in the science of man" (303). Both novels indicate that individuals who consider themselves "competent adept[s] in the different modes in which the human intellect displays its secret workings" are likely to discover that there is much about "the science of the human mind" that they do not understand.

Caleb's motivation for telling his story changes as the act of composition progresses. After having been persecuted for several years by Falkland, Caleb writes his narrative in order to vindicate himself:

> These papers shall preserve the truth: they shall one day be published, and then the world shall do justice on us both. . . . This Falkland has invented against me every species of foul accusation. He has hunted me from city to city. He has drawn his lines of circumvallation round me that I may not escape. He has kept his scenters of human prey for ever at my heels. He may hunt me out of the world.—In vain! With this engine, this little pen I defeat all his machinations. (315)

This passage recalls the paranoid pronouncements in Rousseau's *Confessions* in which he vows to protect his autobiography from his enemies:

> My *Confessions* are not intended to appear in my lifetime, or in the lifetime of the persons concerned. If I were master of my own destiny and that of my book, it would not see the light till long after my death and theirs. But the attempts made by my powerful oppressors, who dread the truth, to destroy every trace of it, compel me to make every effort consonant with the strictest justice and the most scrupulous fairness, in order to preserve them. . . . [S]ince my name is fated to live, I must endeavour to transmit with it the memory of that unfortunate man who bore it, as he actually was and not as his unjust enemies unremittingly endeavour to paint him.
>
> [Mes confessions ne sont point faites pour paroitre de mon vivant ni de celui des personnes interessées. Si j'étois le maitre de ma destinée et de celle de cet écrit it ne verroit le jour que longtems après ma mort et la leur. Mais les efforts que la terreur de la vérité fait faire à mes puissans oppresseurs pour en effacer les traces, me forcent à faire pour les conserver tout ce que me permettent le droit le plus exact et la plus sévére justice. . . . [P]uisqu'enfin mon nom doit vivre, je dois tâcher de transmettre avec lui le souvenir de l'homme infortuné qui le porta, tel qu'il fut réellement, et non tel que d'injustes ennemis [sic]travaillent sans relâche à le peindre.][42]

Like the *Confessions*, Caleb's narrative is, in part, a vindication addressed to the "world" of presumably impartial public opinion.

In the "Postscript" of *Caleb Williams*, however, Caleb discovers that he no longer needs to vindicate himself. After hearing the "artless and manly story" (324) of Caleb's experiences and sufferings, Falkland finally admits that his former servant has told the truth and that he is a murderer. But rather than gloating over his adversary's confession, Caleb abandons his vindication and recasts his tale as a moral exemplum that centers not on himself but on his former persecutor. He thus renounces the kind of paranoid and narcissistic worldview that distorts the last sections of *Confessions*: "I began these memoirs with the idea of vindicating my character. I have now no character that I wish to vindicate: but I will finish them that thy [i.e. Falkland's] story may be fully understood; and that, if those errors of thy life be known which thou so ardently desiredst to conceal, the world may at least not hear and repeat a half-told and mangled tale" (326). His desire to transform his story into Falkland's can be seen as a repudiation of his autobiographical project. As Eric Daffron points out, "Since as confessional literature memoirs inscribe the self, Caleb ostensibly gives up that self for service to another, one that will apparently confirm Falkland's socially sanctioned character."[43]

Despite his "artless" sincerity, Caleb's emotional instability undermines his reliability as a narrator. In fact, he goes insane in the original manuscript ending of the novel, imagining that he is a gravestone (334). Citing late-eighteenth-century medical theory, Peter Melville Logan contends that Caleb is "a nervous narrator" whose hysteria compels him to describe "in the first person the events in the past that produced [his] nervous condition."[44] His contradictory attitudes toward his master reflect his conflicted mental state: "The fluctuating state of my mind produced a contention of opposite principles that by turns usurped dominion over my conduct. Sometimes I was influenced by the most complete veneration for my master. . . . At other times . . . I was . . . watchful, inquisitive, suspicious, full of a thousand conjectures as to the meaning of the most indifferent actions" (122). He also experiences mood swings during the composition of his narrative, declaring that "Writing, which was at first a pleasure, is changed to a burthen" (304).

Moreover, like a number of Godwin's other protagonists, Caleb is prone to self-deception. In *Enquiry Concerning Political Justice*, Godwin writes that "Self-deception is of all things the most easy. Whoever ardently wishes to find a proposition true, may be expected insensibly to veer towards the opinion that suits his inclination." Whereas "the mere basis of evidence"[45] would indicate that Falkland is neither a Caligula (314) nor "godlike" (325), Caleb's fluctuating inclinations lead him to demonize or eulogize his former master. Both *Caleb Williams* and *Confessions* present narrators who prove vulnerable to episodes of "incomprehensible delirium" and whose interpretations of events and evaluations of others are highly subjective. Although sincerity can enhance the mind's transparency, even a sincere narrator may recite a "mangled" tale. Gay Clifford correctly identifies *Caleb Williams* and *Confessions* as autobiographies posing as histories.[46]

But although unreliable as an interpreter of his life story, Caleb provides the reader with many insights into his emotional and psychological development. In his 1832 preface to *Fleetwood*, Godwin asserts that the first-person narration employed in *Caleb Williams* and his later novels is "best adapted" to his "analysis of the private and internal operations of the mind." He wants *Caleb Williams* to "constitute an epoch in the mind of the reader, that no one, after he has read it, shall ever be exactly the same man that he was before."[47] Kristen Leaver argues persuasively that Godwin directed his novel to "an ideal reader" capable of realizing, in the indefinite future, "the political moral of the text."[48] I contend that he also envisioned the "ideal reader" as a mental anatomist. Godwin designed *Caleb Williams* and his other fictional confessions to help the anatomizing reader gain insight into the mind of the narrator and, by extension, into his or her own psyche.

Godwin made sincerity a central theme in his next novel, *St. Leon*.[49] As Clemit notes, the protagonist's "systematic withholding of information foregrounds issues of unreliability in a more problematic manner than Caleb's narrative."[50] Partial sincerity destroys Reginald de St. Leon's marriage, affects his relationship with the reader, and condemns him to eternal loneliness: "No human ear," he writes, "must ever be astonished with the story of my endowments and my privileges" (161). It also transforms his tale into a parody of Rousseau's *Confessions*. St. Leon, a sixteenth-century French aristocrat, gambles away his fortune in Paris. Penniless and nearly insane, he is taken by his wife and family to Switzerland to live in "virtuous obscurity" (72). While there he encounters a dying man, who offers him "the art of multiplying gold, and the power of living for ever" (160) on one condition: St. Leon's alchemical powers must remain a secret to everyone, including his wife, Marguerite, and his children. After his conversation with the stranger, St. Leon returns to his family and finds that his relationship with them has changed: "Marguerite enquired of me respecting the stranger, but my answers were short and embarrassed. . . . I could see that she was hurt at my incommunicativeness, yet I could not prevail upon myself to enter into an explanation of the causes of my taciturnity. . . . I could observe that the children sympathised with their mother, and secretly were surprised at and lamented my reserve" (130). Despite his misgivings, however, St. Leon agrees to accept the stranger's gifts of the philosopher's stone and the *elixir vitae* and to keep his possession of them secret from his family.

St. Leon's lack of complete sincerity leads to a series of tragedies, including the disappearance of his son, the death of his wife, and his separation from his remaining children. His wife suffers most from his secretiveness: "There was no more opening of the heart between [her and St. Leon], no more infantine guilelessness and sincerity, no more of that unapprehensive exposure of every thought of the soul, that adds the purest zeal to the pleasures of domestic life" (179). In St. Leon's and Marguerite's domestic Garden of Eden, the serpent is insincerity. As soon as sincerity is diluted by any admixture of reserve or falsehood, friendship, in the truest sense of the word, becomes impossible. For Marguerite, her husband's "reserve . . . amount[s] to a divorce of the heart" (177), and she slowly pines away "in speechless grief" (200).

St. Leon also fails to be completely candid with the readers of his narrative. Whereas Rousseau makes unconditional openness the underlying principle of *Confessions*, St. Leon refuses to reveal the secret of his powers or even his motives for writing his life story: "Some persons may be curious to know what motives can have induced a man of such enormous wealth, and so every way qualified to revel in delights, to take the trouble of penning his memoirs. . . . The curiosity here mentioned . . . I cannot consent to gratify" (3). Although he is frequently painstaking in his descriptions of his moral failings, errors in judgment, and emotional states, he has little patience with those readers who may want to know more than he tells them: "Such readers I have only to remind, that the pivot upon which the history I am composing turns, is a mystery. If they will not accept of my communication upon my own terms, they must lay aside my book" (214). The secret of his powers is not the only information he withholds; he also refuses to describe the tortures that he has endured as the Inquisition's prisoner: "Let the reader judge of what I had passed through and known within those cursed walls by the effects; . . . I . . . refuse, to tell what I suffered, and how those effects were produced" (347). His narrative never achieves the transparency that should, ideally, characterize a Rousseauistic confession.

A confession necessarily involves an audience, but in St. Leon's case it is far from clear who will read his tale. Because St. Leon is immortal, he cannot avoid controversy and persecution by publishing his memoirs posthumously. In fact, at one point in the narrative, he asserts that he will be his manuscript's only reader: "It is no matter that these pages shall never be surveyed by other eyes than mine. They afford at least the semblance of communication and the unburthening of the mind; and I will press the illusion fondly and for ever to my heart" (162). This statement recalls Rousseau's authorial stance in *Rêveries*: "I am writing down my reveries for myself alone" [je n'écris mes rêveries que pour moi].[51] However, in the section of his memoirs that describes the sufferings of the Spanish Inquisition's victims, St. Leon speculates that his manuscript may someday find an audience: "If these papers of mine are ever produced to light, may it not happen that they shall first be read by a distant posterity, who will refuse to believe that their fathers were ever mad enough to subject each other to so horrible a treatment, merely because they were unable to adopt each other's opinions?" (338). And near the end of his tale, St. Leon suggests that his manuscript will be published following his son's death: "This narrative . . . shall never see the light, till the melancholy hour when Charles de Damville shall be no more" (476). Thus his sense of his audience, who may or may not be members of "a distant posterity," is extremely vague.

St. Leon's frequent allusions to "the reader" and "readers" further call into question the self-referentiality of his narrative. The fact that he has no idea who these readers will be does not prevent him from speculating about and trying to manipulate their reactions to his memoirs. At different points in his confessions, St. Leon asks the reader to "imagine" his sadness (291), to "agree" with him (300), to "forgive" him (316), and not to "condemn" him (433). He recognizes that "The reader may deem it surprising and unaccountable" (329) that he takes pleasure in the company of a *mosca*, or a man assigned by the Inquisition to spy on him, and the story of his sufferings while imprisoned by the Inquisition will, he fears, "drive the most delicate or susceptible of [his] readers mad with horrors" (335). His attempts to manipulate his audience recall Rousseau's numerous appeals to his reader: "Kind reader, sympathize with me in my grief!" [Lecteur pitoyable, partagez mon affliction]; "Suspend your judgement, reader" [Lecteur, suspendez vôtre jugement].[52]

Despite his claim that his narrative is a "history" of his "vices and follies" rather than their "vindication" (259), St. Leon's frequent addresses to his readers indicate that he believes that they will exist and that he seeks their approval and sympathy. In the closing pages of his memoirs, he tries to manipulate the reader's responses to his tale one last time: "That the reader may enter the more fully into my sentiment of congratulation upon the happiness of my son, and rise from the perusal of my narrative with a more soothing and pleasurable sensation, I will here shortly recapitulate the good qualities that had been unfolded in this truly extraordinary young man from his earliest infancy" (477). Rather than simply allowing the reader to draw his or her own conclusions, St. Leon shifts the focus away from himself, choosing to end his narrative with a "sentiment of congratulation."

Unlike Rousseau in *Confessions*, St. Leon lacks faith in his audience's probity. He declares that the torments of a gambler can only be appreciated by those who have suffered them: "No man who has not felt, can possibly image to himself the tortures of a gamester, of a gamester like me" (56). Although he provides a long description of these "tortures," he does not believe that any text can make this state of mind transparent to a reader who is not a "gamester." Later in the novel, after describing his dog's death, he feels that he must respond to "A morose and fastidious reader" who may ask him why he lays "so great a stress upon so petty and insignificant an incident as the death of a dog." But while St. Leon makes some effort to describe the animal's virtues, he concludes that the reader will never realize their true worth: "[The dog's] conduct the reader may in some degree comprehend and appreciate; but I should in vain attempt to delineate those admirable qualities in this faithful domestic, which do not fall within the province of narrative, and which to have justly appreciated you must have been personally and familiarly acquainted with him" (273). St. Leon also believes that his audience can be duped: "The terms I must use may delude the reader into an imagination that I still participate of enjoyment and of hope. Be it so; they may cheat the reader; they cannot cheat myself!" (356–57). Not only does he decide to repress some of his emotional responses to the events of his life, thereby compromising his mental transparency, he suggests that he, rather than the reader, is the most reliable judge of himself. The reader may be deluded or cheated, but St. Leon cannot be misled. He longs for his readers' sympathy but has little faith in their ability to understand him.

Early in his memoirs, St. Leon claims that his narrative will be both sincere and objective: "I am at my present writing totally changed and removed from what I was, and I write with the freedom of a general historian. It is this simplicity and ingenuousness that shall pervade the whole of my narrative" (22–23). Despite this declaration, however, he is far from detached from the tale he is telling, and his sincerity is compromised by his unwillingness to provide important information and his clumsy attempts to manipulate the reader's responses. The fact that he reveals a great deal to the reader, and recounts a number of episodes that reflect badly on him, does not make up for his lapses in candor. As Rousseau asserts in *Confessions*, mental transparency can only exist if one is completely sincere.

Like St. Leon, the protagonist of Godwin's next novel, *Fleetwood: or, The New Man of Feeling*, describes his childhood experiences and education in some detail. Rousseau's *Émile* had a profound influence on Godwin's views on education, and both *St. Leon* and *Fleetwood* reflect the philosopher's belief that traditional educations are often more harmful than beneficial.[53] According to Godwin, "the characters of men are determined in all their most essential circumstances by education." Because education consists of "every incident that produces an idea in the mind, and can give birth to a train of reflections,"[54] it is an important part of any person's mental history. In St. Leon's case, his chivalric education has a destructive influence on his marriage to Marguerite: when the stranger offers him the philosopher's stone and the *elixir vitae*, "The youthful passions of [his] soul" (130) lead him to choose power and fame over domestic tranquillity, and his family falls apart. Casimir Fleetwood's eighteenth-century education, which includes a few years at Oxford and a sojourn in Paris, also has a negative effect. After having spent his childhood happily exploring the Welsh countryside, this "new man of feeling" becomes "an artificial personage, formed after a wretched and contemptible model" (32) at the university. His "education and travels [leave him] a confirmed misanthropist" (137).[55] *St. Leon* and *Fleetwood*, like Rousseau's *Confessions* and *Émile*, emphasize the important role education plays in the formation, or malformation, of character.

Fleetwood also continues Godwin's examination of the possibilities and limitations of sincerity in confessional narratives. Although Fleetwood's memoirs are at least superficially more sincere than St. Leon's—he has no alchemical secrets to keep from the reader—he is extremely reluctant to enter into the details of his transgressions at Oxford and Paris. After having related how his fellow Oxonians drove a student to suicide, he cuts his account of his university experiences short: "It is not my purpose to convert these honest pages into a record of dissipations; far less, of the rude and unseemly dissipations of an overgrown boy" (45). Although he declares that "The proper topic of [his] narrative . . . is the record of [his] errors," he claims that a description of his "dissipations" would somehow undermine the integrity of "these honest pages." Similarly, he is extremely reticent about his affair with a Parisian coquette: "I write no book that shall tend to nourish the pruriency of the debauched, or that shall excite one painful emotion, one instant of debate, in the bosom of the virtuous and the chaste" (54). Later on, he apologizes for the "debaucheries" he does describe: "Most earnestly do I entreat the reader to pardon me, for having thus much interspersed these pages with a tale of debaucheries" (64). In *Enquiry Concerning Political Justice*, Godwin writes that "Vice and weakness are founded upon ignorance and error."[56] Thus Fleetwood's Godwinian confession is "a register of errors" (137) rather than a catalog of sins. However, Fleetwood's censorship of his "dissipations" contrasts sharply with Rousseau's candid descriptions of his sexual experiences, which include masturbation, indecent exposure, and an appointment with a Venetian courtesan.

In fact, in his eagerness to begin the chief subject of his confession, his misjudgment and ill-treatment of his wife, Fleetwood skips over most of his adulthood years:

> It will readily be supposed, that in . . . twenty years of my life I met with many adventures; and that, if I were so inclined, I might, instead of confining myself as I have done to generals, have related a variety of minute circumstances, sometimes calculated to amuse the fancy, and sometimes to agitate the sympathetic and generous feelings, of every reader. . . . But I willingly sacrifice these topics. I hasten to the events which have pressed with so terrible a weight on my heart, and have formed my principal motive to become my own historian. (151)

If Fleetwood truly means to tell the reader "what manner of man" he is, and what his "spontaneous and native dispositions" are (21–22), his decision to omit twenty years of his life is odd, especially since he makes room in his narrative for Ruffigny's long, Rousseauistic account of his childhood (79–128).

As in the case of St. Leon, Fleetwood's lack of complete sincerity extends to his wife as well his readers. At the age of forty-five, Fleetwood marries a much younger woman, Mary Macneil, and communication breaks down between them as soon as they move into his paternal mansion in Wales. Unwittingly, she takes over a closet that is his "favourite retreat" (194), but rather than telling her how much the room means to him, he vows never to "breathe a syllable on the subject" (195). As their married life progresses, Fleetwood's resentments multiply. He invites two distant relations, Kenrick and his half brother Gifford, to visit him and becomes jealous of his wife's affection for Kenrick. The Iago-like Gifford, who has designs on his host's estate, does all in his power to inflame his suspicions. Again, Fleetwood fails to express his feelings to Mary. When she begs him to reveal the cause of his unhappiness, he makes himself "play the dissembler" (254), and when she urges him to "Open [his] bosom to [his] faithful wife," he scolds her for her "officiousness" (255). His inability to communicate sincerely with his spouse makes him vulnerable to Gifford's misrepresentations and nearly costs him his marriage, his sanity, and his life.

According to Fleetwood's narrative, sincerity is absolutely necessary in a marriage, especially in the marriage of a middle-aged man to a young woman. He does not, however, believe that most human beings can ever truly understand each other. After describing his reluctance to allow his wife to occupy his favorite closet, he makes the following observations:

> There is something wonderfully subtle in the operations of the human mind. Do I differ with another, in project for the future, or judgment on our past conduct? I immediately begin to find a hundred arguments to prove, how absurd and unreasonable he is, how just am I. No man can completely put himself in the place of another, and conceive how he would feel, were the circumstances of that other his own: few can do it even in a superficial degree. We are so familiar with our own trains of thinking: we revolve them with such complacency: it appears to us, that there is so astonishing a perverseness in not seeing things as we see them! The step is short and inevitable from complacency in our own views, to disapprobation and distaste toward the views of him by whom we are thwarted. (196)

Here, Fleetwood calls into question both Adam Smith's faith in the powers of imaginative sympathy and Rousseau's belief that if enough information is provided, one can, in fact, put oneself "in the place of another." According to Smith, all humans have the capacity to sympathize with "our brother . . . upon the rack": "By the imagination we place ourselves in his situation, we conceive ourselves enduring all the same torments, we enter as it were into his body, and become in some measure the same person with him, and thence form some idea of his sensations, and even feel something which, though weaker in degree, is not altogether unlike them."[57] Rousseau asserts that he can make himself transparent to the reader through the narration of a single episode in his life, his abortive attempt to make love to a Venetian prostitute: "Whoever you may be that wish to know a man, have the courage to read the next two or three pages and you will have complete knowledge of Jean-Jacques Rousseau" [Qui que vous soyez qui voulez connoitre un homme, osez lire les deux ou trois pages qui suivent vous allez connoitre à plein J. J. Rousseau].[58]

Fleetwood believes, however, that only a friend who is "as another self" (148) can truly sympathize with and understand him. Yet, although he longs for this kind of friend, "in whom [his] sensations are by a kind of necessity echoed and repeated" (150), he never finds such a person. As Steven Bruhm points out, "By the last page of the novel [Fleetwood] . . . still has no way to enter into and identify with someone else's subjectivity."[59] Although he presumably writes his confessional narrative in order to reveal his inner self to his readers, he is apparently unable to believe in the viability of his own project. To a degree, he reflects Godwin's own doubts about the capacity of humans to make themselves transparent to other people: "No one man ever completely understood the character of any other man. My most familiar friend exaggerates perhaps some virtues in me; but there are others which I know I possess, to which he is totally blind."[60] In the final analysis, no friend can be "as another self."

Godwin's subsequent novel, *Mandeville*, is his most Rousseauistic work of fiction.[61] Whereas St. Leon and Fleetwood are extremely selective in their accounts of their lives, Mandeville's narrative is so thorough that when it abruptly breaks off (after three volumes in the original edition), he is only about nineteen years old (248). In his presentation of Mandeville, who defines himself almost completely in terms of his hatred for his rival Clifford, Godwin explores a ruling passion within the context of a confessional narrative. Like Rousseau, Mandeville writes his story in the faith that it will be interpreted by others:

> whoever will give himself the pains to observe it, will find that every historian puts much of his own character into his work; and a skilful anatomist of the soul, before he reaches the perusal of the last page, will have formed a very tolerable notion of the dispositions of the writer. I, who am penning this series of events to which I give my name of Mandeville, shall have shown, and should have shown, if they were the memoirs of a stranger, to a penetrating reader many secrets of my own heart, which modesty, or, it may be, a feeling of moral right and wrong, would have prompted me to conceal, if I had been aware what I was doing. (197)[62]

The self may be a mysterious entity, but Mandeville is confident that a skillful reader can grasp its nature when it is embodied in a text, particularly in a text like his, which purports to conceal nothing.

Mandeville presents this "penetrating reader" with a bewildering variety of possible reasons for his obsessional passion, reasons which at times seem to conflict with each other. He, like Rousseau in *Confessions*, continually wonders how he might have turned out if only things had been somehow different. As Rousseau speculates on the happy life he might have lived if he had been apprenticed to a better master and had remained in Geneva,[63] Mandeville claims that he would have been a better person if he had grown up with his sister, Henrietta, at Beaulieu

Cottage rather than with his valetudinarian uncle at Mandeville house: "had I lived with my Henrietta, . . . I also should have been a human creature, . . . I should then have been amiable; and I should have been happy!" (75). In both cases, there is a sense that the self is constructed by environment and circumstances: if events had dictated otherwise, Mandeville could have been cheerful and unconflicted instead of bitterly paranoid.

Mandeville does, however, provide the reader with some advice regarding the education of children, and here, too, Godwin has his seventeenth-century protagonist "anticipate" the eighteenth-century Rousseau. In fact, Mandeville claims that his narrative, unlike educational handbooks, presents childhood from a boy's point of view:

> All those persons who have produced practical treatises on the art of education, have been men [rather than boys]. The books are always written by those who are the professors of teaching, never by the subjects. . . . It has been necessary for me, to resume the character of my early years, and to forget for the moment that those years have passed away. I have committed to paper what, during those years, passed through my mind; I have nothing to do with either vindicating or condemning that of which I am the historian. I may thus perhaps have performed a task of general utility; it surely is not unfitting, that that which forms one considerable stage in the history of man, should for once be put into a legible and a permanent form. (61)

Although it is not overtly didactic, Mandeville insists that his narrative can serve a practical purpose, or perform "a task of general utility" for those who study childhood development. *Mandeville* also contains some specific pedagogical advice. While the governor, or tutor, of Rousseau's *Émile* never tries to persuade his pupil "of the duty of obedience" [le devoir de l'obéissance],[64] Mandeville's instructor, a religious fanatic named Hilkiah Bradford, requires him to perform menial tasks in order to teach him humility. Like Rousseau, Mandeville concludes that forcing a pupil to obey against his will is ultimately counterproductive: "Where there is absolute command on one side, and unconditional submission on the other, a useful result as to external circumstances may be achieved; but there cannot be a particle of good moral sense implanted by what is thus done under the bare influence of authority" (58).[65]

However, *Mandeville*'s status as an educational treatise is undercut by the fact that Mandeville is, in many ways, a special case. His parents are horribly murdered when he is three, he spends a reclusive childhood under the tutelage of a religious zealot, and he suffers, at least through early adulthood, from an obsessional passion, his hatred for Clifford. What can a "normal" person learn from this study of human pathology? Mandeville recognizes this problem:

> Far be it from me to impute my own feelings during [my childhood], to every youth that is placed under the direction of a preceptor. I know that my feelings were solitary, unsocial, exaggerated, wicked. Still I regard myself on the whole as a member of the great community of man; and I cannot be persuaded that feelings, which were so familiar and habitual with me, do not under some modification exist in the majority of human minds. (61)

Although Mandeville's passions are more extreme and obsessional than those of most people, he believes that his narrative will still strike a chord with his reader. As Baillie argues in her "Introductory Discourse" to her *Plays on the Passions*, "to the expressions of passion, particularly strong passion, the dullest mind is awake; and its true unsophisticated language the dullest understanding will not misinterpret."[66] Likewise, Mandeville's stress on the effect of education on the formation of character and his belief in the therapeutic value of expressing one's emotional torments to another can easily be applied to the lives of most people.

The educational message of *Mandeville* is confused, however, by the bewildering number of factors that go into the formation of Mandeville's character. According to Clemit, in *Mandeville* "Godwin . . . present[s] a dual theory of the growth of the mind. In keeping with his earlier views on the formation of character by external circumstances, he records the impact of historical events on private life from Mandeville's earliest childhood; but Mandeville's long passages of self-analysis emphasize the unaccountable origins of his irrational passions."[67] Mandeville's narrative is even more complex and conflicted than Clemit suggests. In his attempt to explain how his character has been formed, Mandeville mentions the violent deaths of his father and mother, his defective education by a religious fanatic, the historical situation in which he has been placed, his isolated upbringing in a gloomy environment, his social position as a member of the landed gentry, his lack of a friend and confidant, his victimization by a predatory attorney, and the existence of a rival seemingly designed by fate to frustrate his ambitions. Godwin has his protagonist advance theory after theory, but ultimately such speculations are of limited value, as Mandeville recognizes in retrospect: "What a mockery is enumeration in a case like mine! At this distant period it is a sort of consolation to me, to analyse and count up the different ingredients of which my cup was composed; but, at the time itself, it was all one mighty drench of misery, in which nothing was distinguished" (311). In his effort to present a complete view of his character, however, Mandeville persists in enumerating "the different ingredients" of his bitter and antisocial nature, implying that any nonreductive definition of the self must take on the form of a long, detailed, and self-contradictory narrative.

As if to emphasize the problematic character of Mandeville's enterprise, Godwin has his novel break off rather than end. The protagonist's attempted abduction of his sister and his violent encounter with Clifford are described, and then the novel stops, without any further explanation or resolution. *Mandeville* resembles an unfinished memoir, like Rousseau's *Confessions*, rather than a carefully structured work of fiction. Moreover, Mandeville's bizarrely pedantic description of his mutilation, which makes him "monstrous," with "a sort of preternatural and unvarying distorted smile, or deadly grin," suggests that he is trying (and failing) to distance himself from this traumatic event:

> My wound is of that sort, which in the French civil wars got the name of *une balafre*. I have pleased myself, in the fury and bitterness of my soul, with tracing the whole force of that word. It is a *cicatrix luculenta*, a glazed, or shining scar, like the effect of a streak of varnish upon a picture. *Balafré* I find explained by Girolamo Vittori, by the Italian word *smorfiato*; and this again, I mean the noun, *smorfia*, is decided by "the resolute" John Florio, to signify "a blurting or mumping, a mocking or push with one's mouth." (325)

Here the distinction between the narrator and his past self break down as the obsessional hatred, the trauma of disfiguration, is relived.

The pathological last pages of *Mandeville* can be compared to the last sections of Rousseau's *The Confessions*, in which the narrative is overshadowed by Rousseau's growing paranoia and confusion: "The further I go in my story, the less order and sequence I can put into it. The disturbances of my later life have not left events time to fall into shape in my head. They have been too numerous, too confused, too unpleasant to be capable of straightforward narration" [Plus j'avance dans mes recits, moins j'y puis mettre d'ordre et de suite. L'agitation du reste de ma vie n'a pas laissé aux évenemens le tems de s'arranger dans ma tête. Ils ont été trop nombreux, trop mêlés, trop desagéables, pour pouvoir être narrés sans confusion].[68] In his later years, Rousseau became convinced that Diderot and the other *philosophes* were his enemies, and his description of their machinations reflects his growing paranoia:

> It is from this time that I think I can date the formation of a system, subsequently adopted by those who control my destiny with such rapid and progressive success that it would seem a miracle to anyone who does not know how easily anything can establish itself that favours the malignity of man.
>
> [C'est donc ici que je crois pouvoir fixer l'établissement d'un système adopté depuis par ceux qui disposent de moi, avec un progrès et un succçés [*sic*] si rapide qu'il tiendroit du prodige, pour qui ne sauroit pas quelle facilité tout ce qui favorise la malignité des hommes trouve à s'établir.][69]

While Rousseau feels controlled by a malevolent "système," Mandeville comes to regard himself as the victim of fate: "Fate . . . had bound Clifford and me together with a chain, the links of which could never be dissolved" (140). Mandeville, like Rousseau, is partly the victim of his own hyperactive imagination. His belief that Clifford is a "maleficent wizard" (91) has no more basis in reality than Rousseau's delusion that there is a "universal combination . . . formed against him" (*Fleetwood*, 159).

In fact, at the end of the novel Mandeville's insane hatred of Clifford has made him so identify with his rival that he becomes Clifford's monster, Clifford's slave: "now I bore Clifford and his injuries perpetually about with me. Even as certain tyrannical planters in the West-Indies have set a brand with a red hot iron upon the negroes they have purchased, to denote that they are irremediably a property, so Clifford had set his mark on me, as a token that I was his for ever" (325). His obsessional passion has destroyed his sense of having an autonomous self, and Mandeville begins to perceive himself as a purchased slave who must take on his master's name and obey his master's will. For Mandeville, his self and his ruling passion, his hatred and demonization of Clifford, are one. This breakdown in the last chapter of the text leads Mandeville to violate the principle of objectivity he laid down earlier in the narrative: "I make it a law to myself in this narrative . . . , not to relate any thing to the disadvantage of Clifford, without at the same time producing his side of the question, and stating, not merely how I saw the things that exasperated me, but also what they were in themselves" (227). Moreover, his effort, as an old man, to tell his complete and authentic story has ended in confusion, leaving a text almost as mutilated as his face. Despite Mandeville's belief in the educational value of his narrative, it ends without a clear moral message, and his presentation of himself is far from transparent.

In Godwin's *Cloudesley*, Lord Danvers relates his life story (44–249) to another character, William Meadows, who combines it with other sources to form the narrative that is set forth in the book. Ostensibly, he tells his story to Meadows to enable his servant to undertake a mission on his behalf:

> I expect that, when once you engage with me, you should not draw back. I am about to unfold to you the inmost secrets of my soul. I have a tale to relate, the particulars of which are wholly unknown to any man on English ground, and . . . to only one other person existing on earth. I will not confide in you by halves. If I do not disclose to you the whole of my story, my crimes,—I cannot expect that you will serve me to the extent I require to be served. (42–43)

Thus he claims that his motivation for making his confession is different from Caleb's, St. Leon's, Fleetwood's, and Mandeville's: rather than serving as a vindication, a moral exemplum, or an act of penitence, Danvers's narrative has a practical purpose. It will help Meadows to find and save "the true heir to [Danvers's] title" (251). In a way, Danvers's narrative resembles the monster's in *Frankenstein*. It is at least partially designed to correct an injustice, to motivate a specific action (such as the rescue of an heir or the creation of a female monster). In both cases, the narrator gives far more information than the person listening to him needs. His narrative has a therapeutic as well as a practical effect.

Danvers, like Mr. Collins in *Caleb Williams* (10–105) and Frankenstein and his monster, does not address the reader directly—his account is filtered through the consciousness of another person before being presented to the reader. Meadows describes his editing process in the following way:

> I do not pretend to have put [Lord Danvers's narrative] down in his exact words. . . . I feel that I have sometimes taken the liberty to interweave with it circumstances, that were not fully known to me till afterwards. . . . I have given lord Danvers's narrative in the first person: without doing so I should scarcely have been able to introduce the

> language in which he described his feelings of compunction and remorse; and in this it has been my desire to be faithful and minute. After this it would have had a wretched effect, if I had been scrupulous to separate what I learned from his lordship's lips, from the things respecting which my information was subsequently more complete; and thus to have formed two narratives, coincident in point of time, and separated only in the sources from which I received them. . . . Let the reader be satisfied that the story is substantially true. I have not consciously narrated one circumstance, or given words to one thought, that does not truly make a part of this memorable story. (250)

Our assessment of the reliability of Lord Danvers's confession is, then, complicated by the fact that we can never be sure what parts of his narrative are his and what elements are added by Meadows. Meadows would rather represent Danvers's feelings faithfully and avoid the "wretched effect" of two overlapping accounts than record the lord's confession with literal accuracy. Like a Godwinian novelist, he shapes the narrator's story to make it coherent, psychologically convincing, and aesthetically pleasing.

Moreover, Meadows proves far from objective in his estimation of Danvers's veracity. A "stranger, a plebeian, and a beggar" (253), he feels that he has neither the power nor the authority to tell Danvers to return his title and possessions to their owner. He cannot resist his aristocratic master's charisma:

> learning [Danvers's story] as I did from the lips of a man, bearing an ancient title, and commanding ample possessions, a man highly educated, of a cultivated mind, who had figured honourably in the field, and who had stood in the presence of princes, it struck me very differently from what it would have done, if I had met with it in a book, and read it as a memoir of incidents that had passed in a former generation. There was much that was commanding in the presence of lord Danvers, and impressive in his voice and his gestures. He had told me, as I firmly believed, the whole truth, without the reserve of a single particle, and had spoken of his misgivings and compunctions in a manner which . . . made his feelings mine. There is something which can scarcely be resisted in the whole effect of a man, who tells you all and speaks to you as ingenuously as he is bound to speak in the presence of his Creator. When he thus surrenders himself into your hands, it is scarcely possible that you should not give him in return your sympathy and your aid. (252)

Here, Meadows is describing the perfect confession, a memoir that is so transparent, so reflective of the self, that it could be presented to God on judgment day.[70] In fact, Danvers's narrative is more powerful to him than a "memoir of incidents that . . . passed in a former generation" because the narrator accompanies it with his "commanding" presence, and "impressive" voice and gestures. Unlike the reader of his text, Meadows is privy to visual and auditory evidence, which, he claims, authenticates the confession.

Danvers's confession reveals, however, that he has been a fraud for virtually his entire adult life. After the death of his elder brother as the result of a duel in Bavaria, his brother's wife gives birth to a boy and dies three days later. With the help of his brother's servant, Cloudesley, Danvers has a stillborn child buried with his sister-in-law and has it certified that this baby is his brother's son and heir. Cloudesley and a Greek woman raise his real nephew in Italy, while Danvers returns to England to claim Julian's inheritance. The success of his "lying, forgery and fraud" astonishes even him: "How little correspondence is there between the outer seeming and the inner substance, especially where no previous suspicion exists in the spectator and hearer! . . . My disguise was but skin-deep; but it served me instead of walls of brass and towers of adamant" (110). He becomes first Lord Alton and then Lord Danvers and keeps his guilty secret for eighteen years. Although Danvers finally reveals his crime to Meadows, and, like Falkland, makes a public confession shortly before his death, his expressions of "compunction and remorse" are not entirely credible. After all, he declares that Julian's death would be preferable to his own exposure as "an imposter": "Rather than this, I confess . . ., I should be well content that any thing however fatal should overtake him, that he should be a bandit, or an assassin, and that, after having gone through a course of atrocities, he should be swept from the earth by an ignominious death" (252). Lord Danvers's desire to maintain "the outer seeming" of a spotless reputation easily outweighs his feelings of remorse.

In fact, Danvers's narrative, related in complete confidence to a single listener, is closer to a Roman Catholic auricular confession than it is to Rousseau's public *Confessions*. As Thomas McFarland has observed, "one may see Rousseau's self-examination as a blabbing to the secular world of the secrets reserved for the priesthood."[71] Unlike Rousseau, Danvers fears public exposure and thus prefers the older type of confession. He makes Meadows his "priest" and ventilates his guilty feelings: "oh, Meadows, you can little think what a relief it is to me to speak of myself without reserve! . . . For nearly twenty years I have not shewn myself to any human creature in the undress of soul. . . . You are not my adversary; and I flatter myself never will be. It is for this reason that I have found gratification in telling you my story with minuteness, and amplifying the parts that appeared to be of importance" (245). Unwilling to reveal himself publicly "in the undress of soul," or to expose himself, like Rousseau, in a text, Danvers seeks to relieve his pent-up emotions through a private confession, and Meadows initially seems willing to absolve his employer.

Near the end of the novel, however, Meadows reveals that his sympathy for Danvers was short-lived:

> It is possible to have a deep sympathy with a criminal: but for that purpose it is necessary either to have known him long previously, and to have watched the better man in him, or, by actual observation or narrative, to have become familiar with his sufferings and struggles. I had not known lord Danvers long. . . . The noble youth, who was enriched with such extraordinary endowments, who had suffered the injustice and obscurity of so many years, and who had just been discharged from so tremendous a condition, was master of all my affections. The comparison between him and his uncle was too much to the disadvantage of the latter. (284–85)

Meadows proves to be fickle indeed. He not only repudiates his previous declarations of sympathy for Danvers, he even goes so far as to suggest that he has not "become familiar with [Danvers's] sufferings and struggles" through "narrative," when, in fact, his employer has described these "sufferings and struggles" to him in an extremely long and detailed confession. Danvers's sincerity, which Meadows never questions, does not guarantee his servant's long-term sympathy, particularly after Meadows becomes enamoured of his master's victim. In *Cloudesley*, Godwin shows that self-exposure can eventually lead to disgust rather than sympathy: no narrator, no matter how charismatic, can completely control an audience's responses to his or her confession.

Unlike Godwin's other protagonists, the eponymous main character of his last novel, *Deloraine*, benefits from a happy childhood and an excellent education. He is the only son of a father who is "an English gentleman with an estate of three thousand pounds a year," and his tutor is "the most amiable and exemplary of men" (7). Deloraine becomes an intelligent and virtuous young man: "My understanding was of no common order; my taste was pure, vivid and refined; my application and learning worthy of the education I had received; and my dispositions noble and generous, full of affection, and formed for the reception and cultivation of friendship" (9). Whereas St. Leon's reckless ambition, Fleetwood's misanthropy, Mandeville's paranoia, and Danvers's treachery are all rooted in their childhood experiences and education, nothing in Deloraine's upbringing foreshadows his later destiny. He becomes a member of parliament, is a man of fashion, and marries Emilia Fitzcharles. While insincerity and suspicion poison the marriages of St. Leon and Fleetwood, Deloraine claims that he and Emilia are always perfectly frank with each other: "We talked to each other, as a man talks to his own soul" (21). But despite all of these advantages, Deloraine becomes a murderer and a fugitive from justice, "the most forlorn and odious of men" (7). Godwin's last novel suggests that there is not always an obvious connection between an individual's fate and his or her early mental development and experiences. Not even a privileged upbringing and an excellent education can guarantee happiness and mental health.

After Emilia's tragic early death, Deloraine remarries. His second wife, Margaret Borradale, is nearly twenty years younger than he, and, like Fleetwood, he becomes a possessive and obsessionally jealous older husband. He knows that Margaret does not really love him—her heart belongs to her childhood sweetheart, William, whom she mistakenly believes dead. When William suddenly reappears in England, Deloraine desperately attempts to prevent the lovers from being reunited. Despite his precautions, however, William and Margaret accidentally encounter each other and, in a "sort of transporting delusion" (143), embrace. Deloraine sees them together and, without hesitation, shoots William:

> I flew to the spot. I had, I scarcely knew why, loaded pistols on my person. The whole passed with the rapidity of lightning. William had barely time to rise from his posture, and make two steps towards me, when I lodged a bullet in his heart. He fell instantly . . . I assumed in my own person the robe and function of public justice. I interposed not a moment for deliberation and the sifting of evidence. . . . The highest and purest of all laws, as I believed, was with me. I saw my wife and her paramour together. (144)

Horrified by her husband's act, Margaret curses him and falls dead over William's corpse.

Deloraine presents this sudden act of violence as an anomaly in an otherwise exemplary life: "My offence, though clothed with every possible aggravation, was but the offence of an instant. In all that went before, and all that followed, I was guiltless. What a momentous deposit therefore, and committed to how frail a custody, is human life!" (285). During this fatal "instant," he mistakenly believes that "The highest and purest of all laws" justifies his murder of his wife's lover. In retrospect, he suggests that his physical condition influenced his aberrant behavior: "when I formed my acquaintance with Margaret, I was just recovered from a very dangerous illness, and was in the middle point as it were between life and death. This cooperated with many other circumstances, to give to my passion for her a diseased tone and a sickly hue. During the whole period of our married life my mind was never robust and steady of nerve, but fluttering and tremblingly alive to every trivial occurrence" (138–39). His passion for Margaret is from the outset "diseased," and when William reappears, Deloraine responds in an irrational and unbalanced way. The positive effects of his happy childhood and first-rate education are eclipsed by his physical illness, which renders him both hypersensitive and irrational.

Whereas Godwin's other confessional narrators typically recount an entire "train of follies" (*Fleetwood*, 64), Deloraine focuses on one event. His one crime transforms him from a respected member of society to a hated outcast: "Like Cain, I have a mark trenched in my forehead, that all men should shrink from me" (7). By dwelling on this single lapse, and suggesting that it is rooted in his mistaken notions of honor and sickly condition, he deflects the reader's and perhaps his own attention from his obsessional desire to possess and dominate the women in his life.[72] He believes strongly that women should subordinate themselves to men: "Man is the substantive thing in the terrestrial creation: woman is but the adjective, that cannot stand by itself" (29). Although he acknowledges Emilia's intelligence, Deloraine loves her because she seems indistinguishable from himself; he particularly adores her willingness to "confess her error the instant she [is] aware of it" (23). His desire to possess Margaret is even more intense: "I could not bear that she should be out of my sight. I was like a child, with a new and favourite toy, who, if it is withdrawn from him for a moment, vents his displeasure in piteous sobs and piercing cries . . . I tendered her as the apple of my eye" (139). He admits that he would rather see her dead than embraced by another (136). After Deloraine kills William, and shortly before her own death, Margaret finally rebels: "Monster!

. . . was it for this I married you? delivered myself unreservedly into your hands? . . . My life has been all submission, submission to my father, submission to my husband. But it shall be so no longer. Out of my sight, most odious of all created things!" (144). Deloraine's daughter, Catherine, also sacrifices herself for him, accompanying and protecting him as he flees from justice. She declares that she has "no destination in life, no office concentrating all the powers of [her] nature, but that of being devoted to [his] service and advantage" (161). Thus Deloraine is either misleading the reader or deluding himself when he asserts that he has only committed one "offence" in his life: he has also selfishly exploited his wives and daughter.

While Rousseau's *Confessions* tries to enlist the reader's sympathy, Deloraine assumes that his readers, if they even exist, will be repelled by his story: "Why . . . do I pen this history? Who can sympathise with me? Who can endure to peruse the tale?" He believes, however, that his "narrative has its atoning features." First, it is a memorial to his two wives and daughter, who exhibit "whatever is most precious, and admirable, and life-giving in human nature" (285). Second, it is a moral exemplum that teaches the reader that a single crime can condemn an otherwise virtuous person to a life of misery and remorse. Yet, despite these "atoning features," Deloraine gives his "successors" permission to destroy his manuscript. He is unsure whether he wants to reveal himself to the reader as Rousseau does in *Confessions*, or, like Rousseau in *Rêveries*, to write solely for himself: "If [my tale] never see the light, it will yet have served a temporary purpose to myself." Although his narrative has functioned therapeutically as "a sort of diversion [from his] anguish," he believes that he lacks one of the primary inspirations of a writer of confessions: a sympathetic reader. Torn between his conflicting desires to preserve and erase his life story, Deloraine withholds his real name from the reader and ends his narrative with the hope that his tale will in fifty or one hundred years be considered as legendary as "the records of Haroun Al Raschid" (286), the author of *Arabian Nights*. The prospect of complete transparency can hardly be attractive to "the most forlorn and odious of men."

Mary Shelley's most famous confessional narratives are those of Frankenstein and his monster in *Frankenstein*. Like Lord Danvers's account in *Cloudesley*, Frankenstein's story is recorded by the person who listens to it, and the monster's tale, retold by Frankenstein and then written down by Walton, is twice removed from the source. Unlike Danvers, however, Frankenstein reasserts his authorial control over his narrative by editing it: "Frankenstein discovered that I made notes concerning his history: he asked to see them, and then himself corrected and augmented them in many places; but principally in giving the life and spirit to the conversations he held with his enemy. 'Since you have preserved my narration,' said he, 'I would not that a mutilated one should go down to posterity' " (*The Mary Shelley Reader*, 155). Yet, although Frankenstein ostensibly revises Walton's manuscript to make it more accurate (and presumably to increase his own transparency), his life history and the monster's autobiography are, in Barbara Johnson's words, "clearly attempts at persuasion rather than simple accounts of facts."[73] After detailing the monster's crimes, Frankenstein attempts to persuade Walton to "thrust [his] sword into [the monster's] heart" (154), and the monster recites his narrative in order to convince Frankenstein to create a female monster. The fact that Frankenstein and the monster use their narratives to manipulate the emotions and motivate the actions of their listeners should undermine our faith in the transparency of their self-representations.

David Marshall compares the monster's autobiographical impulse to Rousseau's: "Like Rousseau, the monster puts his faith in autobiography, believing that everything depends on his ability to move the heart of his listener: to inflame his passions, to elicit his compassion."[74] "Listen to my tale," the monster says to Frankenstein, "when you have heard that, abandon or commiserate me, as you shall judge that I deserve" (75). Both Godwin and Shelley praised Rousseau's eloquence,[75] and the monster and Frankenstein also possess this trait. Frankenstein tells Walton that the monster "is eloquent and persuasive; and once his words had even power over my heart" (154). According to Walton, Frankenstein's "eloquence is forcible and touching; nor can I hear him, when he relates a pathetic incident, or endeavours to move the passions of pity or love, without tears" (155).

Frankenstein's and the monster's autobiographical outpourings have, however, a limited effect. The monster's narrative motivates his creator to begin work on a female monster, but another "train of reflection" subsequently influences Frankenstein, and he abandons his task, tearing the unfinished "thing" (123) to pieces. As the monster himself realizes, his autobiography is open to a number of interpretations and may inspire condemnation rather than compassion. In fact, his sincerity works against him: by confessing his murder of William and his incrimination of Justine Moritz, the monster makes a case against the creation of another being like himself. Similarly, Walton does not honor Frankenstein's request to kill his creation: "my first impulses, which had suggested to me the duty of obeying the dying request of my friend, in destroying his enemy, were . . . suspended by a mixture of curiosity and compassion" (161). In spite of his indignation towards the creature who destroyed his friend's life, Walton feels "touched by the expressions of his misery" (162). Like *Cloudesley*, *Frankenstein* suggests that although autobiographical accounts can elicit sympathy and motivate action, particularly if they are narrated with eloquence and passion to a receptive listener, their influence can prove ephemeral. In the narrator's absence the confession loses its emotive power, and the listener can be influenced by other charismatic individuals or trains of thought.

In both Frankenstein's and the monster's autobiographical accounts, the narrators attempt to show how external circumstances form their minds and how the trains of thought that these circumstances initiate shape their lives. Frankenstein tells Walton that "nothing can alter [his] destiny," and his "history" will show "how irrevocably it is determined" (25). The monster, abandoned immediately after his creation and hated and attacked by everyone he meets, declares that he is "malicious because [he is] miserable" (107). Anne Mellor correctly asserts that the 1818 edition of *Frankenstein* is less fatalistic than the 1832 edition.[76] In neither version, however, does Frankenstein believe that he completely controls his destiny. He alludes to fate or destiny a number of times in the 1818 edition (*The Mary Shelley Reader*, 25, 29, 31, 37, 134, 156), identifying, for example, natural philosophy as "the genius that has regulated [his] fate" (29). Moreover, his account of his education in both editions focuses on certain events in his mental development that affect the course of his life. For instance, Frankenstein asserts that if his father had explained that "the principles of Agrippa had been entirely exploded" (29), "the train of [his] ideas would never have received the fatal impulse that led to [his] ruin" (30). Other circumstances serve to reinforce Frankenstein's fatalism: in retrospect, he regards the tragic death of his mother from scarlet fever as "an omen . . . of [his] future misery" (32) and believes that his meeting with M. Waldman, a professor at the University of Ingolstadt who encourages him to study modern chemistry, determined his "future destiny" (37).

Likewise, in *Confessions* Rousseau describes how during a walk to visit Diderot at Vincennes his life was completely changed because he happened to read about a prize offered by the Dijon Academy:

> One day I took the *Mercure de France* and, glancing through it as I walked, I came upon this question propounded by the Dijon Academy for the next year's prize: Has the progress of the sciences and arts done more to corrupt morals or improve them? The moment I read this I beheld another universe and became another man. . . . All the rest of my life and of my misfortunes followed inevitably as a result of that moment's madness.
>
> [Je pris un jour *le Mercure de France* et tout en marchant et le parcourant je tombai sur cette question proposée par l'Académie de Dijon pour le prix de l'année suivante: *Si le progrès des sciences et des arts a contribué à corrompre ou à épurer les moeurs*? A l'instant de cette lecture je vis un autre univers et je devins un autre homme. . . . Toute le reste de ma vie et de mes malheurs fut l'effet inévitable de cet instant d'égarement.][77]

Like the accidents of Frankenstein's education, Rousseau's fortuitous reading of *le Mercure de France* profoundly affects his subsequent life. What Godwin calls "the empire of circumstances" plays a role in both confessional narratives.

The monster has even less control over his mental development than Frankenstein does. Several commentators have noted that Shelley's depiction of the monster's development owes a great deal to eighteenth-century sensationalist and associative psychology. While Peter Brooks contends that "his first ideas demonstrate the processes of Lockean sensationalism and Hartleyan associationism," Sue Weaver Schopf argues persuasively that Shelley's "reliance upon Hartley [in the monster's narrative] suggests that [she], like her father, subscribed to the doctrines of mechanistic determinism and that she was a thoroughgoing empiricist, convinced of the essential goodness of human nature but equally certain that early sensative experiences largely determine what we become as adults."[78] The monster tells Frankenstein that his narrative will show how external events formed his character: "I shall relate events that impressed me with feelings which, from what I was, have made me what I am" (86). By the time Frankenstein marries Elizabeth Lavenza, the monster considers himself "the slave, not the master of an impulse which [he] detest[s], yet [can]not disobey" (162). In Percy Shelley's review of *Frankenstein*, he writes that the monster's "crimes and malevolence . . . flow inevitably from certain causes fully adequate to their production. They are the children . . . of Necessity and Human Nature. . . . Treat a person ill, and he will become wicked."[79] His review echoes the monster's own explanation of his "crimes and malevolence": "My vices are the children of a forced solitude that I abhor" (109).

Thus, whereas both Frankenstein and the monster concede that they have committed a number of transgressions, they also suggest that they have been victimized by environmental conditioning, their passions, and unfortunate circumstances. Their narratives are, like Rousseau's *Confessions*, partly vindications. In the famous story of the stolen ribbon, Rousseau admits that his false accusation of a servant girl is a crime, but he pleads that the mitigating factors of his youth and weakness should be taken into account.[80] Similarly, both Frankenstein and the monster offer a number of extenuating circumstances in their narratives that serve to deflect criticism and inspire sympathy. In fact, on his deathbed Frankenstein claims that his creation of the monster was the result of "a fit of enthusiastic madness," and that he has nothing to reproach himself with: "During these last days I have been occupied in examining my past conduct; nor do I find it blameable" (160). And the monster considers himself as much a victim as a criminal: "Am I to be thought the only criminal, when all human kind sinned against me?" (163).[81] They suggest that since they are the products of their social and environmental conditioning, they cannot be held fully accountable for their actions.

Frankenstein seems, however, much more autonomous than Shelley's other confessional narrators. For example, Frankenstein's decision to destroy the female monster can be considered as an act of free will, even though he performs it while "trembling with passion" (123). In contrast, several of Shelley's other protagonists can legitimately claim to be helpless victims, suffering, in some cases, because of their virtues rather than their crimes. While Frankenstein and his monster, like the Rousseau of *Confessions*, present themselves as part victims, part transgressors, the eponymous narrator of *Mathilda*, Beatrice of Ferrara in *Valperga*, Lionel Verney in *The Last Man*, and the unnamed protagonist of "The Parvenue" appear to be victims who bear little, if any, responsibility for the tragic events that have befallen them. After the tragic deaths of her husband and two of their children (William and Clara), Shelley began to conceive of destiny as a "net" made up of innumerable threads or meshes that imperceptibly enshroud its victim. Lionel Verney, the narrator of *The Last Man*, asks: "Who, after a great disaster, has not looked back with wonder at his inconceivable obtuseness of understanding, that could not perceive the many minute threads with which fate weaves the inextricable net of our destinies, until he is inmeshed completely in it?" (257). Similarly, in her last novel, *Falkner*, Shelley describes how tragedy is often rooted in "trivial events":

> Whoever has been the victim of a tragic event—whoever has experienced life and hope—the past and the future wrecked by one fatal catastrophe, must be at once dismayed and awestruck to trace the secret agency of a thousand foregone, disregarded, and trivial events, which all led to the deplored end, and served . . . as invisible meshes to envelop the victim in the fatal net. Had the meanest among these been turned aside, the progress of the destroying destiny had been stopped; but there is no voice to cry "Hold!" no prophesying eye to discern the unborn event—and the future inherits its whole portion of woe. (25)

The narrators of what I will call Shelley's "victim-confessions" are all women with the exception of Lionel Verney, and Verney is "feminine" in his preference for the domestic sphere over the traditionally masculine realms of politics and warfare (see *The Last Man*, 158). I will argue that these victim-confessions reflect Shelley's desire to rework the confessional form established by male writers like St. Augustine and Rousseau so that it can reflect the experiences, aspirations, and socially imposed limitations of women. Unlike Rousseau, Shelley's female protagonists are reluctant to expose themselves to public view and tend to write confessions in order to vent their emotions rather than to seek vindication or self-knowledge. Although their narratives are not entirely free from feelings of guilt, their guilt frequently stems from their belief that they must have done something to deserve their terrible sufferings. In the cases of Mathilda, Verney, and Shelley herself there is also the guilt of the survivor. They are all haunted by the same question: why was I spared while everyone I loved perished?

Two important literary precursors of Shelley's victim-confessions are, of course, Mary Wollstonecraft's *Mary, A Fiction* (1788) and *The Wrongs of Woman* (1798), both of which present the mental histories of women who struggle against injustice, emotional deprivation, and despair in male-dominated societies. Shelley's Mathilda, like Wollstonecraft's Mary and Maria, is presented as an intelligent and sensitive woman who desperately longs for love and sympathy. According to Janet Todd, "All three novels have at their centres the exploration of the identity and subjectivity of women caught within the 'magic circle' of constructed femininity and the claustrophobic nuclear family unit."[82] While Mary is "Neglected in every respect, and left to the operations of her own mind,"[83] Mathilda, whose mother dies after her birth and whose father abandons her to be raised by his cold-hearted sister, is also "a solitary being" (185) who is "entirely thrown upon [her] own resources" (183). In these works, the destinies of the female characters are largely determined by others: Mary is forced to marry a boy of fifteen whom she does not even know, Maria's husband is "a heartless, unprincipled wretch" who has her imprisoned in a madhouse,[84] and Mathilda's life is ruined when her father returns from his travels, is overcome by an incestuous passion for her, and commits suicide. Mary's entries into her "little book,"[85] the memoirs that Maria addresses to her daughter, and Mathilda's life story are, then, narratives by women whose "fate[s] [are] governed by necessity, a hideous necessity" (*The Mary Shelley Reader*, 176). The errors and crimes they have to recount are for the most part those of their parents or their husbands rather than their own.

Whereas Rousseau writes his confession to reveal and, in some ways, vindicate himself to his readers, the narrator of *Mathilda* lacks a sense of purpose. Because she has no desire for public exposure and her narrative is neither a vindication nor a moral exemplum, she, like the protagonist of "The Parvenue," does not know why she must tell her story: "a feeling that I cannot define leads me on and I am too weak both in body and mind to resist the slightest impulse" (175). She asserts that she is a victim rather than a transgressor: "I record no crimes; my faults may easily be pardoned; for they proceeded not from evil motive but from want of judgement; and I believe few would say that they could, by a different conduct and superior wisdom, have avoided the misfortunes to which I am the victim" (176). However, while she can persuade herself that she does not possess an "evil motive," she comes to suspect that the human mind is subject to unconscious impulses, such as the one that leads her to write her life history, and that there may be a "crime . . . in involuntary feeling" (197).

Although Mathilda's desire to discover the secret of her

father's unhappiness in order to help him deal with it is praiseworthy, it leads to disaster when she compels him to admit his incestuous desire for her. In retrospect, she blames herself for forcing him to reveal his feelings for her:

> His paroxisms [*sic*] of passion were terrific but his soul bore him through them triumphant, though almost destroyed by victory; but the day would finally have been won had not I, foolish and presumptuous wretch! hurried him on until there was no recall, no hope. . . . I! I alone was the cause of his defeat and justly did I pay the fearful penalty. I said to myself, let him receive sympathy and these struggles will cease. . . . I will win him to me; he shall not deny his grief to me and when I know his secret then will I pour a balm into his soul and again I shall enjoy the ravishing delight of beholding his smile, and of again seeing his eyes beam if not with pleasure at least with gentle love and thankfulness. (197)

She wants to become his mental anatomist in order to ease his pain, but she fails to recognize, until it is too late, that there may be good reasons for his reticence, and that she may not be the right person to "know his secret." Thus Mathilda finds reasons to feel guilty even though she regards herself as the victim of "hideous necessity." Paradoxically, one source of guilt is her generous impulse to end her father's pain: her filial devotion to him leads to their destruction.

However, Mathilda's narrative, meant to be read after her death by her friend Woodville, is, at least ostensibly, an explanation of her death wish rather than an attempt to deal with her unresolved feelings for her father. While in *Confessions* Rousseau attempts to tell his reader "all that has happened to [him], all that [he has] done, all that [he has] felt," Mathilda sharply focuses her narrative: she aspires neither to complete self-knowledge nor to complete self-exposure. She details her mental development in order to show how her childhood prepared her for destruction: "During the early part of my life there is little to relate, and I will be brief; but I must be allowed to dwell a little on the years of my childhood that it may be apparent how when one hope failed all life was to be a blank; and how when the only affection I was permitted to cherish was blasted my existence was extinguished with it" (182). Her sense of powerlessness is clear: she is only "permitted to cherish" a single affection, and when that is "blasted" she no longer has anything left to live for. Woodville's optimistic belief (both Godwinian and Percy Shelleyan) that one should strive for knowledge in order to free future generations from "what are now the necessary evils of life" (237) does not console her. She feels "polluted by the unnatural love [she has] inspired" (238), and Woodville's suggestion that she can assuage her own griefs by helping others only serves to reinforce her belief that she is a social outcast: "when I saw Woodville and day after day he tried to win my confidence . . . , I was impressed more strongly with the withering fear that I was in truth a marked creature, a pariah, only fit for death" (239). He urges her to "bestow happiness" (238), but she remembers that her attempt to make her father happy resulted in disaster. Although Woodville may be right when he says that "Socrates, . . . Shakespear, [and] *Rousseau*" had a positive influence on "millions" (emphasis added, 237), Mathilda does not see how his vision of male empowerment applies to her.

Like Wollstonecraft's *The Wrongs of Woman*, *Mathilda* shows how women are turned into "monsters" in a male-dominated society.[86] Mathilda rails against a fate that she ironically genders as female:

> Why when fate drove me to become this outcast from human feeling; this monster with whom none might mingle in converse and love; why had she not from that fatal and most accursed moment, shrouded me in thick mists and placed real darkness between me and my fellows so that I might never more be seen; and as I passed, like a murky cloud loaded with blight, they might only perceive me by the cold chill I should cast upon them; telling them, how truly, that something unholy was near? (239)

By revealing his incestuous passion for her, her father has disabled her from establishing relationships with others. Similarly, the monster's "father," Frankenstein, is responsible for making his creation into an "outcast from human feeling." But at least the monster can seek compensation and then vengeance from the man who condemned him to a lonely and loveless existence; Mathilda's father is dead, and she can neither reproach nor forgive him. *Mathilda* is, in some ways, a version of *Frankenstein* told from the point of view of Elizabeth Lavenza, one of the helpless victims of Frankenstein's misguided obsession. It anticipates Theodore Roszak's *The Memoirs of Elizabeth Frankenstein* (1995), in which Elizabeth's narrative closes with her laying on her marriage "bed like the sacrificial lamb awaiting the expiatory stroke."[87] After carelessly exposing herself to cold and wet conditions outdoors, Mathilda contracts consumption and quickly wastes away. Transformed by circumstances and by her father into a "monster with whom none might mingle in converse and love," she happily leaves a world in which her virtues, her filial devotion to her father, and her capacity to love help to destroy her.

As a contribution to "the science of the human mind," *Mathilda* offers insights into the psychology of victimization. It depicts a victim who feels guilty about an error that precipitates a tragedy, even though that error is well-intentioned, and who also feels guilty as the result of being associated with a transgressive and unnatural act, even though she repudiates the act, which is never actually committed. Unlike Rousseau's and Godwin's confessional narratives, however, *Mathilda* casts doubt on the positive influence of sincerity. Mathilda believes that she can help her father overcome his grief if he will confide in her, but his sincere admission of his incestuous passion has a destructive rather than salutary effect. It is even possible, Mathilda speculates, that if her father had been left alone, he could have overcome his obsession (197).[88] Mathilda, who is only sixteen when her father returns from his travels, can neither understand nor help cure his mental disorder. Rather than respect his determination to keep his secret hidden, she badgers him until he makes his fatal confession. In a sense, she "overpower[s] his more sober judgment" by compelling him to reveal feelings that she cannot deal with. *Mathilda* suggests that absolute sincerity is not always desirable. With this judgment, many eighteenth- and nineteenth-century readers of Rousseau's *Confessions* would agree. In fact, Shelley herself considered Rousseau's public reading of *Confessions* an inexcusable lapse in ethics: "We cannot justify his thus dragging the private life of his existent friends before the world: it is the most flagrant dishonesty in civilised society, and ought to be put on a par with picking pockets."[89] For Shelley, sincerity that hurts others can never be justified.

Like *Mathilda*, Beatrice of Ferrara's narrative in *Valperga* is the tale of an imaginative and passionate woman who, despite her desire to do good and her affectionate nature, is psychologically abused and driven to the edge of madness. But although Beatrice's life story is informed by the same kind of deterministic psychology that undergirds Mathilda's account and Rousseau's *Confessions*, Shelley suggests that Beatrice inherited some of her mental characteristics from her mother, Wilhelmina of Bohemia, who dies when her daughter is two years old. A late thirteenth-century heretic, Wilhelmina "secretly form[s] a sect, founded on the . . . belief, that she [is] the Holy Ghost incarnate upon earth for the salvation of the female sex" (130–31). The orphaned Beatrice (Shelley never identifies her father) is briefly cared for by a leper and then is adopted by the Bishop of Ferrara, who hopes that he will be able to raise her as an orthodox Catholic. In spite of his teachings, however, she gives "herself up to contemplation and solitude, and . . . the wild dreams of her imagination." The Bishop fears that "her mother's soul ha[s] descended into her" (136). She inherits her mother's imagination and charisma, but is denied knowledge of Wilhelmina's feminism. As Barbara Jane O'Sullivan has observed, "Breaking the link between Wilhelmina and Beatrice . . . is a political maneuver, aimed at undermining the development of a female subculture that threatens the social stability of the patriarchy."[90]

"Beatrice seems almost born to be a victim" because men limit and thwart her aspirations as a prophet.[91] Dominican inquisitors arrest her for prophesying, and, after she has survived (with the help of some monks) the "*Judgement of God*" (139), Castruccio, the novel's ambitious male protagonist, seduces her and then callously breaks off their relationship: "he was obliged to undeceive her; and the hand, that tore away the ties her trusting heart had bound round itself, at the same time tore away the veil which had for her invested all nature, and shewed her life as it was—naked and appalling" (153). As Shelley points out, Beatrice is the victim of medieval superstitions, her youth, and the fact that she has fallen in love for the first time:

> Unhappy prophetess! the superstitions of her times had obtained credit for, and indeed given birth to her pretensions, and the compassion and humanity of her fellow creatures had stamped them with the truth-attesting seal of a miracle. . . . Beatrice was hardly seventeen, and she loved for the first time; and all the exquisite pleasures of that passion were consecrated to her, by a mysteriousness and delusive sanctity that gave them tenfold zest. (152)

Like Mathilda, Beatrice responds to psychological trauma by isolating and mortifying herself: while Mathilda dresses like a nun and becomes a recluse, Beatrice, "possessed by a spirit of martyrdom" (253), dresses "as the meanest pilgrim" (254) and goes to humble herself before Euthanasia, the woman Castruccio loves.

After leaving Euthanasia, she continues her penitential journey, and the chief of a band of sadists captures her. She later describes the effects of her captivity:

> what I saw, and what I endured, is a tale for the unhallowed ears of infidels, or for those who have lost humanity in the sight of blood . . . It has changed me, much changed me, to have been witness of these scenes; I entered young, I came out grey, old and withered; I went in innocent; and, if innocence consist in ignorance, I am now guilty of the knowledge of crime, which it would seem that fiends alone could contrive. (257)

Beatrice's sense of guilt, like Mathilda's, stems from the knowledge rather than the commission of crime. Her psychopathic captor tortures her until she becomes mad (258), but she finally escapes and, in celebration of her liberation from male tyranny, embraces "the rough trunks of . . . old trees, as if they were my sisters in freedom and delight" (259). An old Paterin, or "one who believes in the ascendancy of the evil spirit in the world" (241), then befriends Beatrice. He converts her to his heresy, and she becomes convinced that God is an evil, sadistic patriarch: "surely God's hand is the chastening hand of a father, that thus torments his children! His children? his eternal enemies!" (243). Whereas Mathilda is victimized by her love-starved childhood and her father's aberrant passion, Beatrice is thwarted, abused, and traumatized by inquisitors, her lover, and a medieval de Sade—men who take away both her freedom and her innocence. Deprived, like Mathilda, of maternal guidance, she can never achieve any measure of autonomy, and she dies still obsessed with Castruccio, the man who spurned her. Her narrative, although it allows her to ventilate her emotions, does not provide her with the self-knowledge that Rousseau seeks in *Confessions* or the kinds of insights that would enable her to avoid her past mistakes.

Like Mathilda, the unnamed female narrator of "The Parvenue" (1837) cannot explain why she feels compelled to relate her "melancholy story" (*Collected Tales and Stories*, 266). She sees herself as a victim, punished not for any crimes she has committed, but for her dutiful and altruistic nature. The daughter of a former land steward, she grows up poor but virtuous. Her saintly mother teaches her "the precepts of the gospel, charity to every fellow-creature, the brotherhood of mankind, [and] the rights that every sentient creature possesses to our services" (267). When her family's cottage burns down, she is rescued by an aristocrat, Lord Reginald Desborough, who soon after proposes marriage to the "untaught, low-born, portionless girl." Although she thinks his proposal "very strange" (268), she accepts, and they are married. Unfortunately, Lord Reginald retains many of his aristocratic prejudices and objects to her many charities, particularly when she gives money to the poor rather than spending it on a gown in order to outshine "all competitors at a fête" (269). Their marriage begins to unravel as she persists in being charitable and providing money to her greedy relatives, who are intent on taking advantage of her selflessness. Her husband finally gives her an ultimatum: "either give up your parents and your family, whose rapacity and crimes deserve no mercy, or we part for ever" (273). Forced to choose between Lord Reginald and her mother, who is dying, she chooses her mother. After her parents' deaths, she writes to her husband, but he spurns her. Heartbroken, she decides to join her sister in America, where she expects a speedy death.

The destiny of the protagonist of "The Parvenue" is predetermined by her upbringing: "a sort of instinct or sentiment of justice, the offspring of my lowly paternal hearth and my mother's enlightened piety, was deeply implanted in my mind, that all had as good a right to the comforts of life as myself, or even as my husband" (269). As in the other victim-confessions I have discussed, the narrator sees herself as a martyr, punished for her virtues in an androcentric world. She believes that she was, in effect, "consumed at the stake a martyr for [her] faith": "for many years I have wasted at the slow fire of knowing that I lost my husband's affections because I performed what I believed to be a duty" (270). Like Mathilda and Beatrice, the parvenue lacks even the limited degree of autonomy enjoyed by Rousseau (as he presents himself in *Confessions*) and by Godwin's and Shelley's male characters. While St. Leon and Frankenstein suffer as the result of their overreaching ambition and Rousseau admits to having committed a number of shameful and immoral acts, the main "error" of Mathilda, Beatrice, and the parvenue is naïveté. Their narratives are indictments of male irresponsibility and ruthlessness rather than self-justifications.

Although Lionel Verney, the narrator of *The Last Man*, is not a female protagonist, he is, like Mathilda and the parvenue, the victim of forces beyond his control. A worldwide plague determines his destiny by exterminating all of humankind except himself. After his last two companions drown, Verney pays tribute to fate's omnipotence: "fate had administered life to me, when the plague had already seized on its prey—she had dragged me by the hair from out the strangling waves—By such miracles she had bought me for her own; I admitted her authority, and bowed to her decrees" (337–38). One of his motivations for writing his narrative is to remember his dead friends and family: "I had used this history as an opiate; while it described my beloved friends, fresh with life and glowing with hope; active assistants to the scene, I was soothed; there will be a more melancholy pleasure in painting the end of all" (192). He also writes for "the reader" (see 57, 59, 193, 291, 318, 331), despite the fact that he is the last person on earth. Verney's confessional impulse is, however, so powerful that he is compelled to imagine a future race of intelligent beings capable of deciphering his writings:

> Will not the reader tire, if I should minutely describe our long-drawn journey from Paris to Geneva? . . . Patience, oh reader! whoever thou art, wherever thou dwellest, whether of race spiritual, or, sprung from some surviving pair, thy nature will be human, thy habitation the earth; thou wilt here read of the acts of the extinct race, and wilt ask wonderingly, if they, who suffered what thou findest recorded, were of frail flesh and soft organization like thyself. Most true, they were—weep therefore; for surely, solitary being, thou wilt be of gentle disposition; shed compassionate tears; but the while lend thy attention to the tale. (291)

Verney first speculates that the reader will be "of race spiritual," but he soon concludes that the reader will be human, an earth dweller, "of frail flesh and soft organization," solitary, gentle, and compassionate. In describing this reader, Verney—who is also solitary, and was, before the deaths of his family members, a gentle and compassionate family man—describes himself. Like many of Godwin's and Shelley's confessional narratives, *The Last Man* is partly an address to the reader and partly an interior dialogue. It has elements of both Rousseau's *Confessions* and his *Rêveries*.

Like Mathilda and the parvenue, Verney is partly a self-projection of Mary Shelley. *Mathilda* can be seen as Shelley's attempt to deal with her conflicted relationship with Godwin, and "The Parvenue" recalls "her pent-up feelings of inferiority and imposition derived from her years as Shelley's mistress, wife and widow."[92] *The Last Man* reflects her feelings of loneliness following the deaths of two of her children (William and Clara), as well as Percy Shelley, Edward Williams, and Byron.[93] In the 14 May 1824 entry in her journal, Shelley wrote: "The last man! Yes I may well describe that solitary being's feelings, feeling myself as the last relic of a beloved race, my companions, extinct before me—."[94] She made her next journal entry after learning that Byron had died: "What do I do here? Why . . . am I doomed to live on seeing all expire before me? God grant I may die young. . . . At the age of twenty six I am in the condition of an aged person—all my old friends are gone—I have no wish to form new.''[95]

While *Mathilda*, Beatrice's narrative, and ''The Parvenue'' explore the psyches of victims, *The Last Man* makes the mind of a lonely survivor transparent. Verney, like Mathilda and the parvenue, longs for death but refuses to commit suicide: ''Why did I continue to live—why not throw off the weary weight of time, and with my own hand, let out the fluttering prisoner from my agonized breast? . . . But this would not do. I had, from the moment I had reasoned on the subject, instituted myself the subject to fate, and the servant of necessity, the visible laws of the invisible God'' (337). In a universe governed by fate, necessity, and God, the only real choice humans have is to resign themselves to their sufferings. Mathilda and Verney also console themselves with the thought that they will rejoin their loved ones in death.

While Verney becomes ''the servant of necessity,'' *The Last Man* contains another character who at least temporarily transcends his circumstances. Adrian is raised by his widowed mother to regain the British throne: ''The ex-queen . . . turned all her thoughts to the educating her son Adrian, second Earl of Windsor, so as to accomplish her ambitious ends; and with his mother's milk he imbibed, and was intended to grow up in the steady purpose of re-acquiring his lost crown'' (13). Despite his mother's efforts to condition him, however, Adrian becomes a republican and a philanthropist: ''He gave not only a brief denial to his mother's schemes, but published his intention of using his influence to diminish the power of the aristocracy, to effect a greater equalization of wealth and privilege, and to introduce a perfect system of republican government into England.'' Adrian's mind, ''gifted . . . by every natural grace, endowed with transcendant [*sic*] powers of intellect'' (30), overcomes his upbringing, whereas Godwin's St. Leon, who is also raised by an ambitious, aristocratic mother, never outgrows the influence of his early education. Of course Adrian is a privileged male and thus more empowered than Shelley's female protagonists, but he nevertheless remains an example in her fiction of an individual who rises above his circumstances.

The issue of sincerity is much less important in Shelley's victim-confessions than in Rousseau's *Confessions*, Godwin's novels, or *Frankenstein* because their protagonists have few, if any, shameful secrets to hide. Mathilda seems the least sincere of these narrators: her sincerity with her father had, after all, dire consequences. She will only reveal the existence of her father's incestuous passion posthumously, through a narrative addressed to her friend Woodville, and her father is never named. In contrast, Beatrice eagerly tells her life story to Euthanasia and, despite the existence of the Inquisition, does not hesitate to confess her heretical beliefs. The parvenue, confused by the "thick clouds" that obscure her "destiny" (*Collected Tales and Stories*, 271), is content to narrate her tale and "let others judge" (266) her. Verney, of course, has absolutely no reason to be insincere: there is no one alive to read his memoirs, and he believes that if another race of intelligent beings comes into existence, they will be reading his memoirs in the distant future, long after his death. Unlike Caleb Williams, who worries that "the world may . . . hear and repeat a half-told and mangled tale" of Falkland's "errors," and Frankenstein, who revises Walton's manuscript to avoid leaving a "mutilated" account of his life "to posterity," Mathilda, Beatrice, and the parvenue have little interest in the world's or posterity's opinion of them. A need for emotional ventilation rather than a desire to set the record straight motivates and inspires their narratives. Shelley's victim-narrators are not ambitious like St. Leon and Frankenstein, or vengeful like Mandeville and Frankenstein's monster. They are more interested in helping their families than in saving humankind or destroying their enemies. In fact, these victim-narrators lack most of the motivations that Rousseau has for making his mind transparent. Their autobiographical narratives have some therapeutic value, but, unlike Rousseau, they do not feel the need to vindicate themselves to posterity, and they have no crimes or errors that they feel require public confession.

The narrators of Shelley's victim-confessions contribute, however, to the "science of mind" by exploring the ways in which victims respond to trauma. Moreover, in *Mathilda*, *The Last Man*, and "The Parvenue," Shelley portrays characters who share neither Rousseau's exhibitionistic impulses nor his desire for complete independence. Shelley attacks Rousseau in her biographical essay for espousing "entire independence, even of natural duties": "the independence that finds duty an unwelcome clog—that regards the just claims of our fellow-creatures as injurious and intolerable, and that casts off the affections as troublesome shackles—is one of the greatest errors that the human heart can nourish; and such was the independence to which Rousseau aspired when he neglected the first duty of man by abandoning his children."[96]

In contrast, Mathilda, Verney, and the parvenue are steadfast in their devotion to their relatives. Whereas Rousseau places his illegitimate offspring in the Foundling Hospital in order to preserve his freedom, the narrators of *Mathilda*, *The Last Man*, and "The Parvenue" sacrifice at least some of their independence in order to perform their duty to their "fellow-creatures." These narrators suffer a great deal, but at least they avoid what Shelley regards as "one of the greatest errors that the human heart can nourish": the pursuit of personal autonomy at the expense of family obligations. Moreover, Shelley's works suggest that given the dominant influence circumstances have over human destiny, the quest for complete independence is futile as well as unconscionable.

Unlike Shelley's victim-narrators, the title character of her last novel, *Falkner* (1837), commits a criminal act: the abduction of Alithea Neville, whom he has loved since childhood, and whom he wants to "free" (*Falkner*, 185) from her unworthy husband. Falkner's crime results in tragedy: Alithea, determined to do her duty as a wife and mother, drowns trying to escape from him. He and his henchman then bury her in a secret grave. "Falkner's Narrative" is written in an attempt to vindicate Alithea, whose mysterious disappearance leads to a great deal of malicious speculation, and to show that Falkner himself is not "quite a monster": "I reveal the secrets of my heart and dwell on the circumstances that led to the fatal catastrophe I record, so that, though a criminal, I do not appear quite a monster" (154). However, although Falkner does not consider himself a monster, he has some resemblances to Frankenstein's creation. Falkner's character, like the monster's, is shaped by abuse and neglect: "Since my birth—or at least since I had lost my mother in early infancy, my path had been cast upon thorns and brambles—blows and stripes, cold neglect, reprehension, and debasing slavery; to such was I doomed" (162). His Rousseauistic narrative is a description of the "train of circumstances, or rather of feelings, that [hurries him] first to error, then to crime" (157). He repeatedly refers to "fate" (153, 174, 177) and considers himself "the slave of headlong impulse" (156). Like the monster, he is driven to criminal behavior by his desperate need for sympathy and love.

Although Falkner will not "arraign [his] Creator" as the monster does Frankenstein, he asserts that his inborn propensities helped to determine his destiny: "The Almighty who framed my miserable being, made me a man of passion" (156). Similarly, in *Confessions* Rousseau assumes that his inherent "degeneracy" affected his behavior. He recalls how he quickly forgot his upbringing by the Lamberciers: "Despite [the most honest education], I must have had a strong inclination towards degeneracy; for I degenerated very rapidly, and without the least difficulty" ["Il faut que, malgré l'éducation la plus honnête, j'eusse un grand penchant à dégénerer; car cela se fit très rapidement, sans la moindre peine"].[97] Unlike Rousseau, however, Falkner never receives an "honest education," and he blames his "evil habits" (163) on the negative influence of his alcoholic father, who physically and verbally abuses him, and the cruel treatment he experiences at school. Following his father's death, he is placed in the home of his coldhearted uncle: "No eye of love ever turned on me, no voice ever spoke a cheering word" (158). From there he is sent away to school, where his "new tyrants" consider him "a little blackguard, quite irreclaimable." At this point in his narrative, Falkner's defiant rhetoric clearly recalls the monster's speeches to Frankenstein: "I declared war with my whole soul against the world; I became all I had been painted; I was sullen, vindictive, desperate" (159).

Desperate "for something to love," Falkner cares for "a little nest of field mice" (162) in his room at school. Unlike the monster, however, he experiences a brief period of happiness: Mrs. Rivers, who serves as his surrogate mother, and her daughter Alithea befriend him. Under Mrs. Rivers's loving guidance, he tries to overcome his "evil habits," but his mistreatment at school undercuts her efforts to socialize him: "I taxed myself to bear with patience the injustice and impertinence of the ushers, and the undisguised tyranny of the master. But I could not for ever string myself to this pitch. Meanness and falsehood, and injustice, again and again awoke the tiger in me. . . . I was doomed" (163). Falkner's school days end when an usher discovers that he has a "little family of mice" in his room and sends a cat after them (164). Falkner throws the cat out of the window and, when the usher attempts to kill the mice with a knife, Falkner wounds his antagonist with his own weapon. Through this violent act, he believes that he has "severed the cords that bound [him] to the vilest servitude" (165).

Falkner's loss of his family of mice is followed by his separation from the Rivers family. He attends "the East Indian military college" (167), and, two years later, Mrs. Rivers dies. Captain Rivers returns to England and violently rebuffs Falkner's request for his daughter's hand in marriage. Vowing to come back to claim Alithea, Falkner sails for India, where he takes the "part [of] the weak, and show[s] contempt for the powerful" (171). He learns the language and respects "the habits and feelings of the natives" (172). In India, his obsession for Alithea grows: "the idea of [her] was so kneaded up and incorporate with my being, that my living heart must have been searched and anatomized to its core, before the portion belonging to her could have been divided from the rest" (172). After ten years in India he inherits his uncle's fortune and returns to England, determined to realize his "tender fancies of domestic union and bliss with Alithea" (173).

Upon his return to England, however, he is thrown into despair when he finds out that Alithea has married Mr. Neville. This discovery proves to be a turning point in his life: "Now began that chain of incidents that led to a deed I had not thought of. Incidents or accidents; acts, done I know not why; nothing in themselves; but meeting, and kindled by the fiery spirit that raged in my bosom, they gave such direction to its ruinous powers, as produced the tragedy for ever to be deplored" (174–75). He meets Mr. Neville by chance, finds him "cold, proud, and sarcastic," and takes a "violent dislike to him" (175). The idea of Alithea's being "bound to that grovelling and loathsome type of the world's worst qualities" (176) is insupportable to him. In retrospect, Falkner considers his abduction of her as an act of madness: "What moved me to this height of insanity—what blinded me to the senseless, as well as the unpardonable nature of my design, I cannot tell; except that, for years, I had lived in a dream, and waking in the real world, I refused to accommodate myself to its necessities, but resolved to bend its laws to my desires" (184). Like the monster, Falkner disregards the value systems of the society that has mistreated and spurned him. Given his "fiery spirit," an unlucky "chain of incidents," and his blindness to the consequences of his actions, his abduction of the woman he has dreamed about for ten years seems almost inevitable.

In fact, Falkner even presents his hasty burial of Alithea, a shockingly sacrilegious act according to the mores of nineteenth-century English society, as the result of his imperfect social conditioning: "I knew little of English customs. I had gone out an inexperienced stripling to India, and my modes of action were formed there. I now know that when one dies in England, they keep the lifeless corpse, weeping and watching beside it for many days, and then with lingering ceremonies, and the attendance of relations and friends, lay it solemnly in the dismal tomb. . . . To hide the dead with speed from every eye, was the Indian custom" (190–91). Falkner describes himself as a cultural outsider for whom hiding "the dead with speed from every eye" makes much more sense than prolonged "weeping and watching." Similarly, Mathilda hints that her father's transgressive impulses may have been strengthened by his eastern travels:

> The burning sun of India, and the freedom from all restraint had rather encreased the energy of his character: before he bowed under, now he was impatient of any censure except that of his own mind. He had seen so many customs and witnessed so great a variety of moral creeds that he had been obliged to form an independant [*sic*] one for himself which had no relation to the peculiar notions of any one country. (*The Mary Shelley Reader*, 188)

As cultural relativists, Falkner and Mathilda's father find it difficult to abide by "the peculiar notions" of English society.

Falkner's decision to commit suicide after burying Alithea may also stem from his Indian experience. In *St. Leon*, the narrator refers to "the Indian doctrine, that the survivor ought to leap into the flames, and perish upon the funeral pyre of the deceased" (295). While St. Leon disapproves of suttee, Falkner "quickly" decides "not to outlive [his] victim" (191). His suicide attempt is thwarted when a child, the orphaned Elizabeth, knocks his pistol out of his hand as he sits, sacrilegiously, on her mother's grave.[98] As Godwin observes in *Enquiry Concerning Political Justice*, the practice of suttee is decidedly "contrary" to European customs: "What can be more contrary to European modes than the dread of disgrace, which induces the Brahmin widows of Indostan to destroy themselves upon the funeral pile of their husbands?"[99] In retrospect, Falkner realizes that in profaning the dead and attempting suicide he has broken two Western taboos, but he argues that his "shocking" (190) behavior must be judged within the context of his ten years of acculturation in India, where his "modes of action were formed."[100]

In Falkner's opinion, the "materials of each mind" determine each individual's actions: "Oh, how vain it is to analyse motive! Each man has the same motives; but it is the materials of each mind—the plastic or rocky nature, the mild or the burning temperament, that rejects the alien influence or receives it into its own essence, and causes the act. Such an impulse is as a summer healthy breeze, just dimpling a still lake, to one; while to another it is the whirlwind that rouses him to spread ruin around" (156). Falkner's narrative serves as a "justification" (153) inasmuch as it shows how "the materials of [his] mind," influenced by external circumstances, shape his conduct. What would have been a breeze to another person is a destructive whirlwind to him. Falkner's adoptive daughter, Elizabeth Raby, finds his "justification" extremely persuasive. For her, to understand is to forgive: "There are few crimes so enormous but that, when we undertake to analyse their motives, they do not find some excuse and pardon in the eyes of all, except their perpetrators." She believes, moreover, that her foster father's "repentance washes away [his] sin" (194).

Falkner cannot, however, pardon himself. He posits the existence of "the voice of conscience implanted in our souls" (156), which infallibly warns us when we are about to do wrong. In her commentary on his narrative, Shelley suggests that he is culpable for ignoring this "voice": "Sympathy is more of a deceiver than conscience. The stander-by may dilate on the force of passion and the power of temptation, but the guilty are not cheated by such subterfuges; he knows that the still voice within was articulate to him. He remembers that at the moment of action he felt his arm checked, his ear warned; he could have stopped, and been innocent" (197). Falkner's "still voice within" does not, however, succeed in overcoming his lifelong obsession with the only person, besides the dead Mrs. Rivers, who has ever been kind to him. Before abducting Alithea, he hesitates and almost abandons his plan, but his "hellish mind" (186) will not allow him to act contrary to his wishes: "I was the same slave of passion I had ever been. I never could force myself to do the thing I hated; I never could persuade myself to relinquish the thing I desire" (186). There is no indication that his conscience can resist "the force of passion," or that it "checks" his arm when he lifts Alithea into the carriage. It is, however, capable of haunting him for the rest of his days.

In her discussion of *Confessions*, Shelley is particularly struck by Rousseau's remorse over his treatment of the servant girl who was dismissed because he wrongly accused her of stealing a ribbon. According to Shelley, "The shadows of our past actions stalk beside us during our existence, and never cease to torment or to soothe, according as they are ill or good, that mysterious portion of mind termed conscience."[101] Her belief in the existence of an innate conscience runs counter to Godwin's view, in *Enquiry Concerning Political Justice*, that at least some individuals are capable of justifying their criminal or vengeful actions with ease: "It is probable that no wrong action is committed from motives entirely pure. It is probable that conscientious assassins and persecutors have some mixture of ambition or the love of fame, and some feelings of animosity and ill will. But the deception they put upon themselves may nevertheless be complete. They stand acquitted at the bar of their own examination."[102] *Falkner* presents, however, the conscience as a powerful force, capable of warning against evil or irresponsible actions and punishing them. Falkner would agree with Godwin's Deloraine that "Conscience is too true a monitor, to suffer her dictates to be baffled" (*Deloraine*, 283).[103]

The consciences of these protagonists compel them to write autobiographical accounts, which, taking the place of auricular confessions, provide them with the opportunity to confront and deal with their guilty memories. Shelley regards the conscience as a faculty of the mind that essentially transcends the circumstances of one's life. In this she parts company with Locke, who argues that "since some men with the same bent of conscience prosecute what others avoid" and because moral principles vary from culture to culture, the conscience is neither innate nor infallible.[104] The negative effects of abuse, injustice, and emotional frustration do not, however, prevent Falkner from developing a conscience that warns him against committing evil actions and makes him feel remorse for his past conduct. Moreover, in her satirical essay, "Roger Dodsworth: The Reanimated Englishman," Shelley declares that "notwithstanding education and circumstances may suffice to direct and form the rough material of the mind, it cannot create, nor give intellect, noble aspiration, and energetic constancy where dulness, wavering of purpose, and grovelling desires, are stamped by nature" (*Collected Tales and Stories*, 48). Both Godwin and Shelley emphasize the power of "the empire of circumstances" to mold human behavior, but in some of Shelley's works her conception of the mind is more essentialist than Godwin's.[105]

Thus Godwin and Shelley use and transform the confessional form pioneered by Rousseau in a variety of ways. Whereas Rousseau's *Confessions* is partly a catalog of crimes and partly a record of victimization, and Godwin's novels are typically registers of the protagonist's errors, several of Shelley's fictional confessions explore the psyches of victims who suffer because of the crimes or errors of others. Both Godwin and Shelley embraced Rousseau's project of making the human mind transparent and were, like their precursor, eager to contribute to "the science of the human mind." But although Godwin, like Rousseau, was an enthusiastic proponent of sincerity, he recognized that it is a difficult virtue to practice. In several of his novels he presents protagonists who claim to be sincere but who hide relevant information about themselves from other characters and even the reader. Shelley is more concerned than her father about sincerity's potentially negative effects. Her novella *Mathilda* suggests that complete openness can be harmful, and in her Rousseau essay she writes that when it reveals the secrets of living people sincerity is as dishonest as picking pockets. In *Enquiry Concerning Political Justice*, Godwin asserts that everyone should "make the world his [or her] confessional."[106] However, in Godwin's and Shelley's fictional works sincerity is frequently undermined by such factors as the desire for sympathy, mistrust, prudishness, or even contempt for the reader. Without sincerity there can be no mental transparency, but complete sincerity can seldom be found in an imperfect world.

For Rousseau, Godwin, and Shelley, the human mind is a complex product of sense impressions, patterns of mental associations, social conditioning, and a multitude of other factors. Their confessional narratives typically present the reader with a great deal of information because virtually no detail in an individual's experience is irrelevant to the construction of his or her mind. Godwin's doctrine of necessity in *Political Justice* states that "if we form a just and complete view of all the circumstances in which a living or intelligent being is placed, we shall find that he could not in any moment of his existence have acted otherwise than he has acted."[107] Some of Shelley's texts hint, however, that there are some aspects of human behavior that transcend "circumstances." Adrian's altruism in *The Last Man* and Falkner's conscience appear to transcend the forces of environmental and social conditioning.

Godwin writes in his "Essay of History and Romance" that the primary goal of a writer of fiction is to "impress the heart and improve the faculties of his [or her] reader."[108] He and Shelley believe that their confessional works can provide readers with insights into the nature of the human mind. To obtain these insights, however, readers frequently must contend with narrators who are emotionally unstable, who withhold information, whose sincerity is questionable, and who seek to manipulate their audience. Readers must also assess the many factors that influence the formation and development of the protagonist's character in order to advance their understandings of "the science of the human mind" in general and of themselves in particular. As Shelley points out in *Fortunes of Perkin Warbeck*, only an exceptional person has the ability to comprehend the "feelings, desires and capacities" of others: "We are all and each of us riddles, when unknown one to the other. The plain map of human powers and purposes, helps us not at all to thread the labyrinth each individual presents in his involution of feelings, desires and capacities; and we must resemble, in quickness of feeling, instinctive sympathy, and warm benevolence, the lovely daughter of Huntley [i.e., Katherine, the sensitive and sympathetic heroine of *Perkin Warbeck*], before we can hope to judge rightly of the good and virtuous among our fellow-creatures" (346–47). Even Katherine's skills as a mental anatomist are, however, limited: while she can "judge rightly of the good and virtuous," the duplicitous King Henry VII (347) easily misleads her. A truly "skilful anatomist of the soul" must recognize the human capacity for both good and evil, sincerity and subterfuge, in order to "thread the labyrinth each individual presents."

2
The Ruling Passions

FOR MANY WRITERS DURING THE ROMANTIC PERIOD, THE STUDY OF the mind is virtually equivalent to the study of the passions; through the passions, the mind can be known, analyzed, and perhaps even regulated. Because the passions are such a powerful determinant of human behavior, a number of Romantic-era writers tend to focus on them rather than on other facets of the psyche. In his 1802 preface to *Lyrical Ballads*, for example, Wordsworth states that he has chosen to examine "Low and rustic life . . . because in that condition, the essential passions of the heart find a better soil in which they can attain their maturity, . . . our elementary feelings co-exist in a state of greater simplicity, and consequently, may be more accurately contemplated, [and] because the manners of rural life germinate from those elementary feelings."[1] For Wordsworth, low and rustic life provides a kind of botanical laboratory in which passions grow to maturity and from which manners germinate. This laboratory is an ideal one because in it we perceive passions in their simplest state and can thus contemplate them "accurately." In *Frankenstein* Mary Shelley explores powerful passions within a very different context. Percy Shelley's preface to his wife's novel praises it for "afford[ing] a point of view to the imagination for the delineating of human passions more comprehensive and commanding than any which the ordinary relations of existing events can yield."[2] This eighteenth- and early nineteenth-century project of anatomizing the passions reflects a widespread interest in defining the mind through the emotions that drive or motivate it.

During the Enlightenment and Romantic periods, the term passion had many meanings and connotations. In *A Treatise of Human Nature*, Hume refers to "calm" as well as "violent" emotions as passions and asserts that reason is passion's "slave," because passions alone are capable of motivating action: "Reason is, and ought only to be the slave of the passions, and can never pretend to any other office than to serve and obey them."[3] Thomas Reid, in his *Essays on the Active Powers of the Human Mind* (1788), criticizes Hume for giving "the name of *passion* to every principle of action, in every degree."[4] Reid's own definition of passion is much more restrictive: "When [the natural desires and affections] are so calm as neither to produce any sensible effects upon the body, nor to darken the understanding and weaken the power of self-command, they are not called passions. But the same principle, when it becomes so violent as to produce these effects upon the body and upon the mind, is a passion, or, as Cicero very properly calls it, a perturbation."[5]

As a young man, Godwin read *De L'Esprit; or, Essays on the Mind and Its Several Faculties* (1758) by the *philosophe* Claude Arien Helvétius.[6] In it, Helvétius states that "Passion are in the moral what motion is in the natural world. If motion creates, destroys, preserves, animates that whole, that without it every thing is dead, so the passions animate the moral world."[7] According to his definition, "Strong-Passion [is] a passion, the object of which is so necessary to our happiness, that without the possession of it life would be insupportable."[8] Whereas Godwin and Shelley often present ruling passions as tragic flaws in their fictional works, Helvétius maintains that without strong passions there would be neither heroes nor great thinkers: "If the generous pride, the passion of patriotism and glory, determine citizens to . . . heroic actions, with what resolution and intrepidity do not the passions inspire those who aim at distinction in the arts and sciences, and whom Cicero calls the peaceable heroes?"[9] "[O]nly a strong passion," he concludes, "being more perspicuous than good sense, can teach us to distinguish the extraordinary from the impossible."[10] In contrast to Helvétius, who believes that all passions stem from self-love, Godwin agrees with the British philosopher Francis Hutcheson "that disinterested benevolence [also] has its seat in the human heart."[11] "Disinterested benevolence" transforms some of Godwin's and Shelley's characters (e.g., Euthanasia, Cloudesley, Catherine Deloraine, and Elizabeth Raby) into "peaceable heroes."

Like Hume, Godwin applies the term passion to a number of states of mind, some of which are "calm" indeed. For instance, in *The Enquirer* he refers to indolence as "one of the most fundamental passions of the human mind."[12] In *Enquiry Concerning Political Justice* (1798 ed.), he notes that "The word passion is a term extremely vague in its signification" and gives the following definitions: "It either represents the ardour and vehemence of mind with which any object is pursued; or secondly, that temporary persuasion of excellence and desirableness, which accompanies any action performed by us contrary to our more customary and usual habits of thinking; or lastly, those external modes or necessities to which the whole human species is alike subject, such as hunger, the passion between the sexes, and others."[13] He also contends that according to the first definition (which is closest to Hume's understanding of the word passion), passion is not irreconcilable with reason:

> In the first sense it has sufficiently appeared that none of our sensations, or, which is the same thing, none of our ideas, are unaccompanied with a consciousness of pleasure or pain; consequently all our volitions are attended with complacence or aversion. In this sense without all doubt passion cannot be eradicated; but in this sense also passion is so far from being incompatible with reason, that it is inseparable from it. Virtue, sincerity, justice, and all those principles which are begotten and cherished in us by a due exercise of reason, will never be very strenuously espoused, till they are ardently loved.[14]

Godwin's treatment of passion is, however, usually more narrowly focused in his imaginative than in his philosophical works. Although he and other Romantic-era writers are fascinated with all kinds of emotions, including what Wordsworth calls the "less impassioned feelings,"[15] they tend to be most concerned with obsessional passion, the "ruling passion" that leads Godwin's protagonist Caleb Williams to pry into Falkland's past, and which compels Falkland to go to any lengths to keep his shameful secret (see *Caleb Williams*, 118, 122, 163, 190, 262). Hays's *Memoirs of Emma Courtney* dwells on the dangers of master passions, and in Ann Radcliffe's *The Mysteries of Udolpho: A Romance* (1794) a dying nun, Sister Agnes, warns Emily St. Aubert against indulging her passions: "beware of the first indulgence of the passions . . . their force is uncontroulable [*sic*]. . . . Such may be the force of even a single passion, that it overcomes every other, and sears up every other approach to the heart."[16] Joanna Baillie dedicated each of her *Plays on the Passions* to exploring "the force of . . . a single passion." In her "Introductory Discourse" to *Plays on the Passions* (1798), she proposes to unveil in her tragedies "the human mind under the dominion of those strong and fixed passions, which seemingly unprovoked by outward circumstances, will from small beginnings brood within the breast, till all the better dispositions, all the fair gifts of nature are borne down before them."[17]

This kind of obsessional passion is defined by Alexander Pope in *An Essay on Man* (1733):

> On diff'rent senses diff'rent objects strike;
> Hence diff'rent Passions more or less inflame,
> As strong or weak, the organs of the frame;
> And hence one master Passion in the breast,
> Like Aaron's serpent, swallows up the rest.
> As Man, perhaps, the moment of his breath,
> Receives the lurking principle of death;
> The young disease, that must subdue at length,
> Grows with his growth, and strengthens with his strength:
> So, cast and mingled with his very frame,
> The Mind's disease, its ruling Passion came;
> Each vital humour which should feed the whole,
> Soon flows to this, in body and in soul.[18]

Rebecca Ferguson has put Pope's concept of passion in its historical context: " 'passion' may be taken to signify impulse, and especially motivational impulse, encompassing also its more modern meaning of 'intense emotion'; it might be defined as denoting the affective or emotional capacity of the soul. . . . 'Passion' is a term which is constantly employed in seventeenth- and eighteenth-century psychologies, steadily departing from the Renaissance faculty psychology and the physiological division of 'humours' towards less confidently rationalistic analysis of the 'perturbations of the mind' such as melancholy, hysteria, and insanity."[19] Whereas Pope regards some passions as allies of reason and virtue (see *An Essay on Man*, 2:97–100), ruling passions defy reason, a "weak queen" that can do no "more than tell us we are fools" (2:150, 152) to obey the passion that overmasters us.

Godwin agrees with Hartley that an individual's passion is the product of the series of impressions (or sensations) and associations of ideas that combine to create the self rather than a "faculty" that can be distinguished from the "essential" self.[20] This means that a strong or habitual passion cannot simply be detached from a particular person's psyche. It is so interwoven into the impressions and associations that make up that individual that its removal must be, at the very least, traumatic in nature. In *Observations on Man*, Hartley describes how a passion can come to take over the self: "if the same Passion returns frequently, it may have so great an Effect upon the Associations, as that the Intervention of foreign Ideas shall not be able to set things to rights, and break the unnatural Bond. The same

Increase of Vibrations makes all the principal Ideas appear to affect *Self*, with the peculiar interesting Concern supposed to flow from personal identity."[21] Thus the protagonist of Hays's *Memoirs of Emma Courtney* declares that when passions are "strengthened, by time and reflection, into habit, in endeavouring to eradicate them, we tear away part of the mind."[22]

According to Hartley, "It is of the utmost Consequence to Morality and Religion, that the Affections and Passions should be analysed into their simple compounding Parts, by reversing the Steps of the Associations which concur to form them. For thus we may learn how to cherish and improve good ones, check and root out such as are mischievous and immoral, and how to suit our Manner of Life, in some tolerable Measure, to our intellectual and religious Wants."[23] Hartley's belief that "the Affections and the Passions" can "be analysed into their simple compounding Parts" is reflected in many late eighteenth- and early nineteenth-century literary works. For example, Emma Courtney maintains that "It is by tracing, by developing, the passions in the minds of others; by tracing them, from the seeds by which they have been generated, through all their extended consequences, that we learn, the more effectually, to regulate and subdue our own."[24] Similarly, Joanna Baillie asserts in her "Introductory Discourse" to *The Plays on the Passions* that by "representing the passions" her tragedies and comedies may allow her readers or audiences to control their feelings before they become obsessional: "in checking and subduing those visitations of the soul, whose causes and effects we are aware of, every one may make considerable progress, if he proves not entirely successful. Above all, looking back to the first rise, and tracing the progress of passion, points out to us those stages in the approach of the enemy, when he might have been combated most successfully."[25]

Mary Brunton was so impressed by Baillie's project that she dedicated her novel *Self-Control* (1811) to the playwright, declaring that Baillie's "portraitures of the progress and of the consequences of passion,—portraitures whose exquisite truth gives them the force of living examples,—are powerful warnings to watch the first risings of the insidious rebel."[26] According to Brunton, however, the purpose of her novel is to demonstrate that "The regulation of the passions is the province, it is the triumph of RELIGION." In Laura Montreville, the heroine of *Self-Control*, "the religious principle is exhibited as rejecting the bribes of ambition; bestowing fortitude in want and sorrow; as restraining just displeasure; overcoming constitutional timidity;

conquering misplaced affection; and triumphing over the fear of death and disgrace."[27] For Hays, Baillie, and Brunton, mental anatomy is necessary to psychological well-being: it can help individuals to identify potentially obsessional passions before they go out of control.

Of course, a model of the self based on the passions has an important limitation—although it recognizes the importance of emotions, it may undervalue the social determinants of human behavior. Perhaps one of the reasons that Wordsworth typically chooses to study passion in the context of rural isolation is that he wants to avoid the complications of urban (or even village) society, which would dilute the purity of the feelings he is examining. Such eighteenth-century thinkers as Adam Smith and David Hume are cognizant of the often antisocial effect of the selfish passions, and thus they put special value on sympathy, an emotion that serves to bind humans together rather than divide them, like the passions of hatred or remorse, into alienated and unhappy individuals.[28] In *The Theory of Moral Sentiments*, Smith argues that sympathy is entirely unselfish:

> Sympathy . . . cannot, in any sense, be regarded as a selfish principle. . . . [T]hough sympathy is very properly said to arise from an imaginary change of situations with the person principally concerned, yet this imaginary change is not supposed to happen to me in my own person and character, but in that of the person with whom I sympathize. . . . How can that be regarded as a selfish passion, which does not arise even from the imagination of any thing that has befallen, or that relates to myself, in my own proper person and character, but which is entirely occupied about what relates to you?[29]

Sympathy is thus defined as the imaginative identification of the self with another. Rather than dwell on his or her own passions and interests, the sympathetic individual considers other people and is therefore able to think and act in a socially responsible and compassionate way.

Hume makes this point even more emphatically in *A Treatise of Human Nature*: "Now as the means to an end can only be agreeable, where the end is agreeable; and as the good of society, where our own interest is not concern'd, or that of our friends, pleases only by sympathy: It follows, that sympathy is the source of the esteem, which we pay to all the artificial virtues [such as justice]. Thus it appears, *that* sympathy is a very powerful principle in human nature, *that* it has a great influence on our taste of beauty, and *that* it produces our sentiment of morals in all the artificial virtues."[30] As an unselfish and extroverted "principle in human nature," sympathy can be contrasted to other, more anti-social passions, passions that insist on the priority of the self, and its desires or antipathies, over social considerations of any kind.

Romantic-era writers tend, however, to explore the alienated rather than the sympathetic self. Rivers (in later versions Oswald) in Wordsworth's tragedy *The Borderers* (1796–97) and Byron's solipsistic Manfred (1817) are good exemplars of this kind of character. Wordsworth describes Rivers as "a young Man of great intellectual powers, yet without any solid principles of genuine benevolence. His master passions are pride and the love of distinction."[31] In a man like Rivers, Wordsworth argues, the "master passions" will always rule the intellect: "Such a mind cannot but discover some truths, but [Rivers] is unable to profit by them and in his hands they become instruments of evil."[32] While the idea behind Baillie's *Series of Plays* is to show the reader (or, in rare performances, the audience) the progress of a passion and suggest the stages at which the passion could have been arrested, in Wordsworth's *The Borderers* there is a degree of skepticism regarding the susceptibility of these master passions to any kind of control.

Smith's warning against solitude could be applied to a great number of Romantic solitaries: "In solitude, we are apt to feel too strongly whatever relates to ourselves: we are apt to over-rate the good offices we may have done, and the injuries we may have suffered: we are apt to be too much elated by our own good, and too much dejected by our own bad fortune. The conversation of a friend brings us to a better, that of a stranger to a still better temper."[33] For a solitary like Byron's Manfred, however, conversation is not a cure for obsessional passion. Even the sympathetic conversation of a stranger, the Chamois hunter, does nothing to dispel Manfred's longing for his dead sister. He sees the Chamois hunter's "humble virtues, hospitable home, / And spirit patient, pious, proud and free," but then he looks "within" and finds that his "soul was scorch'd already!"[34] The passion raging within obscures all external impressions. In her "Introductory Discourse," Baillie writes that "It is a characteristick of the more powerful passions that they will encrease and nourish themselves on very slender aliment; it is from within that they are chiefly supplied with what they feed on."[35] Solitary characters like Baillie's De Monfort, Rivers, Manfred, Mandeville, and Mathilda's father "nourish" their ruling passions "from within," and their obsessions ultimately consume them.

This problem of the ruling passion, of the passion so dominant that it can virtually define an individual's self, fascinated Godwin and Shelley. In this chapter, I will focus on their fictional treatments of ruling passions. I will contend that both writers are concerned with certain key questions: How are obsessional passions formed? To what extent can an individual overcome his or her ruling passion, particularly when that ruling passion has become pathological? Can others "cure" a person who suffers from an obsessional passion? And what does the existence of such master passions tell us about an individual's free will? As I will demonstrate in this chapter, these writers are developing, in a sometimes dialogical fashion, a passionate model of the self, a model that they regard with a mixture of fascination and antipathy.

Godwin makes frequent allusions to the powerful influence of the passions, especially of the ruling passions, in both his nonfictional and fictional works. In his *Autobiography* he writes that reading was the ruling passion of his early years, and, in his "Analysis of Own Character," he discusses his "boyish passion" for poetry.[36] He also declares in "Analysis of Own Character" that it is "the uniform passion of [his] mind to associate with the intellectually great" and that he possesses "a most unequivocal, perhaps unmingled, passion for truth."[37] Similarly, Godwin's *Memoirs of the Author of a Vindication of the Rights of Woman* (1798) focuses on the passions that motivated Wollstonecraft, whom he refers to as "a female Werter [*sic*]," throughout her tempestuous life.[38] For instance, he writes that Wollstonecraft's friendship with Frances Blood was "for years . . . the ruling passion of her mind."[39]

In 1790 Godwin wrote "a tragedy on the story of St Dunstan, being desirous . . . of developing the great springs of human passion."[40] Four years later he published *Caleb Williams*, in which the title character describes how he feels while in the grips of his ruling passion, curiosity: "I seemed to be in a state in which reason had no power. I felt as if I could coolly survey the several arguments of the case, perceive that they had prudence, truth and common sense on their side; and then answer, I am under the guidance of a director more energetic than you" (154).[41] Godwin's misanthropic Mandeville acknowledges the power of passion in even more emphatic terms: "the passions of the human mind laugh at philosophy; and the events that the course of affairs brings forth to torture us, render its boasts as impotent, as the menaces of a man that had lost the use of his limbs" (174). While Godwin asserts in *Enquiry Concerning Political Justice* that "bad passion" can be rooted out of the mind by "truth, a sound and just estimate of things," Williams and Mandeville insist that truth and philosophy are no match for the powerful emotions that control them.[42]

According to Godwin, passions cannot be developed or sustained without the imagination. He contends in his essay "Of Love and Friendship" that "there can be no passion, and by consequence no love, where there is not imagination."[43] Moreover, in his novels Godwin shows how the imagination can intensify a passion until it becomes obsessional, particularly when a character's imagination is powerful but narrowly focused. For example, Caleb William's ruling passion, curiosity, is "dormant" unless his "imagination [is] excited" (4). His master's mysteriousness inspires "ideas that give scope to all that imagination can picture of terrible or sublime" (123), and, as a result, Caleb's desire to learn whether or not Falkland is a murderer turns into an obsession. Similarly, Falkland is devoted to the "the grand and animating reveries of the imagination." After Tyrrel's attack on him destroys his self-image as "a true knight," his imagination becomes dominated by "visions . . . of anguish and despair" (97), and the preservation of his reputation becomes his ruling passion. Caleb's and Falkland's passions become obsessional because they are inflamed by their hyperactive imaginations, which blind them to the irrationality of their actions. As Pope declares in *An Essay on Man*, "Whatever warms the heart, or fills the head, / As the mind opens, and its functions spread, / Imagination plies her dang'rous art, / And pours it all upon the peccant part" (2:141–44). In the same vein, Hume remarks in *A Treatise of Human Nature* that "lively passions commonly attend a lively imagination."[44] Godwin's and Shelley's novels show how the imagination can transform the passion of love into either "erotomania"[45] or jealous hatred, ambition into megalomania, hatred into a persecution complex, and remorse into a death wish.

Godwin asserts that in *St. Leon* he "mixed human feelings and passions with incredible situations" (preface, xxxiii). St. Leon's ruling passion, ambition, is instilled in him by his mother, whom he describes as having "rather a masculine understanding" (3). Like a number of Godwin's and Shelley's other obsessional characters, he is brought up "in the most sequestered retirement" (5) and his perspective on reality is informed by his imagination rather than experience. His mother sends him to witness the meeting of Francis I of France and Henry VIII of England at the Field of the Cloth of Gold in 1520, where he sees "all that was graceful and humane in the age of chivalry." She does not, however, allow him to join King Francis's retinue: "She rightly judged that my passion for the theatre of glory would grow more impetuous, by being withheld for some time from the gratifications for which it panted" (7). By temporarily frustrating St. Leon's ambition, his mother fosters it: "I never shut my eyes without viewing in imagination the combats of knights and the train of ladies" (8). His early education, reinforced by his imagination, implants a ruling passion in him that is never entirely eradicated.

The death of St. Leon's mother only serves to inflame his ambition: "I had been too deeply imbued with sentiments of glory, for it to be possible . . . that I should remain in indolence. The tender remembrance of my mother itself . . . furnished a new stimulus to my ambition." When his uncle comes to recruit him for a military expedition, he responds enthusiastically: "I have a passion pent up within me, that feeds upon my vitals: it disdains speech; it burns for something more unambiguous and substantial" (10). He joins the French forces besieging Pavia, and "The force of education, and the first bent of [his] mind" enable him to overlook "demoniac mischief, barbarity, and murder" (24) that he witnesses there. Following King Francis's defeat, however, his military career comes to an abrupt end. He marries Marguerite de Damville and decides to "cultivate domestic affection" (48) rather than seek power and glory.

But although Marguerite does all that she can to make his life with her and their children fulfilling, St. Leon "retain[s] the original vice of [his] mind" (42). His ambition resurfaces when he leaves his wife to accompany their son to Paris and begins to associate "with some of those noblem[e]n who had been the companions of [his] former dissipation and gaming" (51). He hopes that through gambling he can regain the wealth that he has squandered through his extravagant lifestyle, but he does "not take into the account the ungovernableness of [his] own passions" (53). He becomes "infected with the venom of gaming" (55) and loses vast sums of money. When Marguerite comes to Paris to reclaim him, his love for her is no match for his all-consuming passion: "Instead of being weaned, by the presence of this admirable woman, from my passion for gaming, it became stronger than ever" (66).

In an attempt to regain his family fortune through gambling,

St. Leon loses everything and goes temporarily insane. After paying her husband's debts, Marguerite takes him and their family to Switzerland and tries to reconcile him to the simple life of a "patriot-yeoman" (86). Her efforts to overcome his desire for "admiration and homage" are, however, doomed to failure: "It was in vain that I heard the praises of simplicity and innocence. . . . The lessons of my education had left too deep an impression" (87). Not even the wise, virtuous, and dedicated Marguerite, a student of Leonardo da Vinci and the poet Clément Marot (34), is able to wean St. Leon from his ruling passion.

When a stranger, using the alias Francesco Zampieri, offers St. Leon the philosopher's stone and the elixir of life, he accepts them despite the fact that in order to obtain these gifts he must swear never to reveal their existence to anyone, including his wife. Because his marriage to Marguerite is based on complete openness, his reticence eventually destroys their relationship. He is asked to choose between his ambition and his wife, and he chooses ambition. Zampieri's question, "Was ever gallant action achieved by him who was incapable of separating himself from a woman?," appeals directly to St. Leon's passions: "The stranger touched upon the first and foremost passions of my soul; passions the operation of which had long been suspended, but which were by no means extinguished in my bosom" (126–27). He realizes that the humble, rural existence prized by Marguerite never completely satisfied him: "the curse entailed upon me from the earliest period to which my memory can reach, operated even in the cottage of the lake. I was not formed to enjoy a scene of pastoral simplicity. Ambition still haunted me; an uneasiness, scarcely defined in its object, from time to time recurred to my mind" (177–78).

From this point in the novel to its end, St. Leon's ruling passion takes complete control of him, inspiring him to perform one disastrous "experiment" after another with the philosopher's stone (see 200, 230, 232, 246, 258, 383). He becomes addicted to the practice of alchemy:

> no reading of my story, no mere power of language and words, can enable a by-stander to imagine how deep [alchemical experimentation] was sunk into my heart, how inextricably it was twisted with all the fibres of my bosom. . . . It would have required a miracle, greater than all the consecrated legends of our church record, to have restored me to what I formerly was. If then I could have resolved never henceforth to use the gifts I had received, I yet firmly believe that I

> never could have refrained from the composition and decomposition of simples, and from experiments on the nature of substances, chemical and metallic.

He claims that alchemy engages "the most imperious passions of the human mind[:] wealth, power, and pleasurable sensation" (258). It becomes so intertwined with his identity that he is convinced that not even a miracle could make him refrain from his experiments.

After St. Leon has lost his wife and family, and has been imprisoned for lengthy periods of time by both the Inquisition and the Hungarian partisan Bethlem Gabor, he admits that his alchemical powers have led only to disaster: "I had made a sufficient experiment of the philosopher's stone, and all my experiments had miscarried." Even his philanthropic projects fail: "My . . . trials in attempting to be the benefactor of nations and mankind, not only had been themselves abortive, but contained in them shrewd indications that no similar plan could ever succeed" (434). Near the end of the novel, St. Leon encounters his son, Charles, who, because of St. Leon's use of the *elixir vitae*, does not recognize him. Soothing his "soul with delusive dreams" (437) again, St. Leon decides to devote himself to Charles's service. He meets Charles's beloved Pandora, befriends her, and decides to use the philosopher's stone to bestow a dowry on her. Unfortunately, this scheme, like all his others, ends in disaster. Charles becomes convinced that St. Leon has seduced Pandora and, when he finds out that St. Leon is "a magician, a dealer in the unhallowed secrets of alchymy and the *elixir vitae*" (473), challenges him to a duel. Guided by his passions rather than his reason, St. Leon fails to learn from his mistakes. He is, therefore, condemned to repeat them.

St. Leon calls into question Hartley's belief that by analyzing the passions "into their simple compounding Parts, by reversing the Steps of the Associations which concur to form them . . . we may learn how to . . . check and root out such as are mischievous and immoral." The novel's protagonist analyzes his master passion and explains how it is formed, but he never learns how to check or root it out. In fact, he believes that the "youthful passions of [his] soul, which [his] early years had written there in characters so deep" (130) can never be dislodged. He is simply not "formed to be satisfied in obscurity and a low estate" (101). Although he comes to regard himself "as a monster that [does] not deserve to exist" (363), he cannot bring himself to renounce the philosopher's stone, the elixir of life, or his ambitious "experiments." In fact, *St. Leon* suggests that obsessional passions can become such a dominant force in an individual's mind that not even the intervention of a loved one or a series of heart-rending disappointments can overcome their influence.

Unlike "the passions of a husband and a father" (49), St. Leon's ambition, his desire for wealth, power, and glory, engages his imagination fully. Thus it, rather than the more mundane "domestic and private affections" (xxxiv), becomes his ruling passion. As Hume observes, "When two passions . . . are both present in the mind . . . The predominant passion swallows up the inferior, and converts it into itself."[46] Instead of discouraging St. Leon from pursuing his projects, his "passions of a husband and a father" provide more fuel for his ambition. Zampieri convinces him that, without the philosopher's stone, his "children are destined to live in the inglorious condition of peasants" (127); with it, St. Leon will be able to finance his children's "career of honour" (178). St. Leon is only too ready to accept this argument, and, accordingly, his "predominant passion swallows up" his "domestic affections," converting them into itself. Ironically, his family's poverty becomes St. Leon's excuse for engaging in a series of alchemical experiments that lead to their destruction. Yet, even if St. Leon had perceived a conflict between his obligations toward his family and his ruling passion, Hume's theory of the passions indicates that his predominant passion would have won out against his sense of duty: "The notion of duty, when opposite to the passions, is seldom able to overcome them; and when it fails of that effect, is apt rather to encrease them, by producing an opposition in our motives and principles."[47]

The ending of *St. Leon* suggests, however, that powerful emotions are not always irresistible. St. Leon describes how the "dignity and virtue" of his son Charles allow him to triumph over his passion for Pandora: "Love often entails imbecility on the noblest of mankind: but Charles surmounted the most perilous attacks of this all-conquering passion" (478). Unlike his father, Charles is able to remain true to his principles, even when attacked by an "all-conquering passion." But Charles is an unconvincing exception to the Godwinian rule that education and circumstances determine character. According to St. Leon, his son was essentially born virtuous; he alludes to "the good qualities that had been unfolded in this truly extraordinary young man from his earliest infancy" (477). The series of disasters experienced by his family and the bad example set by his father apparently do not affect

Charles's character in any negative way. Although St. Leon finds a basis for optimism in the life story of his "truly extraordinary" son, he recognizes that it does not square with his "personal experience of human life" (478). It also flies in the face of the deterministic psychology that underpins the novel as a whole.

Like *St. Leon*, *Mandeville* focuses on the protagonist's ruling passion. Whereas St. Leon is driven by ambition, Mandeville is obsessed with his hatred for a schoolboy rival. In his preface to *Mandeville*, Godwin notes that his novel was inspired by "a storybook, called Wieland, written by . . . C. B. Brown" and "some hints in De Monfort, a tragedy, by Joanna Baillie" (8). Like the title character of *Wieland*, Mandeville is a religious fanatic, and his ruling passion, like De Monfort's, is his hatred of a male rival. Mandeville's religious mania takes the form of virulent anti-Catholicism. When Mandeville learns that Clifford, the object of his loathing, "has become reconciled to the church of Rome" (251), his hatred for him intensifies into a "desperate fury" (254). In the language of *A Treatise of Human Nature*, Mandeville's predominant passion, his hatred of Clifford, "swallows up" his "inferior" one, his detestation of Catholicism, "and converts it into itself." His religious bigotry, his aristocratic pride, and his ambition (140) are all absorbed by his obsession: "all my passions seemed to merge in this single passion. . . . no passion ever harboured in a human bosom, that it seemed so entirely to fill, in which it spread so wide, and mounted so high, and appeared so utterly to convert every other sentiment and idea into its own substance" (106). Like St. Leon, Mandeville attempts to trace his master passion to its source, through the chains of associations which shaped it, but he never fully understands it. His uncertainty regarding the exact cause of his hatred for Clifford is cogently expressed in the following statement: "My nature, or my circumstances, seemed to have made hatred my ruling passion" (202).

According to Darwin, "the first impressions made on us by accidental circumstances in our infancy continue through life to bias our affections, or mislead our judgments."[48] In *Mandeville*, the protagonist's psyche never recovers from an experience in his early childhood. At the age of three, he witnesses the brutal murder of his parents by Irish Catholics, and his memories of this tragedy haunt him throughout his life:

> I saw . . . in my dreams, whether by night or by day, a perpetual succession of flight, and pursuit, and anguish, and murder. I saw the

agonising and deploring countenances of Protestants, and the brutal and infuriated features of the triumphant Papist. I recollected distinctly the expiring bodies I had beheld along the roadside in my flight, some perishing with hunger and cold, and some writhing under the mortal wounds and tortures that had been inflicted by their pursuers. . . . This was all the world to me. I had hardly a notion of any more than two species of creatures on the earth,—the persecutor and his victim, the Papist and the Protestant; and they were to my thoughts like two great classes of animal nature, the one, the law of whose being it was to devour, while it was the unfortunate destiny of the other to be mangled and torn to pieces by him. (45)

Mandeville's hatred of "the Papist" is reinforced by his tutor, Hilkiah Bradford, who teaches him "that the Pope is Antichrist" (47) and who inflames his imagination with tales and engraved illustrations of the gruesome fates of Protestant martyrs. It also prefigures his conflicted relationship with Clifford, who becomes, in Mandeville's mind, "the persecutor" who is destined to mangle and devour him.

Mandeville competes with Clifford for an appointment "to the office of secretary to the commander-in-chief" (117) in the royalist forces under Sir Joseph Wagstaff and, when he is denied the appointment, angrily deserts. After his best friend at Oxford hears of his desertion, he breaks off their relationship, and Mandeville, consumed by his jealousy and hatred of Clifford, goes temporarily insane. During his period of madness, the trauma of his parents' deaths is relived. Far from being "obliterated from the tablet of [his] memory" (144), his parents' murders continue to affect Mandeville, shaping his Manichaean world view and his paranoid relationship with Clifford. He suffers from what we would now call "posttraumatic stress disorder," and his violent encounter with Clifford at the end of his narrative, which results in his being mangled by his "persecutor," can be seen as yet another instance of his compulsion to reenact the tragic event that overshadowed his childhood.

Hume asserts that "whenever any object excites contrary passions" a "new emotion" is produced, which "is easily converted into the predominant passion, and encreases its violence, beyond the pitch it wou'd have arriv'd at had it met with no opposition."[49] In Mandeville's case, the violence of his intense hatred for his rival is increased by his powerful attraction to Clifford. In fact, he describes his relationship to his archenemy as a kind of marriage:

> "Marriages," it is said, "are made in heaven." . . . In the same manner as . . . there exist certain mysterious sympathies and analogies, drawing and attracting each to each, and fitting them to be respectively sources of mutual happiness, so, I was firmly persuaded, there are antipathies, and properties interchangeably irreconcilable and destructive to each other, that fit one human being to be the source of another's misery. Beyond doubt I had found this true opposition and inter-destructiveness in Clifford. (140–41)

There is a curious paradox in Mandeville's relationship to the object of his hatred: part of the reason that he hates Clifford is that his rival is attractive and well-liked. The result of his violent feelings toward his enemy is to forge an indissoluble physical union with him through mutilation, a marriage of hatred that is more binding and intense than any other relationship he has.

When Mandeville describes his "brief intoxication" (83) with Clifford early in their relationship, he employs the language of a lover: Clifford "was an extraordinary creature indeed. He seemed both to attract all eyes, and to win all hearts. There was something in him perfectly fascinating and irresistible. His countenance was beautiful, and his figure was airy. . . . There was a vivacity in his eye, and an inexpressible and thrilling charm in the tone of his voice, that appeared more than human" (82). This attraction soon fades, however, as Mandeville becomes jealous of Clifford's eloquence and popularity at Winchester College. Although Clifford does nothing to earn Mandeville's enmity, Mandeville describes him as a malevolent and strangely feminine influence: "Clifford was the maleficent wizard by whom I was hag-ridden, and the night-mare, under whose weight I lay at the last gasp of existence" (91). As Clemit points out in her footnote to this passage, "Nightmare, originally, as here, [was] a female monster supposed to settle upon people and animals in their sleep, producing a feeling of suffocation."[50] Mandeville's initial sense of Clifford's beauty and irresistibility has thus gone through a radical transformation—Clifford becomes, in his mind, a female monster suffocating him, whose presence (and imagined touch) is terrifying and even physically threatening.[51] Moreover, Mandeville thinks of himself as Clifford's conjoined twin:

> I have read of twin children, whose bodies were so united in their birth, that they could never after be separated, while one carried with him, wherever he went, an intolerable load, and of whom, when one died, it involved the necessary destruction of the other. Something

> similar to this, was the connection that an eternal decree had made between Clifford and me. (141)

This decree that they must be joined until death is, of course, yet another allusion to marriage, the sacrament that, in Mandeville's mind, his relationship with Clifford repeatedly parodies. His horror of being joined to Clifford until one of them dies is part of the delusional mythology he creates, in which an "eternal decree" has determined that he must become physically one with the man who so violently attracts and repels him.

Mandeville's hatred of Clifford turns murderous after he learns that his rival intends to marry his sister, Henrietta. This unexpected development seems to confirm his paranoid belief that Clifford is out to destroy him, except in this case Clifford's "aggression" has moved from the social to the domestic realm, striking at the very core of Mandeville's sense of self. The thought of Clifford's marrying his sister, or his own flesh and blood, is too much for him to bear. He tells Henrietta that her union with Clifford would destroy him: "for the sake of this crime, this abhorred mixture, this unnatural pollution, this worse than incest, you would destroy your brother!" (314). Although the fact that Henrietta proposes to marry a Catholic accounts for some of Mandeville's outrage, he seems primarily disgusted by the possibility of an "abhorred mixture" of sister and rival, a grotesque coupling of virtue and corruption. His odd assertion that Henrietta's marriage to Clifford would be a crime "worse than incest" is more than just an expression of religious bigotry. It suggests that his horror of Clifford's sexuality is so extreme that he believes that it would be better for Henrietta to break the incest taboo (presumably with him, her only living relative) than make love to his rival. His homophobic aversion to Clifford could not be expressed any more forcibly.

It is possible, however, to account for Mandeville's emotional conflicts in a number of ways. For example, on an unconscious level Mandeville could be jealous of his sister's possessing the object of his desire, the "beautiful and prepossessing" (96) Clifford. One might also argue that his anger against Henrietta is in a way directed toward himself: his sister is his alter ego who must be prevented from acting out his own transgressive fantasies. But whatever interpretation one chooses, it is clear that the image of Henrietta embracing his arch-enemy drives Mandeville to violence. He gathers together some henchmen and tries to separate the lovers by force. In the ensuing struggle he and Clifford unite in a deadly embrace: "we struck; we grappled; we fell from our horses, and came to ground together." Guided by a "sure instinct" (324), he "conjoins" with his rival, temporarily displacing his sister. His sword fight with Clifford results, however, in his own mutilation, a facial mutilation that links Mandeville and Clifford together forever: "Even as certain tyrannical planters in the West Indies have set a brand with a red-hot iron upon the negroes they have purchased, to denote that they are irremediably a property, so Clifford had set his mark upon me, as a token that I was his for ever." In his effort to prevent the marriage of his sister to Clifford, Mandeville has become joined to his rival as his perpetual slave and "property." The more he struggles against Clifford, the more he is united with him.

According to Mandeville, only a friend could have halted the growth of his obsessional hatred: "No man needs a friend, so much as he who is under the slavery of a domineering passion. . . . I never had a friend. . . . For this want, and this want only, I have become a monument of human misery, and a villain" (145–46). In his case, this friend must be a man; although he is devoted to his sister Henrietta, he feels unable to unburden himself to her. His desperation is so extreme that he ultimately tries to befriend his diabolical nemesis, Mallison, telling this sinister figure things about himself that he could never tell Henrietta: "not the presence of Henrietta herself, and the charm of her society, ever gave such a loose to my tongue. . . . But Mallison was so implicit, bowed so completely to all my judgments, and drank in all my suggestions, that it was a pleasure to talk to so accommodating a pupil" (244). Unfortunately for Mandeville, he is constitutionally incapable of making friends with Clifford, whose generosity and positive outlook on life might have counteracted his constitutional gloominess and misanthropy, and he only befriends men who are either socially maladroit (Waller and Lisle) or coldly manipulative (Mallison). These one-sided friendships tend to be short-lived and psychically destructive, and Mandeville ultimately becomes "a monument of human misery, and a villain." Although he has enough insight to recognize that he needs a male friend, he is psychologically unable to choose a friend who will help him overcome his obsessional and melancholy nature. Because there is nothing to counteract it, Mandeville's ruling passion eventually consumes him, leaving him, at the end of the novel, both psychologically and physically mutilated.

In *Fleetwood* and *Deloraine* Godwin explores obsessional love. Godwin's conception of love, like Mary Hays's, Percy Bysshe

Shelley's, and Mary Shelley's, is influenced by a famous passage in Laurence Sterne's *A Sentimental Journey*: "I declare," says Sterne's persona, Yorick,

> that was I in a desart, I would find out wherewith in it to call forth my affections—If I could not do better, I would fasten them upon some sweet myrtle, or seek some melancholy cypress to connect myself to—I would court their shade, and greet them kindly for their protection—I would cut my name upon them, and swear they were the loveliest trees throughout the desert: if their leaves wither'd, I would teach myself to mourn, and when they rejoiced, I would rejoice along with them.[52]

Godwin has the idealistic Macneil advance a similar conception of love in *Fleetwood*. Macneil thinks of writing a novel in which a "fastidious misanthrope" is "shipwrecked on a desert island, with no companion but one man, the most gross, perverse, and stupid of the crew." No longer able to choose his companions, this misanthropist would learn to love his unattractive associate: "How these two companions would love one another! . . . With what eager anxiety, when any necessary occasion separated them, would they look for each other's return! . . . After some years I would bring back my misanthrope from England. Sir, he would never be able to part with his companion in the desert island. He would believe that there was not a creature in the world . . . so valuable" (163–64).

The passage from *A Sentimental Journey* cited above is quoted approvingly (if not entirely accurately) by the protagonist of Hays's *Memoirs of Emma Courtney*, and Percy Shelley alludes to it in his "On Love."[53] In Mary Shelley's *Mathilda*, the heroine's "warm affections[,] finding no return from any other human heart[, are] forced to run waste on inanimate objects," including "every tree in [her family's] park."[54] Like Sterne's Yorick, Emma Courtney, Macneil, and Mathilda regard love as a powerful, innate human need. They suggest that an isolated and lonely person tends to fall passionately in love with virtually anyone or anything in his or her environment. As Mary Wollstonecraft writes in *The Wrongs of Woman*, "There are beings who cannot live without loving, as poets love."[55]

The title character of *Fleetwood*, a disillusioned "New Man of Feeling," suffers from his inability to sustain a loving relationship. During his residence in Paris he becomes infatuated with "a finished coquette" (53) and "gratuitously ascribe[s] to her a thousand virtues" (57). He soon finds, however, that he has been deluded by his imagination; far from being devoted to him, his mistress has been dividing "her favours with every comer,—a music-master—an artisan—a valet" (60). Fleetwood consoles himself with another mistress who, like her predecessor, proves faithless. As a result of these experiences, he becomes a misogynist: "I felt like the personage of a fairy tale I have somewhere read, who, after being delighted with the magnificence of a seeming palace, and the beauty of its fair inhabitants, suddenly sees the delusion vanish, the palace is converted into a charnel-house, and what he thought its beautiful tenants, are seen to be the most withered and loathsome hags that ever shocked the eyes of a mortal" (63–64).

In *Émile*, Rousseau stresses the importance of a man's first love on his later destiny:

> people . . . do not sufficiently consider the influence which a man's first liaison with a woman ought to have on the course of both their lives. They do not see that a first impression as lively as that of love, or the inclination that takes its place, has distant effects whose links are not perceived in the progress of the years but do not cease to act until death.
>
> [On ne considère pas assez l'influence que doit avoir la première liaison d'un homme avec une femme dans le cours de la vie de l'un et de l'autre. On ne voit pas qu'une première impression, aussi vive que celle de l'amour ou du penchant qui tient sa place, a de longs effets dont on n'aperçoit point la chaîne dans le progrès des ans, mais qui ne cessent d'agir jusqu'à la mort.][56]

Although Fleetwood's first two liaisons have no discernible effect on his mistresses, they exert a powerful influence on him. He judges "of the whole sex from the specimens which [are] brought before [him]" (66) in his youth. Conditioned by his initial relationships with women to be suspicious and jealous, he is ill-prepared, in his mid-forties, to become the husband of Mary Macneil, a much younger woman whose gaiety and flirtatiousness he comes to detest. Before he marries Mary, Fleetwood thinks of her as a goddess: "There was something too aërial, too subtle, too heavenly in her countenance, to be properly the attribute of a terrestrial being. The glories of Elysium seemed to hang around her" (185). When Mary turns out to be more worldly than heavenly, more inclined to enjoy the pleasures of Bath than to sit in the company of her middle-aged husband, he compares her to his two Parisian mistresses and concludes that "all women [are] in the main alike, selfish, frivolous, inconstant, and deceitful" (212). The "distant effects" of Fleetwood's first two love affairs thus prevent him from having a stable and trusting relationship with his wife.

It is, however, when Fleetwood begins to suspect that Mary is having an affair with Kenrick, a young relation of his, that his feelings for her become truly obsessional. Jealousy replaces love as his ruling passion, a jealousy that is inflamed by his imagination. Even when Mary and Kenrick appear to be innocent, he feels compelled to suspect them: "my sick imagination is for ever busy, shaping [their] attitudes and gestures" (235). Fleetwood's "diseased imagination" (237), coupled with his misogynistic tendencies, makes him vulnerable to the machinations of Kenrick's diabolical half-brother, Gifford, who manufactures evidence against his wife. Like Mandeville, Fleetwood is an egoist who has a difficult time understanding the thoughts or the motivations of others. Caught in the grips of a ruling passion, he fails to recognize that Gifford is a lying scoundrel and that Mary is telling the truth when she declares that she is innocent. When Mary responds to Fleetwood's false accusations by calling on her dead parents to witness her husband's brutal treatment of her, he becomes more rather than less abusive: "Bursting as I was with rage and agony, I could not bear any thing that was calculated to excite an opposite passion. It created confusion in my mind; it made me half fear I was doing wrong: and to conquer this fear, I became ten times more furious and peremptory than ever" (259). The "opposite passion" only serves to intensify his obsessional jealousy. After becoming convinced of his wife's infidelity, Fleetwood leaves her. His jealous "transports of passion" following their separation drive him temporarily insane and transform him "almost to a skeleton" (267).

Like *Fleetwood*, *Deloraine* is narrated by a man whose desire to possess and control his wife becomes an obsession. In both cases, the middle-aged protagonist is attracted to a much younger woman, partly because he perceives her as a frail, sickly, childlike woman who must be cared for and protected. Fleetwood describes his relationship with Mary Macneil in the following way: "The very infirmities of her delicate frame had rendered her dearer to me; I was her shelter, her bed-side watch, the physician of her soul. I wanted such an object to engage my care; she stood in need of such a guardian" (249). Similarly, Deloraine is drawn to Margaret Borradale because she is so unhealthy and in need of his paternal care: "she was an imagination only, and a memory. Her body was a corpse, if we can figure to ourselves a corpse, void of every thing offending and repulsive, but which on the contrary was more beautiful, more ravishing, more celestial, than any living mortal could ever be. For the soul that informed this body, was all delicacy, all sensitiveness, tremblingly alive" (95).

While Fleetwood thinks of his wife as "an object" he can care for, Deloraine regards Margaret as "an imagination," or a soul illuminating a corpse. Both characters tend to treat their spouses as daughters rather than wives, and neither of them subscribes to the egalitarian conception of marriage that Mary Macneil espouses in *Fleetwood* when she informs her husband that she will not "sink [her] being and individuality" in his: "I shall have my distinct propensities and preferences. Nature has moulded my mind in a particular way; and I have . . . my tastes, my pleasures, and my wishes, more or less different from those of every other human being. I hope you will not require me to disclaim them. In me you will have a wife, and not a passive machine" (187). Rather than respect their wives' "propensities and preferences," however, Fleetwood and Deloraine attempt to reduce them to "passive machines." As Margaret laments immediately before her death, her "life has been all submission, submission to [her] father, submission to [her] husband" (144). Her exemplary behavior does not, however, prevent Deloraine from brutally murdering the only man she has ever loved.

Thus both *Fleetwood* and *Deloraine* link obsessional love with patriarchal tyranny. But while the protagonist's physical condition is not an important factor in *Fleetwood*, Deloraine's health exerts a major influence on the progress of his ruling passion. Deloraine contrasts his love for his first wife, Emilia, with his dysfunctional passion for Margaret: "When my passion for Emilia took its rise, I was in the full vigour of health; and, when I formed my acquaintance with Margaret, I was just recovered from a very dangerous illness, and was in the middle point as it were between life and death. This cooperated with many other circumstances, to give to my passion for her a diseased tone and a sickly hue" (138–39). Here Deloraine indicates that his association of Margaret with his recovery from a serious illness warped their entire relationship, preventing it from progressing in a healthy way. His necrophiliac fascination with Margaret's corpselike body may also reflect his longing for Emilia, who died when she was about Margaret's age. Deloraine's association of Margaret with death proves prophetic when, after he kills William, she falls dead on her former fiancé's corpse.

Fleetwood and *Deloraine* also differ in their presentations of the consequences of obsessional passion. Whereas Fleetwood's errors in judgment can be rectified, Deloraine's crime is irrevocable. Fleetwood blames many of his mistakes on Gifford's machinations, but Deloraine is solely responsible for his violent action. While Fleetwood is forgiven by his wife and Kenrick, Deloraine is haunted by his memories of his victims and fears, for much of the novel, "the ministers of human justice" (284). His ruling passion has motivated him to commit an act that destroys three lives. Obsessional love is depicted as incestuous, necrophiliac, and pathologically possessive in both works, but in *Deloraine* it becomes homicidal. Godwin's last novel is perhaps his most powerful indictment of "unbridled and ungovernable passions" (*Deloraine*, 203).

Deloraine's love for Margaret, like Fleetwood's love for Mary, is essentially selfish: both men regard their wives as their possessions and become pathologically jealous when their wives show affection for others. Similarly, St. Leon's ambition and Mandeville's hatred are egocentric passions that alienate them from family members and motivate socially irresponsible behavior. Godwin believes, however, that there can be unselfish as well as selfish passions. He claims in *An Account of the Seminary* (1783) that it has "been fully demonstrated by that very elegant philosopher Mr [Francis] Hutcheson, that self-love is not the source of all our passions, but that disinterested benevolence has its seat in the human heart."[57] In *The Theory of Moral Sentiments*, Smith (whose ideas were also influenced by Hutcheson) contrasts selfish passions with sympathy and the other "social Passions," which include "Generosity, humanity, kindness, compassion, mutual friendship and esteem, . . . the social and benevolent affections."[58] A number of the characters in Godwin's novels appear to be motivated by these "social and benevolent" passions: instead of dwelling obsessionally on their own needs and feelings, they are primarily concerned with the well-being and happiness of others.

For instance, Margaret de Damville completely identifies herself with her husband and family. According to St. Leon, "she felt the truest sympathy" for his "sufferings" (83) following his loss of the family fortune, and "Her attachment to her children was exemplary, and her vigilance uninterrupted" (133). In contrast, the title character of *Cloudesley* is guilty of "an act of baseness in lending himself to assist the uncle in stripping [Julian] of his birthright and his name," but he redeems himself by doing everything in his power to promote "the interests and welfare of his pupil": "He cast to earth 'all trivial, fond records;' he cleansed his bosom of all those passions, which till then perhaps had twined their tendrils round his heart, and lived for one thing alone" (240). In *Deloraine*, Catherine Deloraine, whose selflessness rivals Margaret de Damville's, tells her fugitive father that she lives entirely for him:

> I have borne for you, as you say, more perhaps than ever daughter bore for a father. . . . I esteemed you as my only good: to know that you were safe, to hope that all would be well with you, was every thing I asked. . . . The only thing on which I valued myself, and for which I lived, ever since the moment when I became acquainted with your fatal encounter, was my vigilance and my exertions for safety; and, those concluded, my business in this mortal scene is over; that moment I die. (274–75)

The ruling passions of all these characters are sympathetic and unselfish, and the novels' narrators present them as moral paragons.

There is, however, a dark side even to these "social and benevolent" passions, which can become every bit as obsessional as the selfish passions of St. Leon, Fleetwood, Mandeville, Lord Danvers, and Deloraine. A person's total devotion to his or her family, ward, or father can prove self-destructive. Margaret, unable to bear her husband's "reserve" (177) following his bargain with Zampieri, wills herself to a premature death, and Cloudesley decides to sacrifice himself in order to restore Julian's inheritance to him: "He was like what is related of the bee, when its anger is stirred up within, that seizes desperately upon the aggressor, fixes its sting deep in the living vein, and is entirely content to leave its own life in the wound it inflicts" (179). He is murdered while attempting to rescue his ward from a band of robbers. Moreover, Catherine's speech to her father, in which she attempts to convince him not to surrender himself to the authorities, repeatedly alludes to her own death: "death will have laid his grasp on me," "the deed that separates us will to me at least be mortal," "that moment I die" (275). Whereas selfish passions frequently lead to antisocial, even violent behavior, individuals motivated by selfless passions tend to become martyrs. Their identities become so intertwined with the identities of others that they become incapable of perceiving themselves as separate, independent human beings.

The passion-driven characters in Shelley's fictional works also have a difficult time striking a balance between the extremes of selfishness and selflessness. In her short story "A Tale of the Passions" (1823), she presents two characters who semi-allegorically represent selfish and selfless passions. When Despina dei Elisei rejects Guielmo Lostendardo's advances, his love for her turns into hatred, and "the fire of rage . . . burn[s] in his heart, consuming all healthy feeling, all human sympathies and gentleness of soul" (*Collected Tales and Stories*, 16). Lostendardo's "terrible egotism . . . would sacrifice even himself to the establishment of his will" (11). In contrast, Despina's unrequited love for Manfred is completely selfless: she parts "with her heart, her soul, her will, her entire being, an involuntary sacrifice at the shrine of all that is noble and divine in human nature." She devotes herself to Manfred's wife "and never in thought or dream degrade[s] the purity of [her] affection towards him" (12). Like Godwin's Catherine Deloraine, she is eager to sacrifice herself in order to serve the person she loves: "I am animated but by one feeling," she tells Lostendardo, "an aspiration to another life, another state of being. All the good depart from this strange earth; and I doubt not that when I am sufficiently elevated above human weaknesses, it will also be my turn to leave this scene of woe" (13).

Although Shelley presents Despina's transcendent love as heroic and Lostendardo's hatred as demonic, both of these obsessional passions prove destructive. Despina puts herself in Lostendardo's power in order to further the cause of Manfred's son, Corradino, and dies after Lostendardo forces her to witness Corradino's execution. Lostendardo's all-consuming hatred transforms him into a sadistic monster who, apparently stricken by remorse, becomes a monk and dies after "having gained the character of a saint, through a life of self-inflicted torture" (23). In Shelley's fiction, ruling passions are often regarded as pernicious. Lady Brampton, a minor character in *Perkin Warbeck*, cogently describes the destructive effect of passions: "We poor faulty human beings, hurried hither and thither by passion, are for ever jostling against and hurting each other, where more perfect natures would coalesce, and thus succeed where we fail" (37–38). According to her, the passions promote chaotic and antisocial behavior, cause needless suffering, and make any kind of unified action impossible.

In *Frankenstein*, the title character realizes in retrospect that his megalomaniacal ambition to create "a human being" (*The Mary Shelley Reader*, 40) was incompatible with his duties to his family and friends:

> A human being in perfection ought always to preserve a calm and peaceful mind, and never to allow passion or a transitory desire to disturb his tranquillity. I do not think that the pursuit of knowledge is an exception to this rule. If the study to which you apply yourself has a tendency to weaken your affections, and to destroy your taste for those simple pleasures in which no alloy can possibly mix, then that study is certainly unlawful, that is to say, not befitting the human mind. If this rule were always observed; if no man allowed any pursuit whatsoever to interfere with the tranquillity of his domestic affections, Greece had not been enslaved; Cæsar would have spared his country; America would have been explored more gradually; and the empires of Mexico and Peru had not been destroyed. (41)

Frankenstein has become so suspicious of emotion that he advocates constant mental equilibrium: any "passion" or "transitory desire," any alienation from one's "domestic affections," can lead to the creation of a monster, the enslavement of a country, or the destruction of empires. The product of his passionate reveries (156) has, after all, murdered his brother, best friend, and wife.

Shelley believes, however, that there can be good as well as bad passions. In her Preface to *The Poetical Works of Percy Bysshe Shelley* (1839), she honors "the ruling passion of [Percy Shelley's] soul": "To defecate [purify] life of its misery and its evil."[59] She also portrays positive as well as destructive passions in her fiction. In the discarded draft for *Mathilda*, *The Fields of Fancy*, Shelley presents Diotima, "the instructress of Socrates," who, appalled by the "mean passions" of the ancient Athenians, leaves society in order to discover the source of her "unquenshable [*sic*] love of beauty" and pass that knowledge on to others: "if I can teach but one other mind what is the beauty which they ought to love—and what is the sympathy to which they ought to aspire . . . then shall I be satisfied & think I have done enough."[60] While the love of beauty is the "ruling star of [Diotima's] life,"[61] the "strong and ruling passion" of Euthanasia, the Countess of Valperga, is "A hatred and fear of war" (*Valperga*, 98). Adrian, the Percy Shelley surrogate in *The Last Man*, is also passionately idealistic and dedicates himself to aiding the English victims of a global plague. Although he cannot contend with the "vices and passions" of others, he "can bring patience, and sympathy, and such aid as art affords, to the bed of disease" (179). Describing the feelings of Edmund Plantagenet, a character in *The Fortunes of Perkin Warbeck* who dedicates his life to the Yorkist cause, Shelley writes: "Self-devotion is, while it can keep true to itself, the best source of human enjoyment: there is small alloy when we wholly banish our own wretched clinging individuality, in our entire sacrifice at the worshipped shrine" (62).

Some of Shelley's virtuous characters are, however, more devoted to particular individuals than to ideals or impersonal acts of benevolence. These nurturing, supportive characters are, with the exception of Lionel Verney, women. Like Godwin's Marguerite de Damville and Emilia Fitzcharles, they dedicate themselves entirely to the "domestic affections." In *Perkin Warbeck*, the protagonist's wife, Katherine, argues that her passions are "an integral part of [her], and not the worst part of her": "We are not deities to bestow in impassive benevolence. We give, because we love—and the meshes of that sweet web, which mutual good offices and sympathy weaves, entangle and enthral me, and force me to pain and pleasure, and to every variety of emotion which is the portion of those whom it holds within its folds" (400). She loyally supports her husband as he unsuccessfully tries to dethrone Henry VII, and after his execution, she finds fulfillment in raising his nephews.

Shelley wrote to her publisher that Cornelia Santerre and Ethel Villiers, the heroines of *Lodore* (1835), are admirable because they completely dedicate themselves to those they love: "A Mother [Cornelia] & Daughter [Ethel] are the heroines—The Mother who after sacrifising *all* to the world at first—afterwards makes sacrifises not less entire, for her child—finding all to be Vanity, except the genuine affections of the heart. In the daughter I have tried to pourtray in its simplicity, & all the beauty I could muster, the *devotion* of a young wife for the husband of her choice."[62] Similarly, Elizabeth Raby, the heroine of *Falkner*, devotes herself single-mindedly to the happiness of her adoptive father: "All her employments, all her pleasures, referred themselves, . . . to this primary motive, and were entirely ruled by it" (56).[63] As Godwin asserts, "self-love is not the source of all our passions[;] disinterested benevolence has its seat in the human heart." Shelley considers Diotima's "universal love,"[64] Euthanasia's pacifism, Adrian's altruism, Edmund Plantagenet's loyalty, Katherine's sympathy, Cornelia's self-sacrifice, Ethel's adoration of her husband, and Elizabeth Raby's dedication to her foster father praiseworthy because they are benevolent rather than selfish or self-destructive passions.

In *Mathilda*, however, ruling passions devastate both the title character and her father. After the death of Mathilda's mother "a few days after [her] birth" (180), her father abandons her to the care of an aunt and does not return until sixteen years later. During their long separation, their love for one another is nurtured and intensified by their imaginations: while Mathilda's father, who has "the imagination of a poet" (189), "passionately love[s]" her even before they meet (208), Mathilda makes her absent parent "the idol of [her] imagination" and fantasizes about disguising herself as a boy and seeking him "throughout the world" (185). When they meet for the first time, Mathilda sees her father as a magical being who has the power to transport her "from a narrow spot of earth into a universe boundless to the imagination and the understanding" (189), and he believes that she looks "more like a spirit than a human maid" (187). In a Journal entry dated 25 February 1822, Mary Shelley expresses her determination to love others as they are: "let me in my fellow creatures love that which is & not ~~imagine~~ fix my ~~love~~ affections on a fair form endued with imaginary attributes—where goodness, kindness & talent are, let me love & admire them at their just rate neither adding or ~~dim~~ diminishing."[65] The relationship between Mathilda and her father becomes dysfunctional because they become obsessed with each other's "imaginary attributes." Mathilda's father sees his dead wife in his daughter; Mathilda initially is "attracted and enchanted" by her father's "strangeness" (188) and later considers him her "curse" (239). Like Fleetwood, Deloraine, and Hays's Emma Courtney, they fall in love with projections of their imagination rather than with real human beings, and their passions for each other quickly turn obsessional.

Shelley indicates in *Fortunes of Perkin Warbeck* that love is a passion that can be either positive or pernicious depending on a person's "natural propensities" (368): "Love has been called selfish, engrossing, tyrannic—as the root, so the green leaf that shoots from it—love is a part of us—it is our manifestation of life; and poisonous or sweet will be the foliage, according to the stock. When we love, it is our aim and conclusion to make the object a part of ourselves—if we are self-willed and evilly inclined, little good can arise; but deep is the fount of generous, devoted, godlike feeling, which this silver key unlocks in gentle hearts" (*Perkin Warbeck*, 228–29). Whereas the love of Lady Katherine and Richard of York is a "generous, devoted, godlike feeling," the passion that Henry VII feels for Katherine soon turns "poisonous":

> love, an exotic in his heart, degenerated from being a fair, fragrant flower, into a wild, poisonous weed. Love, whose essence is the excess of sympathy, and consequently of self-abandonment and generosity, when it alights on an unworthy soil, appears there at first in all its native bloom, a very wonder even to the heart in which it has taken root. The cold, selfish, narrow-hearted Richmond [Henry VII] was lulled to some slight forgetfulness of self, when first he was fascinated by Katherine, and he decked himself with ill-assorted virtues to merit her approbation. This lasted but a brief interval; the uncongenial clime in which the new plant grew, impregnated it with its own poison. Envy, arrogance, base desire to crush the fallen, were his natural propensities; and, when love refused to minister to these, it changed to something like hate in his bosom. (368)

According to this theory, the reason that Mathilda's father's love for her becomes "poisonous" is that it is contaminated by his "natural propensities": his selfishness and tendency to love obsessionally. A "selfish feeling" (180) motivates him to abandon his infant daughter in England: "He existed from [that] moment for himself only" (181). Like Fleetwood and Deloraine, he first realizes the depth of his passion when he becomes jealous. In a letter to his daughter, he describes how he became aware of his incestuous feelings: "when I saw you become the object of another's love; when I imagined that you might be loved otherwise than as a sacred type and image of loveliness and excellence; or that you might love another with a more ardent affection than that which you bore me, then the fiend awoke within me; I dismissed your lover; and from that moment I have known no peace." He wants to be "all the world" to Mathilda and cannot stand to share her with another (209). In his "madness" he begins to fantasize that his dead wife's "spirit" inhabits his daughter's body: "Diana died to give her birth; her mother's spirit was transferred into her frame, and she ought to be as Diana to me" (210).

Consumed by his possessive jealousy and his necrophiliac fantasy of being reunited with Diana, he is incapable of maintaining a normal relationship with his daughter. For a time, he tries to overcome his passion for her by opposing his melancholy to it: "He contrived in many ways to nurse his melancholy as an antidote to wilder passion" (196). Godwin critiques this theory that one passion can be subdued by another in *Enquiry Concerning Political Justice*: "Miserable indeed would be our condition, if we could only expel one bad passion by another of the same kind, and there was no way of rooting out delusion from the mind, but by substituting another delusion in its place."[66] In the case of Mathilda's father, his attempt to "expel" his passion for his daughter by indulging his grief over his wife's death only succeeds in further confusing his feelings for his daughter with those for Diana. His failure is consistent with Hume's belief that "When two passions . . . are both present in the mind . . . [t]he predominant passion swallows up the inferior, and converts it into itself." Mathilda's father finally decides that he was "miserably mistaken in imagining that [he] could conquer [his] love" (210) for Mathilda, and he commits suicide. His passion for his daughter, like his love for Diana, becomes "entwined with every faculty and every sentiment and [is] only to be lost with life" (178).

After her father's death, Mathilda is stricken by remorse and guilt. Her obsessional passions appear to be as incurable as her father's, and she intensifies them by withdrawing from society. Even the comforting words of her friend Woodville fail to overcome her "old habits of feeling." Her hyperactive imagination fuels her remorse: "to the natural sorrow of my father's death and its most terrific cause, imagination added a ten-fold weight of woe. I believed myself to be polluted by the unnatural love I had inspired, and that I was a creature cursed and set apart by nature" (238). Mathilda's morbid imagination is, like her father's, necrophiliac: she longs to die in order to be able to "unite" with him "in an eternal mental union" (244). Both Mathilda and her father come to believe in "the crime there may be in involuntary feeling" (197); she wills herself to a premature death, and he commits suicide despite the fact that they never actually commit any "crime."[67] In destroying themselves they seek to destroy the passions that have taken over their minds and made them believe that they are "monsters" (201, 239).

Joanna Baillie seems to have exerted a major influence on Shelley's conception of the ruling passions. Baillie's plays on the passions, particularly *De Monfort*, which focuses on hate, possibly inspired an early fictional effort by Shelley (then Mary Godwin), a story or novel entitled *Hate* begun in September 1814. Mary Godwin also read Baillie extensively during late December 1814.[68] One of the passion plays that Shelley read during this period was *Ethwald* (1802), Baillie's two-part tragedy on the passion of ambition, a work that may have helped shape Shelley's treatment of obsessional ambition in *Valperga*. Like Mary Shelley's protagonist, Castruccio, Ethwald's ambition for fame and power consumes him. As one of his followers notes, "nature has form'd [Ethwald's] mind / Too restless and aspiring."[69] In both works, ambition is pursued at the expense of love: after Castruccio seduces and then deserts her, Beatrice goes into a mental decline that ends in madness, and Bertha, Ethwald's rejected former sweetheart, also goes insane. Castruccio even sacrifices his love for his childhood companion Euthanasia when his lust for power leads him to go to war with her beloved Florence.

Ambition is presented in *Ethwald* and *Valperga* as a passion that gradually destroys whatever virtues the protagonists once possessed. What is said of Ethwald could also be applied to Castruccio: "from this mixed seed of good and ill / One baleful plant in dark strength rais'd its head, / O'ertopping all the rest."[70] Of Castruccio, Mary Shelley writes: "Ambition, and the fixed desire to rule, smothered in his mind the voice of his better reason; and the path of tyranny was smoothed, by his steady resolve to obtain the power, which under one form or other it had been the object of his life to seek" (173). She indicates that if the protagonists had been able to resist their ruling passion, much tragedy, and their own corruption, could have been avoided. Ethwald and Castruccio differ, however, in the way in which they meet their fates. While Ethwald degenerates into a paranoid insomniac, Castruccio faces death with "that coolness and presence of mind which was his peculiar characteristic" (325). In some ways Mary Shelley's portrait of obsessive ambition is subtler than Baillie's. She shows that this passion can rage even within an outwardly calm individual, and that a degree of psychological insight (such as that possessed by Euthanasia) may be needed if one is to recognize a would-be Napoleon before it is too late.

Castruccio's ruling passion, like Mathilda's, stems from his childhood. His early experience of cruelty and injustice conditions him to be ambitious and vengeful:

> Little Castruccio saw many of his dearest friends among [the Ghibellines fleeing from Lucca]; and his young heart, moved by their tears and complaints, became inflamed with rage and desire of vengeance. It was by scenes such as these, that party spirit was generated, and became so strong in Italy. Children, while they were yet too young to feel their own disgrace, saw the misery of their parents, and took early vows of implacable hatred against their persecutors: these were remembered in after times; the wounds were never seared, but the fresh blood ever streaming kept alive the feelings of passion and anger which had give rise to the first blow. (11–12)

Despite the pacifistic teachings of his mentor Guinigi, who instructs the youthful Castruccio in the rural virtues, and the exhortations of his beloved Euthanasia, Castruccio becomes completely enslaved by his obsessive need for fame and power: "he fixed his whole soul on the point he would attain, and he never lost sight of it, or paused in his efforts to arrive there" (183). He is able to rationalize his ruthless conduct with ease, and his career as a Machiavellian prince only ends with his premature death as the result of a sudden fever. His master passion resembles an incurable disease that spreads through his psyche until it enfeebles or obliterates every other faculty.

In *Valperga*, *Perkin Warbeck*, and *The Last Man*, Shelley advances the theory that history is driven by the ruling passions of individuals. While in *Valperga* Castruccio's ruling passion inspires him to wreak havoc throughout Tuscany, in *Perkin Warbeck* Henry the Seventh is "actuated . . . by base and bad passions," including his "hatred of the House of York," which is "At first the ruling feeling of his heart" (26–27). Similarly, in *The Last Man* the events of the future, before a catastrophic plague suddenly ends history itself, are shaped by the passions of a handful of people. The major political and military figure of the first part of the novel, Lord Raymond, is "the victim of ambition" (141) as well of his inconstant passion for Perdita. His demonic counterpart is the "imposter-prophet" (281) who, "instigated by ambition," attempts to become the "patriarch," "prophet," or even "deity" (281) of the last survivors of the epidemic.[71]

In opposition to these selfish, passion-driven characters, Shelley presents idealists like Euthanasia (in *Valperga*) and Adrian (in *The Last Man*). She suggests, however, that these altruistic figures are too scrupulous ever to be completely successful leaders: "It is a strange fact, but incontestible, that the philanthropist, who ardent in his desire to do good, who patient, reasonable and gentle, yet disdains to use other argument than truth, has less influence over men's minds, than he who, grasping and selfish, refuses not to adopt any means, nor awaken any passion, nor diffuse any falsehood, for the advancement of his cause" (*The Last Man*, 281). Thus Euthanasia is defeated and banished by Castruccio, and Adrian can assume power only after the plague has exterminated nearly all of his subjects. Even then, he has a difficult time contending with the "imposter-prophet." Those who are governed by their principles are frequently no match for those who are willing "to adopt any means" to further their ambitions.

Valperga also examines the passion of love. Shelley's use of a passage from a Wordsworth poem in the novel suggests that she, like Wordsworth, is wary of love as a ruling passion. After Euthanasia finds out that Castruccio has seduced Beatrice, Mary Shelley quotes from " 'Tis Said, that Some Have Died for Love" in order to convey Euthanasia's heartbreak:

> Thou, thrush, that singest loud, and loud, and free,
> Into yon row of willows flit,
> Upon that alder sit,
> Or sing another song, or choose another tree!
> Roll back, sweet rill, back to thy mountain bounds,
> And there for ever be thy waters chained!
> For thou dost haunt the air with sounds
> That cannot be sustained.
> * * * *
> Be any thing, sweet rill, but that which thou art now.
> (*Valperga*, 191)[72]

In *Valperga*, as in Wordsworth's poem, this expression of passionate grief is followed by sentiments that are more reasonable than passionate. The speaker of " 'Tis Said, that Some Have Died for Love" reacts to the lover's "moan" (line 10) by saying that he would rather be without love than to suffer as the lover has, and the disillusioned Euthanasia soon recovers from her "feverish emotions." After her initial despair, she realizes that Castruccio is incapable "of participating in her own exalted feelings," and she rejects passion in favor of reason: "her imagination furled its wings, and the owlet, reason, was the only dweller that found sustenance and a being in her benighted soul" (191). Although Mary Shelley describes Euthanasia as having "master-passions" (79), they involve her patriotism for Republican Florence and her hatred of war (98)—they are not selfish like Castruccio's. Euthanasia has the capacity to curb her emotions with her reason, and this makes her a kind of ideal in the bloody, medieval world of *Valperga*.

In contrast to Euthanasia, Beatrice is psychically destroyed by her master passion: her complete and unreasoning adoration of Castruccio. Whereas Euthanasia sacrifices her love for Castruccio on the altar of her principles, requiring in a husband "a conformity of tastes to those she had herself cultivated" (191), Beatrice insists that she would love Castruccio even if he were to be proven a villain: "Methinks, it would please me, that my lover should cast off all humanity, and be a reprobate, and an outcast of his species. Oh! then how deeply and tenderly I should love him; soiled with crimes, his hands dripping blood, I would shade him as the flowering shrub invests the ruin; I would cover him with a spotless veil" (250). Her "natural propensities" toward masochism and fanatical devotion poison her love for him. Clearly, Euthanasia's rigid adherence to her moral standards and political principles is far more conducive to psychic survival than Beatrice's devotion to a ruthless tyrant. In *Valperga* Mary Shelley's condemnation of the ruling passions of ambition and love implies an endorsement of reason, a faculty that, even though it condemns Euthanasia to an emotionally deprived and melancholy existence, allows her to avoid the storms of emotion that buffet and finally destroy Beatrice.

As Euthanasia's father warns her, "either [her] judgement or passions must rule" (82), and she uses her judgment in making the major decisions of her life. The favorite daughter of an intellectual father, Euthanasia receives what in Shelley's time would have been considered a masculine education: "I was ever near [my father] reading and conversing with him; and if I have put order in my day dreams, and culled the fruit of virtue and some slight wisdom from my meditations, it is to his lessons that I owe this good. It is he who taught me to fathom my sensations, and discipline my mind; to understand what my feelings were, and whether they arose from a good or evil source" (80–81). Her education emphasizes reason and moral understanding rather than the passions, a lesson that Euthanasia passes on to Castruccio: "rule your own heart; enthrone reason there, make virtue the high priest of your divinity" (178–79). As Mary Wollstonecraft writes, "the understanding, as life advances, gives firmness to the first fair purposes of sensibility—till virtue, arising rather from the clear conviction of reason than the impulse of the heart, morality is made to rest on a rock against which the storms of passion vainly beat."[73] Moreover, Euthanasia is able to study "the polished language of Cicero and Virgil" (18), thus receiving a classical education virtually denied to women of every class during the eighteenth and early nineteenth centuries. Although Euthanasia's life is scarcely a happy one, her "masculine" education effectively prepares her to withstand life's vicissitudes—she possesses "female softness [but not] female weakness" (177).[74]

Beatrice, on the other hand, receives only "a disorderly kind of education."[75] Raised first by her nurse, then by one of the disciples of her heretical mother, and then by a hideous leper, Beatrice ultimately becomes the ward of the Bishop of Ferrara, who attempts to educate her "in the Holy Catholic faith" (136). This unbalanced education, based on faith rather than reason, contrasts sharply with Euthanasia's study of the classics and training in mental discipline, and the bishop soon observes its bad effects:

> I was fearful that her ignorance and enthusiasm might lead her astray, since, in her accounts of her meditations, she often said things of God and the angels that were heretical; and I hoped that a knowledge of the truth would calm her mind, and lead her to a saner devotion. But my labours had a contrary effect; the more she heard, and the more she read, the more she gave herself up to contemplation and solitude, and to what I cannot help considering the wild dreams of her imagination. (136)

When Euthanasia and Beatrice are together, their mental differences become painfully obvious: "Euthanasia was astounded; she was herself so steady in her principles, so firm in opinion and action, slow to change, but resolute having changed, that she was at a loss to understand the variable feelings and swift mutations of the poor, untaught Beatrice" (246). If Euthanasia recalls Wollstonecraft's dream of a well-educated, enlightened woman, Beatrice suggests Wollstonecraft's description of her falsely educated female contemporaries: "All their thoughts turn on things calculated to excite emotion; and feeling, when they should reason, their conduct is unstable, and their opinions are wavering—not the wavering produced by deliberation or progressive views, but by contradictory emotions."[76] For Mary Shelley, as for Wollstonecraft, education is the key in disciplining the passions: because she does not develop her reason, Beatrice is preyed upon by her emotions and ultimately goes insane.

Moreover, Euthanasia's commitment to self-improvement allows her to grow morally and mentally throughout the novel, whereas Beatrice and Castruccio increasingly become the slaves of their ruling passions. Even at "the very prime of life . . . [Euthanasia's] character was always improving, always adding some new acquirements, or strengthening those which she possessed before; and thus for ever enlarging her sphere of knowledge and feeling" (297). According to Wollstonecraft, education is just "the first step to form a being advancing gradually towards perfection" (53), and Euthanasia continues this process even towards the end of her life. Unfortunately, Euthanasia fails to convert anyone else in the novel to her enlightened rationality: when she argues with Castruccio, she finds that "It is difficult to answer the language of passion with that of reason" (172), and although she helps Beatrice keep her ruling passion under control, in Euthanasia's absence Beatrice is "left without a guide to the workings of her own mind" (269) and falls victim to the machinations of a witch.[77] As the only advocate of reason in a world driven by passion and superstition, Euthanasia is doomed to be ignored and misunderstood. In this, she is not unlike Mary Wollstonecraft, and it is likely that in presenting Euthanasia's life of suffering and moral courage Mary Shelley had the author of *A Vindication of the Rights of Woman* in mind.

According to Anne Mellor, *Valperga* "emphasizes the inability of women, whether as adoring worshippers (like Beatrice) or active leaders (like Euthanasia), to influence political events or to translate an ethic of care—whether embodied in the domestic affections or in a political program of universal justice and peace—into historical reality."[78] I would argue, however, that Euthanasia's life is, in a sense, successful. As Euthanasia asserts, "Life is all our knowledge, and our highest praise is to have lived well" (231). Although she has not altered "historical reality," she has, according to her own lofty principles, lived well—she dies at peace with herself. Defeated in battle by Castruccio's henchmen, Euthanasia nevertheless succeeds in conquering her passions and, in this, she rises above Castruccio, who is a slave to ambition. She also serves as an embodiment of Wollstonecraftian rationality and becomes, therefore, a prophetic figure. She may not be politically effective in the fourteenth century, but in a world transformed by "a REVOLUTION in female manners" she would presumably come into her own.[79]

Even in the fourteenth century, however, Euthanasia succeeds in upholding her principles and retaining her sanity; after all, her father has taught her "to look upon events as being of consequence only through the feelings which they excited, and to believe that content of mind, love, and benevolent feeling ought to be elements of [one's] existence; while those accidents of fortune or fame . . . were as the dust of the balance" (82). Thus even when events are out of control, mental serenity is possible—historical chaos can be transcended by those who turn inward and master their passions. If the present looks hopeless, one can still look forward, as Euthanasia does, to a positive future: "what would not this world become, if every man might learn from its institutions the true principles of life, and become as the few which have as yet shone as stars amidst the light of ages?" (82). In essence, Euthanasia discovers a psychological strategy for dealing with tragic reality: she sets out to conquer ruling passions (such as love or ambition), enthrone reason as the dominant mental faculty, and maintain a balance between the conflicting elements of her mind. As a result of her mental discipline, she is able to withstand the pain of disappointed love, the complete annihilation of her castle and childhood home, the tragic death of her dearest friend, and banishment. Although Euthanasia's psychic survival may seem like a minor triumph, it is, unfortunately, the only victory allowed her in a world dominated by male passion.

While Godwin's female characters who are actuated by benevolent passions, Margaret de Damville and Catherine Deloraine, tend to have martyr complexes, Euthanasia manages to balance passion and reason. Her portrait of Euthanasia suggests that Shelley has more confidence than her father in a woman's capacity to live a fulfilled and independent life. Euthanasia does not rely on a husband or a father to provide her with a raison d'être. Shelley can envision an emancipated woman, "free in a physical, moral, and civil sense," who "will emulate the virtues of man [and] . . . grow more perfect."[80]

In the novels that follow *Valperga*, Shelley presents a number of characters who are driven by their passions but who are less monomaniacal than Castruccio and Beatrice. She claims in *Falkner* that emotional inconstancy is more common in men than in women: "In the human heart—and if observation does not err—more particularly in the heart of man, the passions exert their influence fitfully. With some analogy to the laws which govern the elements—they now sleep in calm, and now arise with the violence of furious winds." Thus Falkner's remorse over having caused Alithea's death is intense at some periods of his life, particularly when he comes into contact with her son, Neville, but at other times he "attain[s] a state of feeling approaching to equanimity" (48). The passions of Raymond, the self-destructive political and military leader of *The Last Man*, fluctuate even more than Falkner's:

> The selected passion of the soul of Raymond was ambition. Readiness of talent, a capacity of entering into, and leading the dispositions of men; earnest desire of distinction were the awakeners and nurses of his ambition. But other ingredients mingled with these, and prevented him from becoming the calculating, determined character, which alone forms a successful hero. He was obstinate, but not firm; benevolent in his first movements; harsh and reckless when provoked. Above all, he was remorseless and unyielding in the pursuit of any object of desire, however lawless. Love of pleasure, and the softer sensibilities of our nature, made a prominent part of his character, conquering the conqueror; holding him in at the moment of acquisi-

tion; sweeping away ambition's web; making him forget the toil of weeks, for the sake of one moment's indulgence of the new and actual object of his wishes. Obeying these impulses, he had become the husband of Perdita; egged on by them, he found himself the lover of Evadne. He had now lost both. (106)

Raymond, like a number of Shelley's other male characters, is based on Byron, whom she regarded as both "capricious [and] fascinating."[81] Her fictional portrait of him recalls his own description of his character in a letter to Annabella Milbanke (in which he quotes from Pope's *Essay on Man*): "I am sure that of my own character I know nothing—nor could I if my existence were at stake tell what my 'ruling passion' is—it takes it's [*sic*] colour I believe from the circumstances in which I am placed—there are few which at one period or other of my life have not affected me—but I could not fix on one which like 'Aaron's serpent swallowed all the rest.' "[82]

Likewise, Raymond's ruling passion changes according to "the circumstances in which [he is] placed." While Castruccio is willing to sacrifice his passion for Euthanasia on the altar of his ambition, Raymond is "remorseless and unyielding in the pursuit of any object of desire." Like Byron, he exiles himself from England following the breakup of his marriage and joins the Greeks fighting to liberate their country from the Turks (a struggle that Shelley has continuing in 2092). His former lover Evadne, delirious with fever, predicts his imminent death: "Fire, and war, and plague, unite for thy destruction—O my Raymond, there is no safety for thee!" (131). After hearing this prophecy, the suggestible Raymond falls into a deep depression. Convinced that he is about to die, he rides along through the streets of Constantinople, which has been devastated by the plague, and is crushed by "some falling ruin" (149). In her presentation of Raymond, Shelley suggests that while a single ruling passion may prove psychologically damaging, an individual who is dominated by a variety of sometimes contradictory emotional impulses is doomed to be ineffective as well as miserable. As Neville asks in *Falkner*, "can any agony equal that which convulses the human heart, when writhing under contending passions—torn by contrary purposes[?]" (210). Raymond cannot fix on either ambition or conjugal love as his ruling passion and, as a result, fails to become either "a successful hero" or a faithful husband.

Richard of York, the hero of *Perkin Warbeck*, is much more single-minded than Raymond. Like Castruccio, Richard has been conditioned to seek fame and power: "From his early childhood he had been nurtured in the idea that it was his first, chief duty to regain his kingdom. . . . On the table of his ductile boyish mind, that sole intent was deeply engraved by every hand or circumstance" (337). As Edward IV's surviving son, he is the heir to the throne after Richard III's death, but his Lancastrian enemies claim that both of Edward's sons were executed in the Tower of London and that Richard is actually Perkin Warbeck, the son of a Flemish merchant. Moreover, Henry VII does everything he can to capture and discredit his rival. However, despite a series of disheartening setbacks, Richard perseveres in his struggle to become England's king: "He had been educated to believe that his honour called on him to maintain his claims. Honour, always a magic word with the good and brave, was then a part of the religion of every pious heart. He had been nurst in war—the javelin and the sword were . . . familiar to his hand" (196). Ambition is clearly Richard's ruling passion, but he, unlike Henry VII and Castruccio, possesses a sense of honor and an aversion to human suffering. He is neither suspicious nor ruthless enough to contend with Henry's Machiavellian stratagems or prevent his followers' treachery.

During Richard's abortive final invasion of England, two of his former supporters, Frion and Robert Clifford, conspire to betray him. Shelley laments the power of such contemptible individuals to bring down someone like Richard:

> It is melancholy that circumstance and fortune should have power to reach the very shrine of our dearest thoughts; degrading them from their original brightness to a likeness of the foul aspect of the outer world. . . . Men, whom he had cast from him as unworthy of his regard, could besiege the citadel of his hopes, and garrison it with disgrace; forcing him to occupy himself with ideas as base as those which possessed their own minds. It is the high heart's curse to be obliged to expend its deep and sacred emotions in hatred of, or struggle with things so mean, so very alien to its own aspiring nature. (313–14)

Richard's naive faith in the honesty of others leaves him vulnerable to the meanest of conspirators, and his compassion for his men undermines his determination to continue his struggle against Henry's soldiers: "one of Richard's characteristics was a quick sympathy with his species, and a reverence for all that bore the shape of man. But . . . these qualities . . . inspired him with a severe sense of his duties towards others, and a quick insight into their feelings; thus increasing to anguish the disquietude that agitated him" (316). Richard's character, like Raymond's, has a number of "ingredients" that prevent "him from becoming the calculating, determined character, which alone forms a successful hero," but in his case the ingredients tend to be virtues rather than vices.

This does not mean, however, that his actions are justified. In fact, Shelley declares that Richard's invasion of England from Scotland is neither "disinterested [n]or justifiable": "Oh, narrow and selfish was that sentiment that could see, in any right appertaining to one man the excuse for the misery of thousands" (252). As Betty Bennett observes, Richard "is . . . the product of erroneous education—a man of intelligence, grace, and ability, whose indoctrination into belief in the supreme rights of monarchs [especially the rule of lineal succession] causes him to generate destruction 'from mistake.' "[83] Although Richard possesses a number of virtues, his "narrow and selfish" ambition turns him into "the curse and scourge of [his] own people" (256).

Clifford, Richard's archenemy, is also torn between contrary impulses. Shelley writes:

> No character can be wholly evil; and Clifford's was not destitute of good. . . . He was generous; but that led to rapacity; since, unable to deny himself or others, if he despoiled himself one day, on the next he engaged in the most desperate enterprises to refil [*sic*] the void. He was bold—that made him fearless in doing wrong; and to drown the gentle spirit of humanity, which too often for his own peace sprung up in his heart, he hardened himself to selfishness; then, as his sensitive, undisciplined nature received new impressions, he was cowardly, cruel, and remorseless. (137)

When Clifford becomes infatuated with Monina, his passion, like King Henry's for Katherine, is poisoned by his inability to sympathize with another: "each feeling that expresses the sympathy of our intellectual nature, was never associated to him with the name of woman" (169). A bitter cynic, he has nothing but contempt for emotions like love, friendship, or sympathy. He cannot, however, withstand the passion of jealousy, and Monina's obvious devotion to Richard infuriates him: "the love he despised, and thought he mastered, became his tyrant, when it allied itself to his evil passions" (151). His selfishness nullifies his good qualities, and jealousy, rather than love, becomes his ruling passion. Like Richard, Clifford "desire[s] honour" (320), but "his evil passions" motivate him to commit a series of treacherous acts and ultimately transform him into a prematurely aged man, racked with self-loathing (354).

The object of Clifford's jealousy, Monina, is as selfless as he is selfish. Like Despina, the heroine of "A Tale of the Passions," she devotes herself entirely to the service of a man whom she can never marry: "[Richard's] cause was her life; his royalty the main spring of all her actions and thoughts. She had sacrificed love to it—she taught her woman's soul to rejoice in his marriage with another, because his union with a princess was a pledge to the world of his truth" (291). As in the case of Despina, there is something unhealthy in Monina's complete selflessness. In fact, Shelley's assessment of her is extremely ambivalent: "Monina,—no, there was no evil in Monina; if too much self-devotion, too passionate an attachment to one dear idea, too enthusiastic an adoration of one exalted being, could be called aught but virtue" (304). Rather than seeking her own fulfillment, she dedicates her life to a hopeless cause, and her death in Portugal virtually coincides with Richard's in England.

Although Lady Katherine's love for Richard also tends toward "self-annihilation" (277), her emotions are clearly more balanced than Monina's. She is also more self-sufficient than Perdita, "the victim of too much loving" (*The Last Man*, 156), who chooses to commit suicide and leave her daughter Clara an orphan rather than be separated from the grave of her beloved Raymond. After Richard's death Katherine lives on as the companion of his sister, Queen Elizabeth (the wife of Henry VII), and her children. In the conclusion of the novel she defends her decision to survive her husband and live in his archenemy's court to Edmund, the last of the Plantagenets: "must my living heart be stone, because that dear form is dust, which was the medium of my communication with his spirit? Where I see suffering, there I must bring my mite for its relief" (400). Like Euthanasia, Katherine can find fulfillment in caring for others; unlike Despina, Beatrice, Perdita, and Monina, she refuses to become a martyr to love.

In *Falkner*, Shelley is more optimistic about an individual's capacity to recover from obsessional remorse than she is in *Mathilda* and *The Last Man*. *Falkner* can, in fact, be read as a reply to Godwin's pessimistic *Deloraine*.[84] After Falkner's abduction of Alithea Neville and her subsequent death, his love for his ward, Elizabeth Raby, and her devotion to him alleviate the pangs of his obsessional remorse, rendering it temporarily dormant: "Falkner . . . attained a state of feeling approaching to equanimity." At the end of *Deloraine* the protagonist declares himself "the most atrocious of offenders" (285) and resigns himself to a short and miserable existence. In contrast, Falkner, after he has been acquitted of murder by a jury and has been forgiven by Alithea's son, lives a relatively happy life: "As much happiness as any one can enjoy, whose inner mind bears the unhealing wound of a culpable act, fell to the portion of Falkner" (299). Rather than obsessively dwelling on his past acts, Falkner follows the advice of Mrs. Raby, Elizabeth's aunt: "The whole order of events is inscrutable—one little change, and none of us would be as we are now. Except as a lesson or a warning, we ought not to contemplate the past, but the future certainly demands our attention" (293). Unlike *Deloraine*, *Falkner* suggests that redemption and even a measure of tranquillity may be possible for someone who, under the influence of a ruling passion, has committed a criminal act.

In Godwin's and Shelley's fictional works most ruling passions, whether selfish or selfless, are shown to be harmful or even pathological. Once they are established in the mind and become associatively linked with an individual's identity, they are virtually ineradicable. They typically transform those who are mastered by them either into monsters (see *St. Leon*, 176, 211, 363; *Mandeville*, 44; *Cloudesley*, 134; *Deloraine*, 144; *Frankenstein*; *Mathilda*, 201, 239; and *Falkner*, 154) or martyrs. Even some of Godwin's and Shelley's characters who believe that they are motivated by benevolent principles, such as St. Leon and Frankenstein, are shown to be self-deluded. Godwin and Shelley often contrast, however, a less violent and more social passion to the negative master passions that they feature in their works: friendship. Many of Godwin's characters believe that a friend will provide them with much-needed emotional support and enable them to escape the evils of selfhood. While Fleetwood longs for "the friendship which can best console a man in calamity and wretchedness, whether of mind or external circumstances" (*Fleetwood*, 149), Mandeville claims that the lack of a friend has turned him into a villain: "never has my hand been pressed in the hand of a friend. For this want, and this want only, I have become a monument of human misery, and a villain" (145–46).[85]

Friendships are among the most positive relationships in Shelley's works: one thinks of Frankenstein and Clerval, Mathilda and Woodville, Euthanasia and Beatrice, Adrian and Lionel Verney, and Ethel Villiers and Fanny Derham. Less intense and less driven by the imagination than love, friendship leads individuals to "coalesce" rather than oppose and hurt each other and involves valuing someone for who that person is rather than for his or her "imaginary attributes." Friendship, rather than love, makes individuals mentally transparent to one another (see *Fleetwood*, 148–51). As I will show in chapter 4, although in Godwin's and Shelley's works friends may not be able to "cure" individuals who are under the influence of a ruling passion, they provide them with the opportunity to ventilate their emotions and perhaps even gain some insight into their obsessions. In the next chapter, however, I will explore Godwin's and Shelley's fictional treatments of one of the negative consequences of uncontrolled passions: madness.

3
Episodes of Madness

AS MANY COMMENTATORS HAVE OBSERVED, MENTAL ILLNESS BOTH horrified and fascinated late eighteenth-century English society. A series of reports on King George III's second attack of madness, which began in October 1788 and continued until March 1789, familiarized the public with the symptoms of madness and the methods used to treat it.[1] The public was also interested in less famous mental patients. Michael V. DePorte describes the "entertainment" provided by Bethlehem Hospital (Bedlam) during the seventeenth and eighteenth centuries: "until its doors were shut to the public in 1770, Bethlehem Hospital was a favorite London tourist attraction. . . . The popularity of the place was enormous; according to a recent estimate it drew no fewer than 96,000 visitors a year . . . For a penny one could not only see the inmates, one could tease them to his heart's content."[2] In Henry Mackenzie's *The Man of Feeling* (1771), the narrator observes that "Of those things called Sights in London, which every stranger is supposed desirous to see, Bedlam is one."[3] According to Godwin's Journal, he, Mary Wollstonecraft, and Joseph Johnson (the publisher) toured Bedlam together on 6 February 1797.[4] Wollstonecraft's observations during this visit probably informed her description of the madhouse in which Maria is imprisoned in *The Wrongs of Woman*.

Locke's belief in *An Essay Concerning Human Understanding* that madness is "a weakness to which all men are . . . liable" was shared by a number of eighteenth-century writers.[5] According to Michel Foucault, during

> the second half of the eighteenth century . . . men regained that awareness, which had been so intense in the sixteenth century, of the precariousness of a reason that can at any moment be compromised, and definitively, by madness. Matthey, a Geneva[n] physician very close to Rousseau's influence, formulates the prospect for all men of reason: "Do not glory in your state, if you are wise and civilized men;

> an instant suffices to disturb and annihilate that supposed wisdom of which you are so proud; an unexpected event, a sharp and sudden emotion of the soul will abruptly change the most reasonable and intelligent man into a raving idiot."[6]

Similarly, in Samuel Johnson's *Rasselas* (1759), Imlac declares that "Of the uncertainties of our present state, the most dreadful and alarming is the uncertain continuance of reason."[7] The protagonist of *The Wrongs of Woman* describes how the ravings of lunatics that she hears in her madhouse prison make her fear for her own sanity: "a mental convulsion, which, like the devastation of an earthquake, throws all the elements of thought and imagination into confusion, makes contemplation giddy, and we fearfully ask on what ground we ourselves stand."[8]

For the most part, Godwin's and Shelley's fictional explorations of madness reflect the Enlightenment belief that the mental stability of virtually any human is vulnerable to "an unexpected event, [or] a sharp and sudden emotion of the soul." Their conceptions of insanity are grounded in late seventeenth- and early eighteenth-century medical and philosophical theories, particularly in the writings of Locke and Darwin. Eighteenth-century mad-doctors were divided about and ineffective in their treatments of madness, and in their works Godwin and Shelley explore different therapies that serve to ameliorate rather than cure their characters' mental problems. Most of their psychologically unbalanced characters are difficult to categorize. Are they "quite mad," or do they maintain, at some level of their psyche, a "latent sanity"? Are they completely "other," or are they basically "normal" except for a single pathological tendency or impulse? To what extent can they be treated or cured? This chapter will examine the ways in which Godwin and Shelley pose these questions and suggest answers to them in their works. It will also argue that there is a significant difference in their perspectives on mental illness. Whereas Godwin's novels, with one possible exception, reflect the horror of lunacy felt by many eighteenth-century rationalists, Shelley presents a more positive view of madness, linking it to the poetic imagination.

Although Locke's *An Essay Concerning Human Understanding* was published in 1690, his definition of madness was still cited during the late eighteenth and early nineteenth centuries. It is, for example, quoted approvingly in Samuel Warren's "The Spectre-Smitten," one of the series of remarkable psychological tales that Warren published in *Blackwood's Magazine* from 1830 to 1837.[9] According to Locke, madness results when an individual's reason is misled by his or her imagination:

> [Madmen] do not appear to me to have lost the faculty of reasoning, but having joined together some ideas very wrongly, they mistake them for truths; and they err as men do that argue right from wrong principles. For, by the violence of their imaginations, having taken their fancies for realities, they make right deductions from them. Thus you shall find a distracted man fancying himself a king, with a right inference require suitable attendance, respect, and obedience: others who have thought themselves made of glass, have used the caution necessary to preserve such brittle bodies.[10]

In another influential description of insanity, Hartley asserts that "The Causes of Madness are of two Kinds, bodily and mental," but he does not attempt to "distinguish" between these causes, because he believes that "they are both united for the most part."[11] According to him, "The bodily Cause lays hold of that Passion or Affection which is most disproportionate; and the mental Cause, when that is primary, generally waits till some bodily Distemper gives it full Scope to exert itself. Ageeably to this, the Prevention and Cure of all Kinds of Madness require an Attention both to the Body and Mind."[12] Hartley closes his discussion of madness by asserting that "Religious Considerations are the best Preservative in hereditary or other Tendencies to Madness; . . . However, bodily Labour, with a Variety of mental Occupations, and a considerable Abstemiousness in the Quantity and Quality of Diet, ought always be joined."[13] Hartley's belief that mental illness has both somatic and mental causes informs *Deloraine*, in which the protagonist has "just recovered from a very dangerous illness" (*Deloraine*, 138) when he falls in love with Margaret. Deloraine's "passion for her [has] a diseased tone and sickly hue," and when her former sweetheart returns to England, "the clouds of [his] mind [appear] to thicken on every side" (138–39). Thus his "original, bodily Disorder falls in with an accidental mental one,"[14] and his love for his second wife becomes pathologically possessive and jealous.

William Battie, the founder of St. Luke's Hospital for Lunaticks, was perhaps the most prestigious "mad-doctor" of the mid-eighteenth century. According to Hunter and Macalpine, his pioneering *Treatise on Madness* (1758) is the first study of insanity written "by a psychiatrist who could draw on his experiences with a large number of patients."[15] Battie contends that "*deluded imagination* . . . is not only an indisputable but an essential character of Madness [and] precisely discriminates this from all other animal disorders."[16] He identifies two basic types of madness: "original" ("owing to an internal disorder of the nervous substance") and "consequential" (caused by organic disease or injury to the brain).[17] What sets Battie apart from many of his predecessors is his conviction that contemporary treatments for mental illness were often worse than useless. He is particularly pessimistic about finding cures for original madness: "altho' we may have reason to hope that the peculiar antidote of Madness is reserved in Nature's store, and will be brought to light in its appointed time; yet such is our present misfortune, that either this important secret hath been by its inventors withheld from the rest of mankind, or, which is more probable, hath never yet been discovered."[18] In his opinion, the best treatment may be no treatment at all: "Madness, like several other animal distempers, oftentimes ceases spontaneously, that is without our being able to assign a sufficient reason; and many a Lunatic, who by the repetition of vomits and other convulsive stimuli would have been strained into downright Idiotism, has when given over as incurable recovered his understanding."[19] Battie emphasizes the importance of "Regimen" and "management" in the treatment of the insane: "Every unruly appetite must be checked, every fixed imagination must if possible be diverted."[20] As Hunter and Macalpine observe, Battie's book anticipates "the 'moral treatment' of the nineteenth century."[21]

However, despite his status as the leading "mad-doctor" of his time, Battie's theories were not universally accepted. John Munro, the physician of Bethlem Hospital, immediately wrote a caustic rebuttal of Battie's *Treatise*, entitled *Remarks on Dr Battie's* Treatise on Madness (1758), and Tobias Smollett satirized Battie's landmark work in *The Life and Adventures of Sir Launcelot Greaves* (1760–61), a novel that Mary Shelley read in 1817.[22] In Smollett's novel, the quixotic protagonist is abducted and thrown into an insane asylum by his rival's henchmen. When Sir Launcelot asks the presiding physician if he considers him insane, the mad-doctor's reply is taken, almost verbatim, from Battie's *Treatise*:

> you have heard, no doubt, of what is called a weakness of the nerves, sir,—tho' that is a very inaccurate expression; for this phrase, denoting a morbid excess of sensation, seems to imply that sensation itself is owing to the loose cohesion of those material particles which consti-

tute the nervous substance, inasmuch as the quantity of every effect must be proportionable to its cause; now . . . if the case were really what these words seem to import, all bodies, whose particles do not cohere with too great a degree of proximity, would be nervous; that is, endued with sensation—Sir, I shall order some cooling things to keep you in due temperature.[23]

After the physician leaves, Sir Launcelot "think[s] it [is] very hard that one man should not dare to ask the most ordinary question without being reputed mad, while another should talk nonsense by the hour, and yet be esteemed as an oracle."[24] While Battie was clearly the most influential mad-doctor of his day, it is important to recognize that neither he nor any other eighteenth-century physician was considered an absolute authority on the "science of the mind."

In his *Observations on Chronic Weakness* (1777), another eighteenth-century mad-doctor, Thomas Withers, contends that physicans should "study and humor" patients who suffer from "Dejection of spirits." He writes that the physician's

conversation, which is manly, rational, and untainted with the low deceits of a craft, both sooths and animates the mind. It affords at once entertainment and instruction, social pleasure and rules of health. The physician should study and humor the different dispositions of his patients. . . . He should be able to read internal characters from external signs. . . . He should endeavor to penetrate at once into the mind, and to ascertain with a cautious exactness the ruling passion. He should observe countenances, gestures, words, and actions, and yet seem as perfectly regardless of these things as if he made no observations upon them.[25]

While Withers's advice to physicians employs Pope's psychology of the ruling passions, it also insists that all patients should be studied as individuals. Inasmuch as Withers places a great deal of emphasis on the importance of conversation, he anticipates twentieth-century psychoanalysis.

The poet-physician Erasmus Darwin shared Hartley's belief that the somatic and the mental causes of madness are frequently intertwined. He writes in *Zoonomia* that a fever can either be "a symptom" of madness or its cause.[26] In fact, he contends that insanity can help cure a fever: "I have always esteemed insanity to be a favourable sign in fevers [because] the introduction of an increased quantity of the power of volition [gives] vigour to those movements of the system, which are generally only actuated by the power of irritation, and of association."[27] Conversely, he writes that the presence of a fever in a sufferer from *mania mutabilis* [mutable madness] "is frequently a salutary sign; because, if the life of the patient be safe, when the fever ceases, the insanity generally vanishes along with it."[28] Darwin's theory that fever can signal the end of madness may have informed the episode in Shelley's *The Last Man* in which Adrian's insanity disappears after he recovers from a serious fever (50–51).

Although Darwin was not averse to using such commonly accepted treatments as "venesection, emetics, . . . cathartics[,] large doses of opium, . . . the vertigo occasioned by a circulating swing, or . . . a sea-voyage," he believed that some mentally disturbed individuals are rational enough to see "the fallacy, or the too great estimation, of the[ir] painful ideas" when "contrary ideas" are repeatedly presented to them.[29] Like the model physician described by Withers, Darwin frequently conversed with and humored his patients. He recounts the case of Miss G——: "Miss G—— . . . said, as I once sat by her, 'My head is fallen off, see it is rolled to that corner of the room, and the little black dog is nibbling the nose off.' On my walking to the place which she looked at, and returning, and assuring her that her nose was unhurt, she became pacified, though I was doubtful whether she attended to me."[30] In another case, Darwin helped a patient overcome a delusion by calmly discussing it with him:

> Master ——, a school-boy about twelve years old, after he came out of a convulsion fit and sat up in bed, said to me, "Don't you see my father standing at the feet of the bed, he is come a long way on foot to see me." I answered, no: "What colour is his coat?" He replied, "A drab colour." "And what buttons?" "Metal ones," he answered, and added, "how sadly his legs are swelled." In a few minutes he said, with apparent surprise, "He is gone," and returned to his perfect mind.[31]

According to Darwin, physicians who treat the mentally ill need to "investigate [their patient's] maniacal idea, or hallucination; as it may not only reacquaint [them] with the probable designs of the patient, from whence may be deduced the necessity of confinement; but also may some time lead to the most effectual plan of cure."[32]

There are, however, no professional mad-doctors in Godwin's and Shelley's fictional works. In *St. Leon*, the eponymous narrator relies on his wife to help him through his period of mental illness; Marguerite is his "physician; not by administering medicines to [his] body, but by carefully studying and exerting herself to remove the distemper of mind" (84). Similarly, *Frankenstein* and a number of Shelley's other fictional works suggest that the loving support of a friend can be extremely therapeutic. After Frankenstein loses his reason following the creation of the monster, Clerval cares for him; Mathilda allows herself to be temporarily comforted by Woodville; Beatrice is guided by Euthanasia, and Lionel Verney waits by Adrian's bedside until "No trace of his past insanity remain[s]" (*The Last Man*, 51). Godwin's Fleetwood, however, recovers from his madness without anyone's help. After his bizarre "ceremonies" with the wax effigies of his wife and her supposed lover, he becomes an invalid:

> For fifteen days I never left my bed. For the most part of the time I was really insane, but I was too weak to break out into the paroxysms of insanity, and those about me were scarcely aware of the degree of my derangement. From the moment the physicians were called in, they pronounced that it was impossible I should recover. I gradually wasted away, till I seemed to be arrived at the last gasp. They were mistaken, however; I was reserved for more sufferings, and for stranger adventures. A favourable crisis took place in my disease, and I became slowly and tediously convalescent. (265)[33]

In *Mandeville*, the title character is confined in "a receptacle for lunatics" (143) in which his keepers brutally repress his maniacal rage: "All [of my thoughts] came mixed to my recollection, with the violence, the cords, the harsh language, the blows, it had been judged necessary to employ, for my restraint, or my cure. I had been turned into a coward, the veriest slave that lives, trembling at a look" (144). Mandeville cannot determine whether his attendants are more interested in restraining or curing him; in any case, he remains "for several weeks under the discipline of men, whose trade it is to superintend persons in [his] unfortunate condition" (146) and eventually recovers his sanity.

While Locke theorizes that madmen are overcome by "the violence of their imaginations" and Battie contends that insanity has its basis in the "*deluded imagination*," in Godwin's and Shelley's works the primary cause of madness is generally a ruling passion, which is intensified rather than engendered by the imagination. Caleb Williams is driven to the brink of madness by his master passion of curiosity and his obsessional love/hatred for Falkland—his master's crime and relentless persecution of him are facts, not the products of an over-strained imagination. Similarly, Frankenstein's episodes of madness stem from his emotional responses to the monster's creation and the murders of Clerval and Elizabeth rather than from delusional thinking. In *St. Leon*, the protagonist goes temporarily insane after having gambled away his family's fortune. His mind "sinks under its suffering": "It seems as if the weakness of the human mind alike incapacitated it to support the delirium of joy, and the extremity of sorrow. . . . Oh, how many sleepless days and weeks did I endure! the thoughts frantic, the tongue raving!" (69–70). Adrian, in Shelley's *The Last Man*, is also driven mad by misery. After being rejected by the woman he loves, he collapses both physically and mentally: "By degrees his health was shaken by his misery, and then his intellect yielded to the same tyranny. His manners grew wild; he was sometimes ferocious, sometimes absorbed in speechless melancholy" (32). In the cases of St. Leon and Adrian, madness results when the mind is overwhelmed by powerful emotions. Whereas the Lockean madman is able to "argue right from wrong principles," these characters become completely irrational; their minds "wander without rudder and pilot" (*St. Leon*, 70).

In *Thoughts on Man,* Godwin asserts that

> Horace says, that all men are mad: and no doubt mankind in general has one of the features of madness. In the ordinary current of our existence we are to a considerable degree rational and tractable. But we are not altogether safe. I may converse with a maniac for hours; he shall talk as soberly, and conduct himself with as much propriety, as any other of the species who has never been afflicted with his disease; but touch upon a particular string, and, before you are aware of it, he shall fly out into the wildest and most terrifying extravagances. Such, though in a greatly inferior degree, are the majority of human beings.[34]

Here Godwin's description of madness is clearly influenced by the theories of both Locke and Hartley. Locke argues that "a man who is very sober, and of a right understanding in all other things, may in one particular be as frantic as any in Bedlam."[35] Hartley contends "that mad Persons often speak rationally and consistently upon the Subjects that occur, provided that single one which most affects them, be kept out of View."[36] In the case of the paranoid Englishman described in Shelley's *Rambles in Germany and Italy in 1840, 1842, and 1843*, the "particular string" of associations is unleashed when an Italian suggests that the madman has "as much cause to be as frightened as" himself (111). After hearing this relatively innocuous remark, the maniac takes his pistol out of his pocket.

Godwin's fictional explorations of madness are more numerous and extensive than Shelley's and reflect his fascination with and loathing of this archenemy of reason; nearly all of his protagonists suffer, at least temporarily, from mental illness. In the original conclusion of *Caleb Williams*, Caleb loses his mind after he fails to convince the magistrate that his story is true. Just before the novel's ending, Falkland's persecutions of Caleb have driven him to the breaking point. When Gines, Falkland's henchman, informs Caleb that he is destined to remain under surveillance for the remainder of his life, Williams experiences "an instantaneous revolution in both [his] intellectual and animal system" (313). He decides to accuse Falkland of murder before a magistrate and awaits his hearing in "a state little short of frenzy[, his] body . . . in a burning fever with the agitation of [his] thoughts" (318). In the published ending, Caleb's "artless and manly story" (324) is validated after Falkland confesses his guilt, and he retains his sanity. In the manuscript conclusion, however, Falkland insists on his innocence, the magistrate accuses Williams of insulting him with a "bare faced and impudent . . . forgery" (330), and Caleb becomes mentally ill. Caleb's sanity thus depends on whether Falkland confirms or refutes his allegations, on circumstance rather than physical debility or an uncontrollable imagination. As Matthey declares, "an unexpected event, a sharp and sudden emotion of the soul will abruptly change the most reasonable and intelligent man into a raving idiot."

In the discarded ending, Caleb describes his tortured mental state. He temporarily loses his sanity after the magistrate rejects his story but subsequently (and mysteriously) regains a "portion of reason" (331). Like Locke and Battie, Caleb believes that madness results when an individual's imagination becomes uncontrollably delusional. Thus in order to avoid going completely insane, he makes a conscious effort to restrain his "visions":

> Wild and incoherent visions perpetually succeeded each other, dragged my attention this way and that, and allowed me not a moment's respite. I had no sleep; day and night it was still the same; the same torture and racking of the faculties. If at any time the pictures that glided along before my terrified imagination moved with a slower pace, the idea then occurred of mystery, of something which the understanding was incessantly anxious to penetrate, it turned it on this

> side and on that, it tried to enter by a thousand paths, but always returned empty, wearied, dissatisfied and unrewarded. (33031)

This conflict between the imagination and the understanding continues, despite Caleb's best efforts: "At present I by no means find myself satisfied with the state of my intellects. I am subject to wanderings in which the imagination seems to refuse to obey the curb of judgment" (331). He decides to record his experiences, which he believes are "pregnant with instruction to mankind" (332).

It becomes, however, apparent that the greatest threat to his reason comes not from his deluded imagination, but from his manipulative keeper, Jones (who was renamed Gines in the published version of the novel). In fact, Caleb wonders how he has "ever recovered any portion of reason . . . under [Jones's] discipline": "He would continue with me for hours still inventing new methods of exasperation. I have no distinct conception of what he practised on me during the period of my insanity; but I am persuaded that no distracted slave of superstition ever annexed such painful ideas to his dreaded Beelzebub, as I annexed to the figure and appearance of this man" (331). Instead of being cared for by a mad-doctor, Caleb is tortured by Falkland's agent, who is more interested in prolonging than curing his mental illness. His final mental collapse appears to be the result of drugs, probably administered by either Jones or his other keeper: "I just now feel a sensation unexperienced before. During the whole of my restraint sleep has been a stranger to me; its visits have been rare and of short duration. I feel now a benumbing heaviness, that I conceive to have something in it more than natural" (332–33). His final entry, entitled "Postscript No. II," consists of drug-induced ravings. While in *Valperga* Euthanasia posits a link between madness and the poetic imagination (263), in the manuscript ending of *Caleb Williams* insanity is associated with a diminished, lethargic, and incoherent imagination. Caleb becomes virtually catatonic, comparing himself to a log and a "GRAVE-STONE" (334), his memory becomes a "BLANK" (333), and he loses the ability to distinguish between dream and reality. By first tormenting and then drugging his emotionally vulnerable victim, Jones succeeds in driving Caleb completely insane.

Unlike the insane Caleb of the unpublished conclusion of *Caleb Williams*, the eponymous narrator of *St. Leon* is lovingly cared for during his madness. His exemplary wife, Marguerite, carefully watches for and encourages "the gleams of [his] returning reason" (74). After having gambled away his family fortune, St. Leon's behavior is first hyperkinetic and then catatonic: he runs through the streets of Paris and then sits "from morning till night in one immovable posture . . . [f]or several days together" (71). This "period of inactivity and stupor" is followed, in turn, "by a period of frenzy" (73). His "paroxysms" become so violent that a male servant is assigned the task of preventing him from "effecting some desperate mischief" (74). However, despite the severity of his mental illness, St. Leon is eventually cured by his wife, who is easily the most effective amateur mad-doctor in all of Godwin's fiction. Like Withers's judicious physician, Marguerite studies and humors her patient's "different dispositions" and is "able to read internal characters from external signs." According to St. Leon, her personal attachment to him makes her much more vigilant than a hired attendant could ever be:

> I was greatly indebted for the recovery which speedily followed to the affectionate anxiety and enlightened care of this incomparable woman. It is inconceivable to those who have never been led to a practical examination of the subject, how much may be effected in this respect by an attachment ever on the watch, and an understanding judicious to combine, where hired attendance would sleep, and the coarseness of a blunt insensibility would irritate, nay, perhaps, mortally injure. (74–75)

One of Marguerite's strategies is to stimulate her husband's "paternal affection" by bringing their twelve-month-old daughter to him: "Her innocent smiles, her frolic and careless laughter, produced a responsive vibration that reached my inmost heart" (76). Whereas Battie argues for the professionalization of the "mad business," *St. Leon* suggests that a personal attachment between a caretaker and his or her patient can be extremely beneficial, especially if the caretaker is as sensitive and judicious as Marguerite.

However, although St. Leon regains his sanity, his moods continue to fluctuate drastically. At times he is "dejected and forlorn," but then he rouses himself from his "stupor" and runs with suicidal fury up and down the Swiss mountainsides (82). He insists, however, that he is no longer insane:

> The state of mind I am here describing was not madness, nor such as could be mistaken for madness. I never forgot myself, and what I was. I was never in that delirium of thought, in which the patient is rest-

> less and active without knowing what it is that he does, and from which, when roused, he suddenly starts, shakes off the dream that engaged him, and stands astonished at himself. Mine was a rage, guided and methodised by the discipline of despair. I burst into no fits of raving; I attempted no injury to any one. (83)

In this passage St. Leon anticipates the late nineteenth-century distinction between psychoneurosis (in which the patient is mentally disturbed but has some control over his or her speech and actions) and psychosis (in which the patient is completely out of touch with reality).[37] A similar distinction is made in *Mathilda*, in which the protagonist is "on the verge of madness" after the suicide of her father: "Oft when I have listened with gasping attention for the sound of the ocean mingled with my father's groans; and then wept until my strength was gone and I was calm and faint, when I have recollected all this I have asked myself if this were not madness" (218). Like St. Leon, Mathilda equates sanity with the ability to avoid "raving" and control one's behavior rather than with mental and emotional stability: "I never was really mad. I was always conscious of my state when my wild thoughts seemed to drive me to insanity, and never betrayed them to aught but silence and solitude" (219). St. Leon's and Mathilda's careful analyses of their own minds lead them to devise a rudimentary nosology in which complete madness is distinguished from another type of mental illness, which is nondelirious ("conscious") but nonetheless debilitating. It could be argued, however, that the effects of St. Leon's psychoneurosis, or his "methodised" rage, are far more devastating than the consequences of his madness. After his insanity has been "cured," he becomes obsessed with the acquisition of power and wealth, strikes a bargain with a mysterious stranger to obtain the philosopher's stone and the elixir of life, rejects his wife as a confidante, alienates his son, abandons his other children, and becomes a social outcast. Similarly, Mathilda's "wild thoughts," although they never "really" render her insane, drive her to seek relief from her suffering through death. Clearly, raving lunacy is not always the most destructive type of mental illness in Godwin's and Shelley's fiction.

Fleetwood contains Godwin's most dramatic portrayal of madness. Driven frantic by his conviction that his wife has been impregnated by Kenrick, his distant cousin, Fleetwood obtains life-sized wax models, which he dresses in his wife's clothes and Kenrick's regimentals. He brings in "a cradle, and a chest of child-bed linen'' to represent their illegitimate child and plays the tunes that Kenrick and Mary danced to at Bath on a barrel organ. As he performs this bizarre ''ceremony,'' his mental condition swiftly deteriorates:

> I have a very imperfect recollection of the conclusion of this scene. For a long time I was slow and deliberate in my operations. Suddenly my temper changed. While I was playing on my organ one of the tunes of Kenrick and Mary,—it was a duet of love . . . ,—my mind underwent a strange revolution. I no longer distinctly knew where I was, or could distinguish fiction from reality. I looked wildly, and with glassy eyes, all round the room; I gazed at the figure of Mary; I thought it was, and it was not, Mary. With mad and idle action, I put some provisions on her plate; I bowed to her in mockery, and invited her to eat. Then again I grew serious and vehement; I addressed her with inward and convulsive accents, in the language of reproach; I declaimed, with uncommon flow of words, upon her abandoned and infernal deceit; all the tropes that imagination ever supplied to the tongue of man, seemed to be at my command. I know not whether this speech was to be considered as earnest, or as the Sardonic and bitter jest of a maniac. But, while I was still speaking, I saw her move—if I live, I saw it. She turned her eyes this way and that; she grinned and chattered at me. I looked from her to the other figure; that grinned and chattered too. Instantly a full and proper madness seized me; I grinned and chattered, in turn, to the figures before me. It was not words that I heard or uttered; it was murmurs, and hissings, and lowings, and howls. . . . I dashed the organ into a thousand fragments. I rent the child-bed linen, and tore it with my teeth. I dragged the clothes which Mary had worn, from off the figure that represented her, and rent them into long strips and shreds. I struck the figures vehemently with the chairs and other furniture of the room, till they were broken to pieces. I threw at them, in despite, the plates and other brittle implements of the supper-table. I raved and roared with all the power of my voice. (264–65)

Although Fleetwood's madness is driven by passion, it is shaped by his ''deluded imagination.'' Unable to ''distinguish fiction from reality,'' he confuses the wax figures with the people whom they are meant to represent. The wax model of Mary appears to come to life and act the part of the ''Impudent harlot'' (259) that he fancies his wife to be. As his insanity progresses, his imagination degenerates: at one point he is able to upbraid the model of Mary with ''all the tropes that imagination ever supplied to the tongue of man,'' but afterwards he becomes incoherent, expressing himself with ''hissings, . . . lowings, and howls.'' His address to Mary seems to be only partly mad because he alternately believes that the wax figure "was, and . . . was not, Mary," and it is unclear whether the speech is "earnest, or . . . the Sardonic and bitter jest of a maniac." But while partial madness can actually enhance the imagination, "full and proper madness" can render its victim completely incoherent. Lacking the structure provided by language, Fleetwood's thoughts become chaotic, and he expresses himself with animalistic noises and violent actions. Freed from the restraints of social conventions and mores, he performs a "ceremony" in which he symbolically commits infanticide, rape, cannibalism, and multiple homicide. His delusions are so powerful that, even after having regained his sanity, he still believes that the wax figure of Mary moved. *Fleetwood* presents madness as a powerful, debilitating illness that has the power to reduce a well-educated "New Man of Feeling" to a savagely transgressive and inarticulate beast. It is an illness from which he nearly dies: only after "A favourable crisis" (265) is he able to recover, "wasted almost to a skeleton" (267).

Because after his initial bout of madness Fleetwood is "too weak to break out into . . . paroxysms of insanity[,] . . . those about [him are] scarcely aware of the degree of [his] derangement" (265). In *Mandeville*, however, the protagonist's insanity, which Mandeville describes as "that sort of madness, which expresses itself in fury" (144), leads to his confinement. The "fury" of this arrogant, Oxford-educated aristocrat is consistent with Darwin's theory that "The violence of action accompanying insanity depends much on the education of the person; those who have been proudly educated with unrestrained passions, are liable to greater fury; and those, whose education has been humble, to greater despondency."[38] Since *Mandeville* is set during the seventeenth century, Godwin is careful to make the treatment of Mandeville's madness reflect the accepted medical practice of that era. "[T]he violence, the cords, the harsh language, [and] the blows" (144) inflicted on Mandeville by his keepers recall the treatments of madness advocated by the seventeenth-century physician and anatomist Thomas Willis, which included "threatnings, bonds, or strokes" along with "punishments, and hard usage in a strait room."[39]

During his period of insanity, Mandeville relives the brutal murders of his mother and father:

> Ireland, and its scenes of atrocious massacre, that one might have expected to be obliterated from the tablet of my memory, presented

> themselves in original freshness. My father and my mother died over again. The shrieks, that had rent the roofs of Kinnard fourteen years before, yelled in my ears, and deafened my sense; and I answered them with corresponding and responsive shrieks. I forgot the lapse of time that had passed between; I did not advert to the circumstance, that I had then been a child; and I put forth my virile strength, and uttered my firmer expostulations and threats, to save the lives of him who begot, and her who bore me. (144)

According to Hartley, madness is caused by the abnormal magnification of "a particular Set of Ideas."[40] In Mandeville's case, malicious rumors casting doubt on his honor and social ostracism at Oxford have triggered the mental reenactment of a series of excruciatingly vivid associations. Shelley's *Perkin Warbeck* also presents a character who is overcome by traumatic memories. Meiler Trangmar's sons have all died in the Lancastrian cause, and the last of them is tortured to death in front of his father. As a result, Trangmar is "haunted by memories which pursued him like the hell-born Eumenides": "often he uttered piercing shrieks, as the scenes, so pregnant with horror, recurred too vividly to his mind" (103). Similarly, Shelley's Beatrice of Ferrara's reason is repeatedly threatened by recollections of her past imprisonment and torture. Mandeville's memory of his parents' murder is, however, unlike Trangmar's and Beatrice's memories in an important way: while Trangmar and Beatrice remember traumatic occurrences that transpired during their adulthoods, the event that Mandeville vividly recalls took place when he was only three and has not been consciously rehearsed in his mind. Hartley states that "The Memory is often much impaired in Madness,"[41] but Mandeville's account of his delirium indicates that his memory has actually been enhanced by his mental illness. In positing the existence of a repressed memory that has the power to revisit his protagonist with nightmarish intensity after having been "forgotten" for fourteen years, Godwin anticipates Freud.[42]

While Mandeville's madness "expresses itself in fury," Julian Cloudesley's insanity is melancholic. This again recalls Darwin's theory that an individual's education determines the type of madness from which he or she will suffer: because Julian's "education has been humble," he is liable "to greater despondency." Like Fleetwood, Julian is a "man of feeling," and his sorrow following the death of his guardian is pathological in its intensity:

> Julian . . . surrendered all his faculties to the agony of grief. His thoughts were disordered and wild; he fell in a short time into complete delirium. He 'saw more devils than vast hell can hold;' he knew not where he was, nor what he was. He would not eat; he would not speak. Sometimes he comforted himself with the agitation of a madman, and uttered his voice in piercing shrieks; at others, he would subside into a state without motion, without perception, and, as it seemed, without life. Whoever spoke to him, he heeded it not; whatever noise, whatever crash occurred near him, he perceived it not. But there was apparently a perpetual working of the inner senses, too feeble to produce any action of the limbs or features, too incoherent and unpronounced to be a subject of after-recollection. When he awoke out of one of these paroxyms, he appeared like a man recovered from an ecstasy; he stared about him for a time, and knew nothing. He did not shed a tear, though his countenance was the picture of despair. He slept neither night nor day. (235–36)

Rather than confining Julian, Borromeo, his new guardian, allows the young man's mental disorder to take its course: "He left him in the care of the servant of the deceased. He was of [the] opinion that nature knew her own time, and that both appetite and sleep, particularly to a person at that time of life, would return, when the frame could no longer subsist without sleep and food" (236). Lord Danvers, the narrator of this portion of the novel, contends that appeals to reason are often worse than useless in the case of grief-inspired madness:

> When a fancied wise man and a monitor approaches him who is absorbed in grief and will not be comforted, and this person is expected to tell the mourner of the uselessness of his sorrows, and to undertake to rouse the man of reason and firmness within him, the mourner would, if it were possible, "take the wings of the morning, and dwell in the uttermost parts of the sea," rather than encounter the words that should be spoken. (237)

Here Godwin may be taking himself to task for his insensitive response to Mary Shelley's sorrow following the death of her daughter Clara in 1818. Acting the part of "a fancied wise man and a monitor," he wrote:

> I sincerely sympathize with you in the affliction which forms the subject of your letter, and which I may consider as the first severe trial of your constancy and the firmness of your temper that has occurred to you in the course of your life. You should, however, recollect that

> it is only persons of a very ordinary sort, and of a pusillanimous disposition, that sink long under a calamity of this nature.[43]

In contrast, *Cloudesley* expresses a very different attitude towards grief: Julian Cloudesley's "filial sorrow" (241) is presented as sacred and awes the harsh and misanthropic Borromeo. Julian needs "to love and be loved" (242), and when Borromeo fails to provide him with the emotional support he craves, he runs away to join St. Elmo and his outlaws.

Godwin's presentation of insanity in *Cloudesley* is somewhat more positive than in his other novels. Although Julian's madness is debilitating, his "agitation" provides some comfort, presumably because it allows him to ventilate some of his feelings in "piercing shrieks." His sufferings are also temporarily alleviated by "sweet and soothing and consolatory imaginations" (238) that his guardian is still alive. *Cloudesley* also suggests that grief can overcome individuals who are far from "ordinary" and "pusillanimous" and that a "wise" man's philosophical notions are likely to prove more repellent than comforting.

In *Deloraine* Godwin has his eponymous narrator encounter a madman on the road from Bruges to Ghent. Deloraine is being pursued by Travers, who has been searching for him in Bruges in order to arrest him for the murder of his friend. Travers has, however, learned that a "singular," "flurried," and "ghastly"-looking man bound for Osnabruck has been observed in a bookshop and mistakenly concludes that this strange individual is the man he is seeking. As Deloraine flees with his daughter, this "false Deloraine" (217) joins them, babbling nonsensically, and Deloraine realizes that unless he can rid himself of his double, Travers will soon be on his trail. The false Deloraine is a "poor, deranged creature" who nevertheless appears "sufficiently reasonable amidst all his incoherence, to be able to give dangerous information respecting [the protagonist's] motions." He tells Deloraine that he has "many reasons for choosing these public highways": "it enables me to pick up followers; for a king without subjects is but a shadowy monarch. I know my own greatness; but there are those who would gladly clip my wings. They once tried it, by shutting me up in a house with bars to the windows, and spikes to the walls; but I gave them the slip" (218). Like the religious maniac in Warren's "The Spectre-Smitten," the lunatic in *Deloraine* is a Lockean madman; his desire for followers is logically derived from his delusion that he is a king. Deloraine finally rids himself of his insane alter ego by acting like one of his keepers:

> I rode up close to his side, and said to him in an emphatical manner:
> Harkye, sir, I have no more time for trifling!—I know you for an escaped lunatic; and it is therefore my duty to seize you, and convey you to a place of safety.—And, saying this, I stretched out my hand, as if intending to arrest him.
> This proceeding of mine had the desired effect. The maniac suddenly drew his steed several yards apart from me, and then,—after having indulged in a portentous and fearful laugh, and exclaiming, I am not mad enough however to be seized by you—urged his horse to the top of his speed, and was presently far a-head of us on the road to Ghent. (218)

Deloraine shares the lunatic's terror of being apprehended, and, in reaching out his hand to arrest the madman, he acts out his own worst fear. While the maniac is capable of being "sufficiently reasonable" in certain situations, he himself experiences episodes of psychotic behavior. Earlier in the novel, his obsessional jealousy drives him to murder, and, after parting from the false Deloraine, he experiences "a frenzy of the soul":

> My visions were wild, incoherent, tormenting, beyond the power of words, to describe; my soul was tumultuously hurried along in restless ecstasy; I felt that every thing which presented itself to my inner sense was inconsistent, contradictory, impossible, yet, impossible, as it was, I was compelled to believe it. . . . My blood was fevered; my brain was maddened; my hours were full of delirious imaginations, which again were sobered and reduced to compulsory steadiness by the near apprehension of some fatal violence. (219)

Like the lunatic, his "inner sense" is torn between his reason, which recognizes that his visions are "inconsistent, contradictory, impossible," and his "delirious imaginations," which compel him to believe the unbelievable. And like the maniac, who responds swiftly when Deloraine threatens to arrest him, he is able to overcome these "imaginations" and steady himself in order to avoid danger or capture. In his final novel Godwin further blurs the distinction between madness and sanity. Deloraine and his fellow traveler are kindred spirits rather than mental opposites: they share the same fears and are both capable, in certain situations, of either sane or insane behavior.

In *Rambles in Germany and Italy*, Mary Shelley describes a "strange and disagreeable" encounter with a mad Englishman:

> Suddenly . . . the Englishman said to [his Italian companion], "Are you not afraid of being set upon? Are you not afraid of being assassinated?" The other, who . . . had no idea of his malady, replied, "No, why should he?" "Do you not know that we are watched, and there is treachery everywhere about us?" "No," said the other, "and if there were, you have as much cause to be frightened as I." "But I am armed," said the madman, "this is loaded," and he drew a pistol from his pocket, and still more excited by the sight of the weapon, began to shriek "Tradimento! Tradimento!" ["Treason! Treason!"] . . . [M]y companions were summoned to see if they could do anything with their countryman.
>
> There he stood on the steps before the gate of the villa leading down to the lake, shrieking "Tradimento;" he kept every one at bay with his pistol, which was cocked, capped, and ready. . . . After three or four hours, however, he grew less watchful. As the people talked to him, he allowed them insensibly to approach nearer, till one fellow getting behind, threw up his arm with the pistol, and then throwing his arms round him, took him prisoner. His pistol was double-loaded. But with all his madness he was aware, that if he had fired it, his power was at an end; and this latent sanity saved, perhaps, his life.
>
> . . . Poor fellow! he is quite mad. He had given English lessons at Milan for some years, and earned a sufficient livelihood. His insanity has taken the turn of believing, that the Austrian police want to poison him. He said he never went to the theatre but a police officer was behind, who scattered a poisonous powder over him. He will not take any food in consequence; neither touch bread nor water. . . . A doctor had been sent for from Menaggio at the first moment; of course, he could do nothing. . . . The next morning, having taken an aversion to all those with whom he had been friendly the preceding day, he consented to go back to Milan, under the escort of a police officer. I saw him as he got into the boat; he was a spare man, with an adust [sunburnt? gloomy?], withered face and unquiet eye; but not otherwise remarkable. (111–12)

Shelley cannot decide exactly what to make of this madman, who, despite his aberrant behavior, appears hauntingly normal. At one point she declares that he possesses a "latent sanity," but almost immediately afterward she laments that he "is quite mad." She also notes that before the Englishman's sudden cries of "Tradimento," his Italian fellow traveler had no idea that he was mentally ill; although the maniac has an "unquiet eye," his physiognomy is "not otherwise remarkable."[44] Abandoned to "the miserable wanderings of his own mind" (112), the madman faces a bleak future: the doctor, "of course, . . . could do nothing."

Thus Shelley, like Godwin, suspects that insanity may be more normative than exceptional. She writes in *Lodore* that "all people who live in solitude become to a certain degree insane. Their views of things are not corrected by comparing them with those of others; and the strangest want of proportion always reigns in their ideas and sentiments" (298). She suggests that this is invariably true, regardless of an individual's background and temperament. In *Falkner* she observes that "It has been said that every clever person is, to a certain degree, mad. By which it is to be understood, that every person whose mind soars above the vulgar, has some exalted and disinterested object in view to which they are ready to sacrifice the common blessings of life" (55). These sentiments recall the teachings of Helvétius, who, as I noted in chapter 2, exerted a profound influence on Godwin. Helvétius writes in *De l'Esprit: or, Essays on the Mind and Its Several Faculties* that

> an ardent passion for glory . . . is the soul of men of genius and talents in every kind; to this desire they owe the enthusiasm they have for their art, and which they sometimes carry so far, as to consider it as the only occupation worthy the mind of man; an opinion for which sensible persons call them madmen; but they are considered in another light by the knowing, who, in the cause of their madness, discern that of their abilities and success.[45]

However, although Shelley shares Godwin's belief that madness is a relatively common state of mind, their attitudes toward insanity are far from identical. I would argue, in fact, that Shelley's attitude toward insanity is far more positive (and perhaps less morbidly curious) than Godwin's. She maintains that madness, if it promotes "some exalted and disinterested object," can be beneficial. Philosophers, martyrs, poets, philanthropists, and heroes may all possess a "certain degree" of insanity. One of Shelley's most virtuous characters, the Percy Shelley-like Adrian of *The Last Man*, temporarily succumbs to madness in his youth, but he later becomes the leader and benefactor of his plague-ravaged country. Euthanasia's description of the human mind in *Valperga* places madness near "Poetry and Imagination" in the mind's "inner cave": "This [cave] is the habitation of the madman, when all the powers desert the vestibule, and he, finding no light, makes darkling, fantastic combinations, and lives among them. . . . But it is here also that Poetry and Imagination live" (263). Moreover, Mathilda's father, who is driven temporarily insane by his incestuous desire for his daughter, is said to have "the imagination of a poet" (189).[46] In drawing this connection between madness and poetry, Mary Shelley may have been influenced by Percy Shelley's poem "Julian and Maddalo: A Conversation" (written 1819), in which he presents a "Maniac" whose insane monologue is considered poetic by Julian and Maddalo (who represent, respectively, Shelley and Byron):

> the wild language of his grief was high,
> Such as in measure were called poetry;
> And I [Julian] remember one remark which then
> Maddalo made. He said: "Most wretched men
> Are cradled into poetry by wrong,
> They learn in suffering what they teach in song."
> (ll. 541–46)[47]

Frankenstein depicts a man with "genius and talents" who could easily be pronounced insane by "sensible persons." Following the creation of the monster, Frankenstein is overcome with "a nervous fever," but, unlike Julian Cloudesley, he has a friend, Henry Clerval, to nurse him through his illness: "surely nothing but the unbounded and unremitting attentions of my friend could have restored me to life. The form of the monster on whom I had bestowed existence was for ever before my eyes, and I raved incessantly concerning him" (46). After the monster murders Clerval, Frankenstein again loses his reason:

> I lay for two months on the point of death: my ravings, as I afterwards heard, were frightful; I called myself the murderer of William, of Justine, and of Clerval. Sometimes I entreated my attendants to assist me in the destruction of the fiend by whom I was tormented; and at others, I felt the fingers of the monster already grasping my neck, and screamed aloud with agony and terror. . . . [N]o one was near me who soothed me with the gentle voice of love; no dear hand supported me. (131–32)

His last episode of madness takes place after his creation kills Elizabeth and his father dies as the result of "an apoplectic fit." In this case, Frankenstein's insanity is described as a sleep from which he awakens to reason:

> What then became of me? I know not; I lost sensation, and chains and darkness were the only objects that pressed upon me. Sometimes, indeed, I dreamt that I wandered in flowery meadows and pleasant vales with the friends of my youth; but awoke, and found myself in a dungeon. Melancholy followed, but by degrees I gained a clear conception of my miseries and situation, and was then released from my prison. For they had called me mad; and during many months, as I understood, a solitary cell had been my habitation. (146)

According to Battie, "confinement alone is oftentimes sufficient" to cure madness,[48] and after languishing for "many months" in his "solitary cell," Frankenstein recovers his reason. However, although Battie argues that those suffering from mental illness "ought strictly to be forbidden . . . the visits . . . of affecting friends,"[49] it is clear that Clerval's loving care of Frankenstein, to which he responds with "sentiments of joy and affection" (46), is far more salutary than the chains and darkness of an asylum.

In *Valperga*, Beatrice's fatal bout of madness begins when her friends are absent. The "witch" Mandragola drugs her with a potion containing Jusquiamo (henbane), which, as Shelley writes in a footnote, "was the principal ingredient in these intoxicating draughts. They had the property of producing madness" (281n). Yet, what seems to make her madness fatal is the fact that she is overcome by conflicting passions. Kneeling "in frantic expectation" (282), Beatrice awaits her beloved Castruccio, but when she sees him he is with Tripalda, one of the "fiends" (257) who tortured her earlier in the novel: "The presence of Tripalda was to her the sign of diabolical interference; she believed him dead; that it was his spirit which then appeared; and, if so, it was also an unreal form, the resemblance of Castruccio alone, that she beheld." Unable to "sustain the sensations" (282) of both love and terror, she falls into convulsions. Similar scenes are described in Byron's *Don Juan* and Godwin's *Deloraine*. In *Don Juan*, a vein bursts in Haidée's head when her father's men cut down her beloved Juan, and she dies shortly thereafter (canto 4:59). Byron claims in his footnote to this passage that "This is no very uncommon effect of the violence of conflicting and different passions."[50] In *Deloraine*, Margaret Borradale falls dead after Deloraine unexpectedly kills William, the man she has always loved. She cannot "sustain the sensations" of her rekindled passion for William, her horror at his murder, and her subsequent hatred for her husband. As in the case of Haidée, the apparent cause of death is a ruptured blood vessel. According to Hartley, madness results from "violent Vibrations" in the brain: "after Madness the Brain is often found dry, and the Blood-vessels much distended; which are Arguments, that violent Vibrations took place in the internal Parts of the Brain, the peculiar Residence of Ideas and Passion."[51] When Haidée's and Margaret's passions cause their blood vessels to rupture, death ensues. While ruling passions engender irrational behavior and mental instability in all of Shelley's and Godwin's novels, in *Valperga* and *Deloraine* "conflicting and different passions" are shown to be deadly.

Compared to Godwin's detailed representations of madness, which typically read like case studies, Shelley's description of Beatrice's insanity is sketchy. She is reluctant to dwell on her character's sufferings: "Why should I describe the scenes that ensued during the following days? Descriptions of unmixed horror cannot be pleasing. . . . Some have seen, most have read the descriptions of, madness" (284–85). This reticence suggests that she finds the symptoms of insanity more repulsive and less interesting than Godwin typically does in his fiction.

Shelley does not present Clorinda, a mentally ill character in *Lodore*, as sympathetically as she does Beatrice. Like "The Bride of Modern Italy" (1824), which also features an Italian woman named Clorinda, the novel's inset tale of the ill-fated marriage between the daughter of a Neapolitan nobleman and an upper-class Englishman was inspired by Percy Shelley's infatuation (memorialized in *Epipsychidion* [1821]) with the nineteen-year-old Teresa Viviani, the unwilling inmate of a Pisan convent. But whereas "The Bride of Modern Italy" exploits the comic possibilities of this kind of situation, *Lodore* explores its potential for tragedy. Clorinda is paranoid, violent, and manic-depressive. She refuses to go to husband's homeland because she is "sure" that she will be "disliked," "censured," and "perhaps taunted" there. Although she loves Horatio, she says that she "could strike him dead, if [she] only knew that [the thought of returning to England] lived for a second in his heart" (169). During a trip to Rome, "some jealous freak" inspires Clorinda to attack her husband with a knife. According to Horatio, "Her repentance is as violent as her rage" (171)—her moments of manic violence are followed by episodes of extravagant remorse. However, even in the case of this potentially homicidal character, Shelley associates madness with a highly developed aesthetic sensibility: "Music . . . and the heavenly strains which filled the churches with an atmosphere of sound more entrancing than incense—all these were hers; and her own voice, rich, full, and well-cultivated, made a temple of melody in her own home" (170). Clorinda also possesses "the imaginative talent of her country" (169).

Horatio hopes that "time, reason, . . . steadiness of conduct on [his] part," and motherhood will "subdue" (171) Clorinda, but when he dotes on their daughter she grows "jealous even of her own child" (278). The mention of Horatio's former love, Lady Lodore, causes "one of her most violent paroxysms of rage" (278), and her mental state deteriorates further when his father tells her that her husband must go back to England. She returns home, and her child is hidden from her as she "raves through her house like a maniac." Horatio finally arrives, and she succumbs, like Haidée and Margaret Borradale, to a ruptured blood vessel: "he entered; her eyes were starting from her head, her frame working with convulsive violence; she strove to speak—to give utterance to the vehemence pent up within her. She darted towards him; when suddenly, as if shot to the heart, she fell on the marble pavement of her chamber, and a red stream poured from her lips—she had burst a blood vessel" (279). Her broken blood-vessel seems to be the result not of contending passions but of her inability to relieve the pressure of her emotions by giving "utterance to the vehemence pent up within her."

This paroxysm proves not, however, to be fatal. During her convalescence, Clorinda agrees to go to England, and Horatio happily accepts. But her fragile self-control evaporates when one of her husband's sisters mentions Lady Lodore, and she again becomes speechless: "she could not speak—she knew not what she felt, but that a fiery torture was eating into her, and she must fly, she knew not whither." She falls into a final depression, gives birth to a stillborn infant, and dies. Clorinda is, Shelley asserts, "the victim of uncontrolled passion" (282); her "passions [are] at once so fiery and so feeble as to excite contempt" (176). Despite the "electric sympathy" (169) that Horatio feels for others, he cannot sympathize with Clorinda's fear of England, which he believes is based on an "unreasonable . . . distaste" (279). After her death he resists the temptation to "give way to unavailing remorse" because he can find no "just cause for repentance" (283). Unlike the false Deloraine and Beatrice of Ferrara, Clorinda remains intractably "other"—she is too xenophobic, unreasonable, and violent to elicit much sympathy from her English husband, his family, or even Shelley, and Horatio's attempt to cure her through his own "steady" conduct seems halfhearted at best. Notwithstanding Shelley's endorsement of Horatio's conduct, there is some truth in Clorinda's sad conclusion that "Her husband [is] not her friend, for he [is] not her countryman" (280).

But while motherhood does not improve Clorinda's mental state, fatherhood helps Lord Lodore and the title character of *Falkner* cope with emotional traumas. Lodore's young daughter Ethel effectively preserves her father's sanity following his separation from Lady Lodore: "He occasionally felt that he might become mad, and at such moments, the presence of his child brought consolation and calm; her caresses, her lisped expressions of affection, her playfulness, her smiles, were spells to drive away the fantastic reveries that tortured him" (69–70). The child improves his mood and grounds him in reality, distracting him from his "fantastic reveries." In *Falkner*, the orphaned Elizabeth Raby prevents the title character from committing suicide by pulling his arm as he attempts to shoot himself. Later in the novel, his love for her gives him a reason to live. She is "the cure; . . . her smiles—her caresses—the knowledge that he benefit[s] her, [is] the life-blood of his design [to travel throughout continental Europe]" (32). Similarly, in *St. Leon* the depressed protagonist is consoled by his twelve-month-old daughter (76), and the remorseful title character of *Deloraine* comes to depend on his adult daughter Catherine after his murder of William. These characters are not "cured" by the devotion of their daughters, but their relationships with their offspring are therapeutic and save them from madness or suicide.

Several years after Mary Shelley's encounter with the English madman in Italy, she heard from her stepsister Claire Clairmont about Oswald Turner, whose father, Thomas, had been one of Godwin's protégés in his youth. Clairmont wrote to Shelley in 1842 that Oswald's excessive studying was ruining his health: "Oswald . . . is painfully languid and weak—nor is it to be wondered at when one considers the life he leads—no amusement[,] nothing except Mathematics and Chemistry; fatiguing his brain for hours, days and months . . . Oswald is young it is true, but very old in character, . . . besides the nature of his pursuits and his want of the success he desires . . . depresses him terribly."[52] By 1844 Oswald had become "quite a confirmed lunatic."[53] Clairmont describes his plight in a 9 December 1844 letter:

> Oswald Turner has been many months in a mad-house[.] I pity him so much but I trust he will come out again quite cured. Oswald talked such horrors of Octavia, took such a hatred to Robecchi and many other people, and wore a costume so pretty and fanciful that he ex-

> cited attention in the streets and so they could not keep him at home any longer. He has done some wonderful things since his confinement: guarded in the strictest way he managed to escape three times—he climbed a high wall . . . where there was not a place of a hair's breadth to put his foot on and jumped into the street and walked quietly into his grandmother and asked for some tea. . . . The second time he persuaded one of his keepers with bland eloquence that he was not mad and promising him much money he connived at his escape. . . . it is over study, intense application to mathematics that has hurt his brain. . . . But every one hopes that rest[,] seclusion, no books, regular diet and the absence of all excitement will cure him.[54]

In an 1845 letter Clairmont writes:

> Another symptom which they think the highest sign of madness is his constantly asserting that his Mother surprized some of his Chemical secrets and betrayed them to the world. . . . Struck by Frankenstein and the idea of creating human Beings, he endeavoured to prove its truth—every body allows his immense skill in Chemistry—he worked much at this idea and was night and day employed in experiments.

According to Clairmont, this is far from conclusive proof that Oswald is mad: "I think him every eccentric but not sufficient to justify his being shut up in a mad-house—unless what they say of his homicidal propensities be true. Magnetism [hypnotism] I have no doubt would cure him."[55] Life imitates, or parodies, art; a compulsive student like Frankenstein, Oswald attempts to enact the character's famous experiment. He exemplifies the link between genius and madness explored in Shelley's fiction. Shelley's response to Clairmont's news about Oswald is, however, somewhat phlegmatic: "Poor Oswald! Madness being in his family he could not escape. . . . I think all the care his relatives took absolutely necessary—unfortunately they relaxed for a moment—& he is in a mad-house."[56] By 1845 Shelley was apparently less intrigued by abnormal psychological states than she had been earlier in her career; despite the fascinating connection between Oswald's madness and her most famous novel, she dismisses his aberrant behavior as a regrettable instance of hereditary insanity. But her defense of Oswald's relatives, whose interference Clairmont condemns but which Shelley thinks is "absolutely necessary," is consistent with her long-held view that victims of mental illness should be monitored and cared for by friends and family rather than by outsiders.

Whereas Shelley's fiction presents an ambivalent view of insanity, Godwin's novels (with the exception of *Cloudesley*) suggest that mental illness is an unmitigated calamity. The protagonist of Godwin's *St. Leon* rejects the notion that madness can provide a relief from misery: "Where is the cold and inapprehensive spirit that talks of madness as a refuge from sorrow? . . . when the masts and tackle of the intellectual vessel are all swept away, then is the true sadness" (70). Fleetwood's behavior during his bout of madness suggests that although insanity can temporarily stimulate the imagination, it ultimately denies its victim the linguistic ability necessary for communication and can lead to death. Mandeville's insanity "expresses itself in fury" and is brutally controlled by his attendants: "My teeth were ground almost to pieces; my head shook, and my mouth scattered foam, like that of a war-horse in the midst of the din of arms" (144). Frankenstein is, however, consoled by his "delirium": "he enjoys one comfort," Walton writes, "the offspring of solitude and delirium: he believes, that, when in dreams he holds converse with his friends, and derives from that communion consolation for his miseries, or excitements to his vengeance, that they are not the creations of his fancy, but the real beings who visit him from the regions of a remote world" (155). Similarly, Shelley's Lionel Verney, the last man in an "empty world," longs for the "refuge" of madness:

> I would not believe that all was as it seemed—The world was not dead, but I was mad. . . . Every house had its inmate; but I could not perceive them. If I could have deluded myself into a belief of this kind, I should have been far more satisfied. But my brain, tenacious of its reason, refused to lend itself to such imaginations—and though I endeavoured to play the antic to myself, I knew that I, the offspring of man, during long years one among many—now remained sole survivor of my species. (*The Last Man*, 327).

Shelley recognizes, of course, that insanity can be irreversible or even lead to death: the Englishman in *Rambles* is apparently incurable and the psychotic episodes experienced by Beatrice of Ferrara and Clorinda prove fatal. But she also suggests that there is an element of madness in visionary idealism and the poetic imagination and that insanity can provide consolation in cases of extreme emotional suffering.

Neither Godwin nor Shelley, however, is as pessimistic about treating mental illness as their American contemporary Charles

Brockden Brown, whose novels they read voraciously.[57] In Brown's *Wieland; or, The Transformation* (1798), the religious mania that incites the title character to murder his wife and family continues unabated until a ventriloquist, whose voice Wieland believes to be the utterances of a supernatural agent, convinces him that he has been deluded by projecting the following "sounds . . . from above": "Man of errors! cease to cherish thy delusion: not heaven or hell, but thy senses have misled thee to commit these acts. Shake off thy phrenzy, and ascend into rational and human. Be lunatic no longer."[58] But instead of becoming "rational and human," Wieland responds to the ventriloquist's revelation by committing suicide. As the narrator's uncle pessimistically but accurately observes earlier in the novel, Wieland's "malady will end but with his life."[59] Similarly, Clithero Edny's homicidal mania in Brown's *Edgar Huntly; or, Memoirs of a Sleep-Walker* (1799) is seen as incurable: the eponymous narrator's friend Sarsefield regards Clithero "as a maniac, whose disease [is] irremediable, and whose existence [can]not be protracted, but to his own misery and the misery of others."[60] Edgar Huntly's clumsy attempts to rehabilitate Clithero only serve to make matters worse.

In contrast, Godwin and Shelley explore psychological therapies in their works which, although they do not necessarily "cure" the sufferer, sometimes prove salutary. As we have seen, both writers were interested in the positive influence children can have on adults who are struggling with mental illness. They also indicate that the care provided by a loved one is far superior to the kind of treatment administered in madhouses. Music helps to console mentally unstable characters in *Valperga* and *Deloraine*: Beatrice seeks "consolation in music" (248), and the singing of Deloraine's daughter mitigates his sufferings: "Catherine was an accomplished singer, and played divinely on her instrument, so that, when the evil spirit was upon me, . . . she called forth the talent with which she was endowed, and the 'evil spirit departed from me' " (206). In the next chapter I will discuss the type of therapy that is most thoroughly explored in Godwin's and Shelley's fiction: word or language therapy, both oral and written.

4

The Therapeutic Value of Language

THE "TALKING CURE,"[1] OR THE "INTERCHANGE OF WORDS BETWEEN the patient and the analyst" that takes place in psychoanalysis,[2] has over the last hundred years become widely accepted as a treatment for mental stress or illness. In contrast, during the eighteenth and early nineteenth centuries "mad-doctors" or "Antimaniac Physicians" favored other "cures," such as bleeding, purging, or vomiting, when dealing with psychological disorders. The therapeutic value of conversation was, however, at least partially recognized by the philosopher Adam Smith, and Godwin and Shelley explored this concept extensively in their writings. They present a number of traumatized characters who desperately need to tell their tales and relieve their pent-up emotions through conversation with a sympathetic listener. These characters tend, however, to be inhibited, especially when confiding to a member of the opposite sex, and in most cases the relief they feel after having ventilated their emotions is fleeting. Oral self-expression is a palliative rather than a cure. Moreover, in Godwin's *Mandeville* and Shelley's *Valperga* the lack of a professional "listener" (such as a priest who has the authority to hear confessions) leaves those who are friendless, or who do not have access to a friend to whom they can bear their souls, vulnerable to psychological manipulation and madness.

Godwin and Shelley consider the therapeutic value of both written and oral self-expression in their fiction. In *Fleetwood* the protagonist recognizes that "There are some kinds of writing in which the mind willingly engages, in which, while we hold the pen in our hand, we seem to unburden the sentiments of our soul, and our habitual feelings cause us to pour out on the paper a prompt and unstudied eloquence" (64). For characters like Lionel Verney in *The Last Man* and the title character in *St. Leon*, writing is the only available emotional outlet. Godwin and Shelley suggest, however, that oral self-expression is more therapeutic than pouring out "the sentiments of [one's] soul" on paper.

In *The Theory of Moral Sentiments*, Adam Smith describes how conversation can further moral and emotional "self-command":

> In solitude, we are apt to feel too strongly whatever relates to ourselves; we are apt to over-rate the good offices we may have done, and the injuries we may have suffered: we are apt to be too much elated by our own good, and too much dejected by our own bad fortune. The conversation of a friend brings us to a better, that of a stranger to a still better temper. The man within the breast, the abstract and ideal spectator of our sentiments and conduct, requires often to be awakened and put in mind of his duty, by the presence of the real spectator: and it is always from that spectator, from whom we can expect the least sympathy and indulgence, that we are likely to learn the most complete lesson of self-command.[3]

One is tempted to see in this description of the salutary effects of conversation an anticipation of Freudian psychoanalysis. Yet, although Smith's listening stranger may appear to prefigure the twentieth-century psychoanalyst, and his "man within the breast" sounds like an eighteenth-century version of the superego, his primary concern is moral rather than psychological. In Smith's view, the main virtue of conversation is that it promotes self-command: mental discipline is more important than consolation or emotional relief. Moreover, the listener need not be a professional counselor—any unsympathetic person, even an enemy, will do.

William Godwin, who read *The Theory of Moral Sentiments* in 1797 and 1798, agreed with Smith that conversation can help an individual achieve self-command.[4] But he also believed that conversation serves other functions, allowing people to ventilate strong emotions, benefit from the sympathy of others, and, through confession, free themselves from the burden of guilt. Thus, in his *Life of Geoffrey Chaucer*, he praises the Roman Catholic practice of auricular confession because "There is nothing which operates more powerfully to mollify and humanise the heart, than the habit of confessing all our actions, and concealing none of our weaknesses and absurdities."[5] According to Godwin, "There is no more restless and unappeasable propensity of the mind than the love of communication, the desire to pour out our soul in the ear of a confident [*sic*] and a friend."[6] Because the Catholic priest combines, at least in theory, a sympathetic attitude with "a superior nature which appears to us inaccessible to weakness and folly," he is the ideal person to hear "the little story of our doubts and anxieties." Moreover, the priest "hears us with interest and fatherly affection, . . . judges us uprightly, . . . advises us with an enlightened and elevated mind, . . . frees us from the load of undivulged sin, and enables us to go forward with a chaste heart and a purified conscience."[7] Whereas Smith's listening stranger offers to those who are suffering from adversity or benefiting from prosperity a disinterested perspective on their thoughts and feelings,[8] Godwin's priest provides his penitents with much more: emotional ventilation, moral judgment, advice, and relief from guilt.

In *Caleb Williams* the title character wants Mr. Collins, who has "contributed more than any other to encourage and assist [his] juvenile studies" (307), to hear the narrative of his sufferings. Collins returns to England after managing Falkland's plantation in the West Indies for ten years, and during his absence Caleb has become a social pariah, unrelentingly persecuted by their mutual employer. Thus Caleb longs for Collins's sympathy and companionship:

> The greatest aggravation of my present lot, was, that I was cut off from the friendship of mankind. I can safely affirm, that poverty and hunger, that endless wanderings, that a blasted character and the curses that clung to my name, were all of them slight misfortunes compared to this. I endeavoured to sustain myself by the sense of my integrity, but the voice of no man upon earth echoed to the voice of my conscience. "I called aloud; but there was none to answer; there was none that regarded." To me the whole world was as unhearing as the tempest, and as cold as the torpedo. (308)

However, because Collins feels that "At [his] age [he] is not fit for the storm" (309) that would result from Caleb's revelations, he is reluctant to listen to this "justification."

Caleb belatedly realizes that instead of deploring Collins's absence he should have made Falkland his confidant. Near the end of his public accusation of Falkland he admits that he has made a "mistake": "I am sure that, if I had opened my heart to Mr. Falkland, if I had told to him privately the tale that I have now been telling, he could not have resisted my reasonable demand. . . . It is . . . impossible that he could have resisted a frank and fervent expostulation, the frankness and the fervour in which the whole soul was poured out" (323). But while a private outpouring of the soul would have reconciled the two adversaries, Caleb falls into a deep depression following his public account of his employer's wrongdoings. At its conclusion, Caleb's "heart [is] pierced," and he is "compelled to give vent to its anguish" (323). He feels like a murderer because he has destroyed Falkland's reputation and therefore his life. Neither his interview with Collins nor his narrative before the magistrate provides Caleb with the peace of mind that auricular confession, in Godwin's view, offers Catholic penitents. Collins is unwilling and perhaps unable to play the role of confessor, and Caleb's recital of his sufferings is, unlike auricular confession, public. It thus has legal and social consequences that could have been avoided if Caleb had told his tale to Falkland "privately." The manuscript ending of *Caleb Williams* suggests, however, that Caleb's public narrative, because it is validated by Falkland, has a beneficial effect. In the manuscript, Falkland denies Caleb's allegations, the magistrate declares them a "forgery" (330), and Caleb goes mad. Although Caleb is full of self-hatred and remorse in the novel's published conclusion, at least Falkland's corroboration of his story allows him to retain his sanity.

Caleb also seeks consolation through writing: "For some time I had a melancholy satisfaction in writing. I was better pleased to retrace the particulars of calamities that had formerly afflicted me, than to look forward, as at other times I was too apt to do, to those by which I might hereafter be overtaken" (303). For him, recording a disastrous past is consoling only because it prevents him from anticipating a potentially worse future. After he develops "a disgust for life and all its appendages," writing "is changed [from] a pleasure . . . into a burthen," and he decides to "compress into a small compass what remains to be told" (304). According to him, the therapeutic effect of writing is extremely limited. Unable to open his heart to a sympathetic listener or to find relief through setting down his "justification," Caleb becomes "truly miserable" (325). Despite the fact that he is a student of language who studies "the manner in which words [are] used" while doing research for his "etymological analysis of the English language" (294), Caleb never learns how to use words to ease his mental sufferings.

But while Caleb is finally able to tell his life story to an attentive audience, writing is St. Leon's only medium of self-expression:

> I wanted some friendly bosom into which to pour out my feelings, and thus by participation to render my transports balsamic and tolerable. But this was for ever denied me. No human ear must ever be astonished with the story of my endowments and my privileges. . . . Sense-

> less paper! be thou at least my confidant! To thee I may impart what my soul spurns the task to suppress. The human mind insatiably thirsts for a confidant and a friend. It is no matter that these pages shall never be surveyed by other eyes than mine. They afford at least the semblance of communication and the unburthening of the mind; and I will press the illusion fondly and for ever to my heart. (161–62)

St. Leon realizes that writing can only "afford . . . the semblance of communication and the unburthening of the mind"; it can never truly be a substitute "for a confidant and a friend." There are some experiences that he will not even put down in his narrative. For example, he passes over the mental and physical torments inflicted on him by the Spanish Inquisition (347). In his view, the idea that writing can provide any kind of lasting consolation or emotional ventilation is an "illusion" indeed. It is better to suppress his terrible experiences than to relive them on "Senseless paper." He discovers that not even the possession of inexhaustible wealth and immortal life can make up for his inability to talk about his true feelings:

> I was endowed with the faculty of speech, but was cut off from its proper and genuine use. I was utterly alone in the world, separated by an insurmountable barrier from every being of my species. No man could understand me; no man could sympathise with me; no man could form the remotest guess at what was passing in my breast. I had the use of words; I could address my fellow-beings; I could enter into dialogue with them. I could discourse of every indifferent thing that the universe contained; I could talk of every thing but my own feelings. This . . . is . . . true solitude. Let no man, after me, pant for the acquisition of the philosopher's stone! (465–66)

Because he has sworn never to reveal his alchemical powers and because priests (particularly in Spain) can turn out to be agents of the inquisition, St. Leon cannot ease his guilt and ventilate his emotions through auricular confession. Nor is this Catholic sacrament an option for the protagonist of *Mandeville*. His parents are murdered by Catholic rebels in Ireland when he is three, and he is educated by an anti-Catholic bigot, Hilkiah Bradford, who believes that

> Auricular confession, and the sacraments of absolution, [is] a stupendous device for subjecting the consciences of all, men, women, and children, to [the church of Rome's] despotic authority. . . . The first encouraging men to sin by the hopes of forgiveness, and then granting them absolution, [is] a nice game, by which the power of the

> clergy over their illiterate followers [is] increased to an incalculable degree. (49–50)

Mandeville's guardian, a reclusive uncle, abandons him to the care of Bradford, and the tutor's strict discipline fills Mandeville with a fury that he cannot ventilate:

> I said little; but this circumstance only deepened the effect on my mind. 'Give sorrow words', says the great master of the human soul [Shakespeare]. Whatever sentiment finds its way to the lips, and vents its energies through the medium of language, by that means finds relief. . . . But my silent nature was an ever-living and incessant curse to me. My displeasures brooded, and heated, and inflamed themselves, at the bottom of my soul, and finding no vent, shook so my single frame of man, like to an earthquake. (59–60)

Although Mandeville recognizes the importance of speech therapy, his "aversion" (61) to Bradford prevents him from accepting his tutor as a counselor or confidant. Unable to "give words" to his conflicted emotions, he becomes extremely paranoid, first imagining that "every thing around [him is] engaged in a conspiracy against [him]" (60), and then developing an obsessional hatred for Clifford, a schoolboy rival who, without intending to, becomes for Mandeville "the night-mare, under whose weight [he lies] at the last gasp of existence" (91).

After Bradford's death, Mandeville seeks the company of Waller, a fellow pupil at Winchester school, because he knows that Waller will never penetrate his reserve: "It was disdain, and the unsociableness of my nature, that dictated this choice. I could not unbosom my thoughts; I could not come into contact with another being of the same species as myself" (96). Much to Mandeville's dismay, Waller falsely accuses him of owning a book of prints satirizing Charles I, disgracing him in the eyes of his schoolmates and ending their friendship. Later, at Oxford, Mandeville tries to deal with his bitterness by forming "a misanthropical club" with a student named Lisle. As the only members of this club, he and Lisle spend time cursing together, but Mandeville denies himself the relief of unloading "the secret sorrows of [his] bosom" (132). In retrospect, he realizes that confessing his obsessional hatred of Clifford would have been a liberating experience for him: "Oh, if I could have pronounced the name of Clifford, if I could have told the griefs that had flowed to me from him, if I could have given vent to the various emotions he had excited within me, I should have become a different man" (133).

Unfortunately, Lisle, like Waller, turns on Mandeville, repudiating him after learning that Mandeville has deserted forces engaged in a royalist rebellion against Cromwell.

After Lisle's rejection, Mandeville goes through a period of madness and ends up in a lunatic asylum, where he is subjected to "the violence, the cords, the harsh language, the blows, . . . judged necessary to employ, for [his] restraint, or [his] cure" (144). He argues that conversation with a friend is far more therapeutic than physical restraint:

> No man needs a friend, so much as he who is under the slavery of a domineering passion. A friend is like Time, the master of us all, or like boundless Space. He removes us to a due distance from the object, which we see falsely and distorted only because we are too near to it. . . . The mere communication and common discussion with a sober and healthful mind, of what sovereign power are they!

According to Mandeville's definition, this "genuine friend" would be patient, sincere, sound in judgment, full of love for Mandeville, yet courageous enough "to dare on all occasions to tell [him] all the truth that [his] welfare require[s]." This ideal confidant, who Mandeville admits is "exceedingly rare," would combine "purity of heart [with] fervour of spirit" (145). Mandeville's "genuine friend" is, in some ways, a version of the confessor that Godwin describes in his *Life of Chaucer*; he is not the disinterested stranger advocated by Smith in *The Theory of Moral Sentiments*. Unfortunately for Mandeville, he yearns for a being whom he is unlikely to encounter in seventeenth-century Protestant England.

Mandeville declares that he "never had a friend" (145) capable of saving him from madness. His sister Henrietta cannot be such a friend because he cannot "bare [his] bosom in her sight" for fear that she "would censure [his] crimes, or . . . despise [his] weakness" (174). Like a number of Godwin's other male characters, Mandeville prefers to confide in a member of his own sex. Caleb Williams yearns to tell his tale to Mr. Collins; Fleetwood takes Gifford as his "pernicious confidant" (*Fleetwood*, 236); and the heartbroken Julian Cloudesley seeks the companionship of his transgressive male friends. Although Mandeville and Henrietta are siblings, they have been raised separately and have received different educations. Because they have grown up in different spheres they are unable to communicate freely with each other, and Mandeville is afraid that if he confesses his pathological jealousy of Clifford to his sister she will either censure or despise him. Henrietta has no way of understanding how or why her brother's humiliation at an all-male public school has transformed him into an intensely bitter and paranoid misanthrope.

The person who ultimately becomes Mandeville's confidant is neither genuine nor priestly, but he is, like the protagonist, the product of a public school and Oxford education. As his name suggests, Mallison, or "evil son," is the very opposite of the paternalistic friend idealized by Mandeville. Whereas a genuine friend would, according to Mandeville's own definition, be willing to tell him unpleasant truths, Mallison is a manipulative flatterer. However, because Mallison's "mind [is] totally vacant of all moral discernment," Mandeville feels free to be himself in his presence:

> If I had at any time an attack of pain, if I was wretched, or was peevish, I no more thought of suppressing the first symptoms of these conditions in the presence of Mallison, than if I had been alone. I played the querulous fool without constraint, and spread out my nature before him in its most pitiful and degrading imperfections. (244–45)

In retrospect, however, Mandeville realizes that the object of Mallison and his coconspirator is "to reduce [him] to so helpless and pitiable a state of mind, that [he] might finally be a passive instrument in their hands" (256). After building up Mandeville's self-esteem through flattery, Mallison infuriates him by declaring that his archenemy has converted to Catholicism, and that this conversion has been approved of by Charles II and the exiled royalists. This reawakens both Mandeville's obsessional hatred for Clifford and his virulent anti-Catholicism: "It was as if my brainpan had been laid open, and all the conceptions and knots of ideas which had been stored there, were given to irretrievable confusion" (252). He becomes even more frenzied when he learns that his sister has fallen in love with his hated rival.

By the end of the novel, Mallison and his uncle have succeeded in goading Mandeville into attacking Clifford, and their victim is left both physically and mentally scarred. Although Mandeville's conversations with Mallison, as long as Mallison remains passive and nonjudgmental, provide him with a temporary relief, he needs a counselor who will not take advantage of his vulnerability. By the time he finally reveals his feelings to Henrietta, he is so deranged that at the end of his harangue he confuses Clifford with "the Duke of Savoy" and Henrietta with "his queen" (316).

As a result, she decides to marry his archenemy. In his review of *Mandeville*, Percy Shelley condemns Henrietta for proceeding "unshrinkingly to her nuptial feast from the expostulations of Mandeville's impassioned and pathetic madness."[9] In his opinion, her failure to be the confidante her brother so desperately needs is reprehensible. As soon as he begins to rave, she gives him up as a lost cause. Lacking a "genuine friend," or someone who would, like the Roman Catholic priest described in Godwin's *Life of Chaucer*, hear his "story of . . . doubts and anxieties" and advise him "with an enlightened and elevated mind," Mandeville becomes Mallison's helpless puppet.

In *Cloudesley* Julian is "utterly averse to oral communication" (238) following the death of the title character, whom he mistakenly believes to be his father. For him, the earth contains "nothing that he value[s], and no one that he love[s]." He does, however, commit "his thoughts to paper . . . almost every day," composing "memorandums" that he destroys, throws aside, or locks "in his escritoire" (238). Unlike those of Caleb and St. Leon, his writings are spontaneous and unsystematic, brief descriptions of feelings rather than long narratives. In one note, he describes his emotional isolation from others: "The eyes of all I meet are hard, and glittering, and indifferent, the eyes of the stranger. They look on me, and pass by on the other side" (239). Borromeo, who replaces Cloudesley as Julian's guardian, longs to "express sympathy" for his charge, but he lacks "the organ. He [can]not find words to convey the feelings of his mind. . . . his stubborn features [refuse] to transmit the sentiments that [live] in his bosom" (241). There is, therefore, "not a human creature near [Julian] to whom he [can] open his heart" (243).

Julian's "memorandums" provide him with little or no consolation, so he flees Borromeo's residence and is nearly executed as a robber along with his bandit friends. In *Cloudesley*, Godwin argues against Smith's view that a "spectator, from whom we can expect the least sympathy and indulgence" is better suited than a friend to teach us "the most complete lesson of self-command." Because he lacks the vocabulary and facial expressions of a sympathetic listener, the austere Borromeo completely alienates Julian. As a result, he fails to teach his ward "self-command," and Julian, "his systems of reasoning . . . strangely discomposed" (268), repudiates "all that [is] soundest in argument" and perversely allies himself to the chief of the robbers "because he [is] an outlaw" (269).

Godwin's assessment of the therapeutic value of oral and written self-expression is slightly more optimistic in *Deloraine*. After murdering William, Deloraine is "cut off from human society; . . . destined to be hunted as a beast of prey, and to be looked upon by all men with horror and execration." Fortunately for him, his daughter, Catherine, decides to accompany and care for her fugitive father. She is able "to animate and encourage [him] in [his] deepest despondency" (162). They entertain each other with accounts of their "personal . . . adventures," and Deloraine "occasionally" forgets his "sorrows" (206). In contrast to Caleb Williams and Mandeville, who desire male confidants, Deloraine believes that rivalry inhibits communication between male friends and that only men and women in love can be completely open with one another. Of his first wife, he writes: "with a female, and that female the object of my growing partiality and preference, every new agreement of sentiment and approbation brings us nearer to each other, . . . dissolves our several identities, and . . . mingles us in heart and spirit, with a feeling that we can never thereafter be divided" (13).

Deloraine's theory is undercut, however, by his failure to communicate honestly with his second wife, Margaret Borradale. He decides to hide from her the fact that William, the great love of her life whom she believes drowned, is still alive. Maddened with jealousy and terrified that William might suddenly appear before his wife, he forces himself to pretend that nothing is wrong. While in Margaret's presence, he is indifferent and serene; after leaving her, he erupts:

> My limbs had been bound down, my features composed, my voice compulsively softened to soothing and encouraging accents; and now in revenge I assumed all the violence and contortions of a madman, I stamped with my feet, I spread my arms with wildness and ferocity, and roared like a savage beast, who has just escaped from the toils that controled [*sic*] him. I found ease in these strange ebullitions of an agonising mind. (120–21)

These repressed feelings are subsequently vented in his murder of William. Deloraine's inability to communicate freely with his wife, the rigid and unnatural control he exerts over his limbs, features, and voice while in her presence, leads him to commit an act of "terrific violence" (144).

Writing his life history provides Deloraine with "a sort of diversion to [his] anguish" and serves as a "relief" from the "all-devouring monotony" (286). However, although Deloraine is able to experience forgetfulness, diversion, and relief through speaking with his daughter and recording his experiences, by the end of the novel he is "burnt up with continual fever" (285), sleepless, and racked with guilt. Here, as elsewhere in Godwin's and Shelley's fiction, language therapy promotes psychic survival but cannot, in itself, eliminate mental suffering. *Deloraine* suggests, however, that this kind of therapy can play a preventive role: if Deloraine had ventilated his jealous feelings in conversation, he probably would not have murdered William.

Whereas Godwin explores the human need for oral and written self-expression through his conflicted and self-conscious male characters, Shelley's fictional investigation of language therapy often focuses on traumatized female characters. For example, the eponymous heroine of *Mathilda* refuses to tell her friend Woodville of her dead father's incestuous passion for her because she fears words, especially the word "incest," and, perhaps partially as a result of this self-censorship, she lives out her life in a state of chronic depression. Ellen-Clarice of "The Mourner" also refuses to talk about her traumatic experience, and the result of this refusal is depression and premature death. Although Mathilda and Ellen-Clarice leave written records of their sufferings, these records are to be read posthumously, and thus have little or no therapeutic effect. In contrast, Beatrice, the brutalized prophet of *Valperga*, relates her tale of suffering to the sympathetic Euthanasia, but this narration provides only temporary relief.[10]

Frankenstein's garrulous monster recounts his misadventures and sufferings to a much less compassionate listener. As Marc A. Rubenstein notes, "the author permits the monster an improbable series of digressions as he relates how he has passed the months since he wandered away from Frankenstein's laboratory."[11] There is, however, a psychological reason for the narrative, which Rubenstein touches on when he compares the monster to a "patient in psychoanalysis"[12]—the monster feels the need to work through and even validate his experience, and Frankenstein is the only person who will listen to him. Although Mary Shelley presents characters who are skeptical about the therapeutic value of verbal self-expression, she acknowledges the human need to put suffering into words, and the short-term relief that words can provide. Moreover, Shelley suggests that, in the case of extreme trauma, writing is sometimes more viable than speaking as a form of language therapy.

Mary Shelley's somewhat skeptical attitude toward the power of words was probably influenced by Percy Shelley's views on language.[13] In "On Life," Percy writes: "How vain is it to think that words can penetrate the mystery of our being"; he goes on to argue that "the misuse of words and signs" prevents "the mind" from acting freely.[14] His frustration with the inadequacy of language is forcibly expressed in his note to "On Love": "These words are inefficient and metaphorical—Most words so—No help—."[15] Moreover, in *A Defense of Poetry*, Percy Shelley asserts that over time words decline into "signs for portions or classes of thought [i.e., abstract ideas] instead of pictures of integral thoughts"—if poets do not intervene to revitalize them, the language becomes "dead to all the nobler purposes of human intercourse."[16] Percy's concern about the inadequacy and abstraction of language is also expressed in his poetical works. In *Prometheus Unbound*, Prometheus repudiates his curse on Jupiter, declaring that "words are quick and vain" (IV.i.303), a sentiment that is echoed by the Maniac in "Julian and Maddalo," who exclaims "How vain / Are words!" (ll. 472–73). These declarations that words are "vain" can be compared to many of the pronouncements in Mary Shelley's fiction regarding the effectiveness of language. For example, her meditation on the failure of words to improve the human condition in her historical novel *The Fortunes of Perkin Warbeck* recalls Percy's views on language's limitations:

> Oh, had I, weak and faint of speech, words to teach my fellow-creatures the beauty and capabilities of man's mind; could I, or could one more fortunate, breathe the magic word which would reveal to all the power, which we all possess, to turn evil to good, foul to fair; then vice and pain would desert the new-born world!
> It is not thus: the wise have taught, the good suffered for us; we are still the same. (275)

Moreover, Clifford, the villain of *Perkin Warbeck*, soothes "his evil passions with words," thus exemplifying "the misuse of words and signs" that Percy Shelley warns against in "On Life": "It was some relief to this miserable man to array his thoughts in their darkest garb, soothing his evil passions with words, which acted on them as a nurse's fondling talk to a querulous child" (168). As I will demonstrate, many of Mary Shelley's works seem to support her husband's view that words are essentially inadequate, too metaphorical and easily misused to provide a reliable mode of self-expression.

In his essay "Of the Study of the Classics" in *The Enquirer*, Godwin's attitude toward language is much less skeptical than his daughter's. He asserts that language can be used effectively by "the man who is competent to and exercised in the comparison of languages. . . . Language is not his master, but he is the master of language. Things hold their just order in his mind, ideas first, and then words. Words therefore are used by him as the means of communicating or giving permanence to his sentiments; and the whole magazine [storehouse] of his native tongue is subjected at his feet."[17] Unfortunately, monolingual individuals are not "accustomed to refine upon words, and discriminate their shades of meaning" and thus they "think and reason after a very inaccurate and slovenly manner."[18] Although Godwin believes that those who are "competent . . . in the comparison of languages" use words with precision and clarity, even his well-educated characters often fail to communicate effectively. As we have seen, despite his etymological studies Caleb Williams completely miscalculates the effect of his speech before the magistrate in both the manuscript and the published endings of *Caleb Williams*.

Like Godwin, Mary Shelley recognizes the human need to communicate and is aware of the psychological ramifications of words, whether spoken or unspoken. Perhaps more than any of her other characters, Frankenstein's monster realizes the importance of oral communication.[19] His hideous and terrifying appearance inspires fear and hatred in others, but when he overhears cottagers conversing with one another, he learns that relationships can have a linguistic basis: "I found that these people possessed a method of communicating their experience and feelings to one another by articulate sounds. I perceived that the words they spoke sometimes produced pleasure or pain, smiles or sadness, in the minds and countenances of the hearers. This was indeed a godlike science, and I ardently desired to become acquainted with it" (83). He has complete faith in the "godlike" powers of language, which he thinks will create a bond between him and the cottagers: "I formed in my imagination a thousand pictures of presenting myself to them, and their reception of me. I imagined that they would be disgusted, until, by my gentle demeanour and conciliating words, I should first win their favour, and afterwards their love. These thoughts exhilarated me, and led me to apply with fresh ardour to the acquiring the art of language" (85). However, language fails to live up to the monster's expectations: although he succeeds in impressing the blind De Lacey, De Lacey's son Felix returns and violently attacks the monster before he can say a word in his own defense. His need to communicate with other intelligent beings remains unsatisfied.

The monster refuses, however, to give up his quest to form a relationship through language, and he asks Frankenstein to create a female monster: "my virtues will necessarily arise when I live in communion with an equal. I shall feel the affections of a sensitive being, and become linked to a chain of existence and events, from which I am now excluded" (109). But when Frankenstein destroys the unfinished female monster, the monster is condemned to perpetual linguistic isolation. He is convinced that he will never experience the consolation of expressing his thoughts and feelings to a sympathetic "equal." Only in the last scene of the novel, after Frankenstein has died, can the monster express his powerful emotions to a compassionate listener, and the extravagance of his language does seem to give him some relief: " 'But soon,' he cried, with sad and solemn enthusiasm, 'I shall die, and what I now feel be no longer felt. Soon these burning miseries will be extinct. I shall ascend my funeral pile triumphantly, and exult in the agony of the torturing flames' " (164). Before Walton, the monster can play his final part "with sad and solemn enthusiasm." Although language cannot in and of itself enable the monster to have the relationships he craves, he can finally experience the satisfaction of confessing his crimes and articulating his miseries before a man who, if not totally sympathetic, is at least torn between "curiosity and compassion" (161). However, despite his last impassioned monologue, the monster is irrevocably cut off from the linguistic community.

Mary Shelley's speculations about language and therapy may have been influenced by "The Rime of the Ancient Mariner," which Coleridge recited at her house when she was a child.[20] In the epigraph to her short story "Transformation" (1830), she quotes from the section of Coleridge's poem in which the Ancient Mariner is compelled to tell his tale:

Forthwith this frame of mine was wrench'd
With a woful agony,
Which forced me to begin my tale,
And then it set me free.
Since then, at an uncertain hour,
That agony returns;

And till my ghastly tale is told
This heart within me burns.
Coleridge's Ancient Mariner.
(*The Mary Shelley Reader*, 286)

"Transformation" begins with the protagonist wondering about his motivation for narrating his story:

> I have heard it said, that, when any strange, supernatural, and necromantic adventure has occurred to a human being, that being, however desirous he may be to conceal the same, feels at certain periods torn up as it were by an intellectual earthquake, and is forced to bare the inner depths of his spirit to another . . . in spite of strong resolve—of a pride that too much masters me—of shame, and even of fear, so to render myself odious to my species—I must speak. (*The Mary Shelley Reader*, 286)[21]

This passage describes both the innate human need "to bare the inner depths of [one's] soul" and the sense that the consequences of this self-exposure could well be devastating and could, in fact, make one appear "odious" to one's entire species. These contradictory urges to reveal and conceal are typical of a number of Shelley's traumatized characters and create a dialectic that Mary Shelley explores extensively in the figures of Mathilda and Beatrice, both of whom are modeled on Percy Shelley's tragic protagonist Beatrice Cenci. Like Beatrice Cenci, Mary Shelley's heroines can find no words to heal their psychic wounds. Both Mathilda and Beatrice Cenci are confronted with the horror of father-daughter incest, and Mathilda also resembles Beatrice in her fear of forbidden words, or, more specifically, in her repression of words signifying incest, the "guilt that wants a name" (*Mary Shelley Reader*, 239). Thus, a comparison of *Mathilda* and *The Cenci* allows us to see how Mary Shelley's treatment of the theme of logophobia builds on her husband's dramatic portrayal of posttraumatic word repression.

In Percy's *The Cenci*, after Cenci has struck and cursed Beatrice, Lucretia asks her what is wrong, and the stunned Beatrice forces herself to say: "It was one word, Mother, one little word" (II.i.63). That unspeakable word has, however, put Cenci in the position of power. Whereas before it was Cenci who left Beatrice uttering "inarticulate words" (II.i.112), after Cenci's threat it is she who is afraid to speak. Moreover, following her father's rape of her, Beatrice is unable to give the act a name. In response to Lucretia's questions she repeatedly equivocates: "What are the words which you would have me speak?" (III.i.107); "Of all words, / That minister to mortal intercourse, / Which wouldst thou hear?" (III.i.111–13). All victims of incest, she suggests, are compelled to leave "it . . . without a name" (III.i.117). As Anne McWhir notes, Beatrice's repression of the word incest results in the word's revenge: "rejected as a way of dealing with passion, [the word] returns as a means of suggesting perverse, excessively literal action."[22] Because she could not give her horror a name, Beatrice feels compelled to have her father murdered.

Like Beatrice, Mathilda struggles with unutterable words, but, unlike Beatrice, Mathilda precipitates her own tragedy by begging her father to speak "that dreadful word" (201). While Beatrice's mistake may be her refusal to give Cenci's crime a name, Mathilda's initial error is to insist that her father tell her his dark secret, and his confession of incestuous passion is what leads to their destruction. Mathilda passionately demands that her father "Speak that word," and his "strange words" (200) are fatal to him and, eventually, to her. In fact, in the scene in which Mathilda confronts her moody and evasive father, "word" and "words" are repeated with obsessive regularity. She replies to her father's "terrific words": "the sword in my bosom [is] kept from its mortal wound by a hair—a word!—I demand that dreadful word; though it be as a flash of lightning to destroy me, speak it" (201). Her father resists uttering the "strange words" of his confession, but Mathilda's "words [he] cannot bear" (200), so his secret is extracted: "My daughter, I love you!" In his subsequent ravings he tells her that he foolishly believed that "these words . . . would blast her to death" (201). Unfortunately, those words, once uttered, can never be taken back, and they inevitably lead to the father's death and Mathilda's decline. Thus, after learning the fatal consequences of certain words, Mathilda becomes, like Beatrice Cenci, logophobic: her thoughts become "too harrowing for words" (219), and, although her narrative is ostensibly written for Woodville, she is never able to tell him her story directly: "I never dared give words to my dark tale" (239).

In its skepticism about the therapeutic value of spoken words, *Mathilda* is somewhat different from the section of *The Fields of Fancy*, an earlier draft of *Mathilda*, in which Diotima persuades Mathilda to tell her story. In *The Fields of Fancy*, Mathilda asks: "Are there in the peaceful language used by the inhabitants of these regions [the Elysian Gardens]—words burning enough to paint the tortures of the human heart—Can you understand them? or can you in any way sympathize with them[?]"[23] Yet, even in *The Fields of Fancy* the implication is that a tale like Mathilda's can be told only in some visionary realm; on earth, Mathilda chooses to repress the words that might help her to exorcize her mental demons. Her tale is left as a manuscript to be read posthumously.

In fact in the final chapters of the novella Mathilda makes the mental error that Percy Shelley, following Locke, describes in his notes to *Queen Mab*: "the vulgar mistake of [confusing] a metaphor for a real being, . . . a word for a thing."[24] She has an almost superstitious awe of words, which seem to have the power to destroy. While she is searching for her suicidal father, Mathilda gazes at "a magnificent oak" in the midst of a lightning storm and declares to her servant that "if the next flash of lightning rend not that oak my father will be alive." Her father is dead, and the tree is accordingly obliterated: "I had scarcely uttered these words than a flash instantly followed by a tremendous peal of thunder descended on it [and] the oak no longer stood in the meadow" (213). While the word incest has the power to damn Mathilda to mental hell, her words in this scene appear to have the power to command the forces of heaven. In light of these events, it is not surprising that Mathilda changes from a woman who demands that her father "Speak that word" to a secretive recluse. Mathilda's logophobia is such that she refuses (while alive) to reveal the secret of her despair to Woodville, although he begs her to allow "complaint and sorrow [to] shape themselves into words" (231). She remembers all too clearly her devastation after her father shaped his "complaint and sorrow" into language.

However, although Mathilda represses the words that would explain the cause of her sorrows, she nevertheless finds a kind of consolation in complaining to Woodville, in clothing her "woe in words of gall and fire" (231). Moreover, Woodville's soothing conversation shows Mathilda the positive power of words: "Woodville's words had magic in them" (232), she writes, admitting that "His words are sweet" (234). Unfortunately, however, "the influence of Woodville's words [is] very temporary" (240), and in his absence Mathilda again succumbs to despair. As long as she fails to "give words to [her] dark tale," she will not be able to exorcize it, and death comes to her as a relief. Mathilda recognizes the "magic" of language but comes to believe that its consolatory effect is too ephemeral to provide any lasting benefit. Moreover, Mathilda's remorse over her father's death leads her to blame herself for his unnatural passion: "I alone was the cause of his defeat and justly did I pay the fearful penalty" (197). In fact, Mathilda even questions her motivation for writing her story: "Perhaps a history such as mine had better die with me, but a feeling that I cannot define leads me on and I am too weak both in body and mind to resist the slightest impulse" (175). Although her conscious mind seems to favor repression, her unconscious, or that "feeling that [she] cannot define," compels her to narrate her life. She can accept the fact that incestuous passion can be written about, but she refuses to believe that it can be *spoken* about. As I have observed, however, written confession in Shelley's fiction invariably fails to mitigate the confessor's sufferings—in Mathilda's case, death comes as a relief.

Ten years after she composed *Mathilda*, Shelley returned to the themes of father-daughter love and linguistic repression in a short story entitled "The Mourner." In "The Mourner" a young woman, Clarice Eversham, is obsessively devoted to her father: "He appeared to her like an especial gift of Providence, a guardian angel—but far dearer, as being akin to her own nature" (*Collected Tales and Stories*, 92). When she and her father are caught in a shipwreck, she refuses to leave him when the women are being put on boats, even though the angry captain expostulates with her: "You will cause your father's death—and be as much a parricide as if you put poison into his cup—you are not the first girl who has murdered her father in her wilful mood" (94). She remains with her father because she has the "fearful presentiment" (93) that if she leaves him he will die; ironically, however, she does indirectly cause his death when the one boat that returns for them has room for only one person. Her father tosses her aboard it and is drowned (like Mathilda's father). During the homeward voyage Clarice hears reproaches from her fellow passengers who, rather harshly, conceive "a horror of her, as having caused her father's death" (94). In essence, "The Mourner" is a reworking of *Mathilda* without the incest theme: like Mathilda, Clarice responds to her father's death by isolating herself and ultimately dying in that isolation. Clarice even goes so far as to change her name to Ellen and pronounce her earlier self (Clarice) dead. She befriends Horace Neville, who, like Woodville, is a Percy Shelley surrogate (the names of both characters end in "ville"), and who, again like Woodville, must persuade her not to commit suicide.

As Ellen, Clarice is characterized by "wordless misery"—instead of telling Neville her story, she generalizes on the subject of sorrow: "She recited no past adventures, alluded to no past intercourse with friend or relative; she spoke of the various woes that wait on humanity'' (89). This relatively abstract form of therapy does not alleviate her suffering, and she occasionally begins to tell her story, but then she breaks off: ''Sometimes she gave words to her despair . . . and every pulsation of her heart was a throb of pain. She has suddenly broken off in talking of her sorrows, with a cry of agony—bidding me to leave her'' (89). This fragmentary type of language therapy does not seem to help in the least, and she soon falls ill, refusing medical help and doing ''many things that tended to abridge [her life] and to produce mortal disease'' (91). Her ultimate confession, like Mathilda's, is in the form of writing, but even here she fragments the word that describes her ''crime.'' In her final letter she asks Neville to give the following message to her erstwhile lover, Lewis Elmore: ''Tell him . . . it had been destruction, even could he have meditated such an act, to wed the parrici——. I will not write that word'' (98). Like Mathilda, she has made ''the vulgar mistake of [confusing] . . . a word for a thing.'' She represses the word parricide just as Mathilda represses the word incest, but neither woman is truly guilty of what she accuses herself. They leave writings that will be read posthumously and seek to escape both life and fearful words in death. Like Mathilda, Ellen-Clarice prefers written revelations to oral confessions, even though she is unsure of the justification for her final document. As Ellen-Clarice muses, ''Perhaps it is a mere prevarication to write,'' but write she does, and she seems to gain some measure of consolation from the fact that she has bid those who loved her ''a last farewell'' (98). Again, whereas spoken words are rejected as a possible form of communication, written words are at least posthumously acceptable.

Moreover, in both *Mathilda* and ''The Mourner,'' the psychologically unbalanced female protagonists are provided, in a sense, with amateur psychoanalysts: the Percy Shelley surrogates, Woodville and Neville, are faithful and supportive listeners who intervene successfully when their friends contemplate suicide. The auditors are clearly present—what is wanting is that one indispensable element, speech. The brusque way in which Mathilda and Ellen-Clarice reject the catharsis of oral self-expression—that catharsis that Coleridge's Mariner must repeatedly experience—suggests a somewhat masochistic desire to preserve their lonely sufferings from outside observation and interference. In memory of their dead fathers, they do not want to be relieved of their guilt until they expiate that guilt in death.

While Mathilda and Ellen-Clarice are traumatized by their inability to deal with their dead fathers, Beatrice of *Valperga* is emotionally shattered by her lover's rejection and her subsequent abuse by a band of sadists. Her sufferings, like those of Percy's Beatrice Cenci, have a physical as well as an emotional component,[25] but unlike Mathilda and Ellen-Clarice, she deals with her terrible memories in an outspoken way. After being seduced by Castruccio, Beatrice wanders as a penitential pilgrim, troubled by a recurrent dream that features a flood, "a dreary, large, ruinous house," and a mysterious and evidently traumatic event: "Then something happened, what I cannot now tell, terrific it most certainly was . . . there is something in this strange world, that we none of us understand" (*Valperga*, 256). Her dream becomes reality when she actually catches sight of "an old, large, dilapidated house islanded in the flood" (257), and she faints. When she awakens, she finds herself in the house of a Cenci-like psychopath who is like a "god of evil" (258). As she represses the horrific event of her dream, she refuses to specify all of what happens to her in that house of torture: "It was a carnival of devils, when we miserable victims were dragged out to—Enough! enough!" (257). Although she speaks about her subsequent madness, she feels unable to dwell on it: "But I must speak of that no more; methinks I again feel, what it is madness only to recollect" (258). In telling Euthanasia of her terrible experiences, she proves far more willing than either Mathilda or Ellen-Clarice to speak of what troubles her, but there are obvious limits to what even she is able to articulate: she partially censors her accounts of her dream, the abuse she suffered, and her subsequent insanity.

Compassionate, patient, wise, and morally upright, Euthanasia has all of the qualities that Mandeville lists in his definition of a "genuine friend." According to Thomas Reid, "the anatomist of the mind [can only] examine . . . his own mind . . . with any degree of accuracy and distinctness. . . . He may, from outward signs, collect the operations of other minds; but these signs are for the most part ambiguous, and must be interpreted by what he perceives in himself."[26] In Euthanasia's case, her lifelong habits of self-analysis have prepared her to become Beatrice's counselor: "Euthanasia was so self-examining, that she never allowed a night to elapse without recalling her feelings and actions of the past day; she endeavoured to be simply just to herself, and her soul had so long been accustomed to this discipline, that it easily laid open its dearest secrets" (251). Like a twentieth-century psychoanalyst, she is willing to listen and respond to the narratives of her "patient." For her part, Beatrice is eager to express her inmost thoughts to Euthanasia, and when her friend attempts to stifle her Paterin heresies, she exclaims: "Oh! let me speak: before all others I must hide my bursting feelings, deep, deep. Yet for one moment let me curse!" (242). In general, however, the countess recognizes the therapeutic value of Beatrice's sometimes rambling speeches: "Euthanasia was glad to hear her suffering friend talk, however wildly; for she observed that, when she had exhausted herself in speech, she became calmer and happier; while, if she brooded silently over her cares, she became almost insane through grief" (247–48).

Although in telling the story of her life Beatrice is forced to remember traumatic events, her narrative has a calming effect on her: "her heart was too big to close up in secrecy all the mighty store of unhappiness to which it was conscious; but, having now communicated the particulars to another, she felt somewhat relieved" (262). But while this seems like an unambiguous affirmation of the therapeutic value of spoken words, the qualifying "somewhat" indicates that Beatrice's cure is not complete, and it turns out to be temporary indeed. In fact, like the modern analysand who becomes overly dependent on his or her psychoanalyst, Beatrice is lost when Euthanasia leaves her alone in Lucca: "she was left without a guide to the workings of her own mind" (269). She encounters a corrupt priest named Tripalda, one of her former torturers, and falls senseless; she dares "not speak to any . . . and the deep anguish she [feels is] no longer mitigated by the converse with her friend" (270). As long as she has Euthanasia as a confidante, Beatrice is able to maintain her sanity.

Thus Beatrice, unlike Mandeville, is able to bear her soul to a sympathetic and insightful friend. She has, moreover, another advantage over Godwin's protagonist: as a Catholic, she can find relief for her emotional and spiritual conflicts through the sacrament of confession. In fact, her confessor, Padre Lanfranco, proves to be as capable as Euthanasia in managing Beatrice's moods: "It would seem that this old man humoured warily and wisely her disturbed understanding; for she appeared at peace with herself and others" (267). Shelley suggests that the sacrament of confession, when performed wisely and benevolently, can be extremely therapeutic.

Beatrice's words provide relief not only to Beatrice but also to her listener, Euthanasia. Both Beatrice and Euthanasia feel a special kinship for one another because they have both loved, and had their hearts broken by, Castruccio. Under Beatrice's influence, Euthanasia is able to break out of her state of emotional paralysis: "Beatrice again awoke [Euthanasia] to words, and these two ladies, bound by the sweet ties of gratitude and pity, found in each other's converse some balm for their misfortunes" (248). Beatrice, unlike Mathilda and Ellen-Clarice, tells her story to a sympathetic woman and confesses to a priest, who functions as a medieval mad-doctor. However supportive Woodville and Neville may appear, they are neither female nor clerical, and the women they attempt to console refuse to confide in them.[27] Together, however, the two patriarchal influences on Mathilda and Ellen-Clarice—first the excessively loving and guilt-inspiring fathers, second the younger men who seek to "save" them from their suicidal depressions—work effectively to silence these extremely sensitive women. But in *Valperga*, Castruccio, the oppressive masculine influence in that novel, allows his female victims to find at least a temporary peace in each other's company.

In Euthanasia's absence, however, Beatrice describes to Fior di Mandragola her recurrent dream of the flood-islanded house, which now includes a confrontation with a doppelgänger: "I was transported into a boat which was to convey me to that mansion . . . a woman sate near the stern, aghast and wild as I. . . . It was myself; I knew it; it stood before me, melancholy and silent; . . . I can tell no more" (274–75). As in its earlier incarnations, this dream is inconclusive, and word repression is again suggested: "a few moments, and I distinctly remembered the words it spoke; they have now faded" (275). Unfortunately, Mandragola, unlike Euthanasia, uses Beatrice's words to manipulate her, misinterpreting the dream as a divine sign of Beatrice's mystical powers, and promising Beatrice that she will be able to use these powers to command Castruccio, whom Beatrice still loves. Exposing one's inner self to the wrong person can be psychologically devastating: the witch raises false hopes in Beatrice and then makes her swear never to reveal what has transpired.

As in the cases of Mathilda and Ellen-Clarice, Beatrice decides to remain silent because of the man she loves, and this silence proves fatal. When Euthanasia returns, she notices a change in Beatrice: "She was much disappointed . . . to find her friend far worse both in body and in mind, than when she left her. More than all wildness of words and manner, she feared her silence and reserve, so very unlike her latest disposition" (278). Beatrice approaches Euthanasia for comfort but cannot speak: "I have sworn, and I will not tell—. . . I shall sleep now; so not a word more" (279). Later the witch drugs her with henbane and arranges for her to encounter Castruccio on the road. When Castruccio and her former abuser Tripalda approach, Beatrice falls down in convulsions and later dies, insane. She is no longer able to separate nightmare from reality.

Thus Shelley balances her presentation of positive language therapy, Beatrice's narration before the loving and sensitive Euthanasia, with an example of how baring one's psyche before a manipulative and unscrupulous person can lead to madness. Just as Mandeville's friendless condition is taken advantage of by Malison, the absence of a responsible counselor leaves a vacuum in Beatrice's life, which a psychological manipulator hastens to fill. Moreover, Beatrice's dependence on Euthanasia and her rapid decline into insanity after she decides to stop confiding in her friend suggest that, although spoken words can be therapeutic, a traumatized person's prognosis depends on the availability of a sympathetic and supportive listener. In an oppressively patriarchal world, a psychologically disturbed woman needs another woman (or, in Beatrice's case, an indulgent priest) to hear her. In *Mathilda* and "The Mourner," women refuse to tell their emotionally-charged stories to men, no matter how well-intentioned the men may be, but Beatrice gains at least a temporary respite when she relates her tale to Euthanasia. Similarly, Lady Katherine allows Queen Elizabeth, the oppressed and isolated wife of Henry VII in *Perkin Warbeck*, to vent her bitterness: "After years of silence, to utter her very inner thoughts, her woman's fears, her repinings, her aversions, her lost hopes and affections crushed: she spent her bitterest words; but thus it was as if she emptied a silver chalice of its gall, to be refilled by Katherine with heavenly dew" (346).

In *Perkin Warbeck* and *Lodore*, Shelley continues her exploration of language's power to effect positive change. In *Perkin Warbeck*, for example, Monina de Faro uses words to entrance the treacherous Robert Clifford:

> They spoke of the desolate waste of waters that hems in the stable earth—of the golden isles beyond: to all these subjects Monina brought vivid imagery, and bright painting, creations of her own quick fancy. Clifford had never before held such discourse. . . . The melodious voice of Monina, attuned by the divine impulses of her spirit, as the harp of the winds by celestial breezes, raised a commotion in his mind, such as a prophetess of Delphi felt, when the oracular vapour rose up to fill her with sacred fury.

Yet, Monina only succeeds in enchanting (and, significantly, feminizing) Clifford for a moment: "A word, a single word, was a potent northern blast to dash aside the mist, and to re-apparel the world in its, to him, naked, barren truth" (151). Her praise of Richard of York (Perkin Warbeck) inspires Clifford's jealous hatred, and "a single word" is enough to recall him to his evil nature. Although Monina is, like Woodville in *Mathilda*, a poetic and spellbinding speaker, both characters fail in their efforts to use words to inspire others. Not even the most powerful and imaginative discourse can wean Clifford and Mathilda away from their self-destructive passions. In *Perkin Warbeck*, Shelley suggests that words cannot convert—they can only reinforce tendencies and beliefs already present. Thus, Monina is able to inspire Edmund Plantagenet because he thinks as she does: "Her bold, impetuous language had its effect on Edmund: it echoed his own master passion" (294).

Fanny Derham, a minor character in Shelley's *Lodore*, believes passionately in the power of words to cause change. She declares her convictions to Ethel Villiers, the novel's heroine:

> Words have more power than any one can guess; it is by words that the world's great fight, now in these civilized times, is carried on; I never hesitated to use them, when I fought any battle for the miserable and oppressed. People are so afraid to speak, it would seem as if half our fellow-creatures were born with deficient organs; like parrots they can repeat a lesson, but their voice fails them, when that alone is wanting to make the tyrant quail. (213)

Moreover, when Ethel and her husband are in need of help, Fanny's conversation with Ethel's estranged mother, Lady Lodore, saves her friend from much suffering. However, Shelley repeatedly undercuts Fanny's idealistic sentiments by presenting her as other worldly and unrealistic. After the speech quoted above, Fanny asserts that "while [she] converse[s] each day with Plato, and Cicero, and Epictetus, the world . . . passes from before [her] like a vain shadow" (214). When Fanny inherits a fortune, she cannot grasp its significance:

> Fanny was too young, and too wedded to her platonic notions of the supremacy of mind, to be fully aware of the invaluable advantages of pecuniary independence for a woman. She fancied that she could enter on the career—the only career permitted her sex—of servitude, and yet possess her soul in freedom and power. (284)

Thus, although Shelley presents a character in *Lodore* who steadfastly believes in the power of language, Fanny is too inexperienced and bookish to be taken as a reliable authority on this subject. In fact, Shelley suggests that life will test Fanny's idealism: "One who feels so deeply for others, and yet is so stern a censor over herself—at once so sensitive and so rigidly conscientious—so single-minded and upright, and yet open as day to charity and affection, cannot hope to pass from youth to age unharmed" (313). Here as elsewhere Shelley is skeptical about the efficacy of words, particularly when they are employed by a naive idealist.

In Shelley's *Falkner* the title character attempts to come to terms with his guilt through writing a long, confessional narrative that explains his role in the death of Alithea Neville. He gives this document to his adoptive daughter, Elizabeth Raby, and Alithea's son, Gerard Neville, to examine. In it he describes his abduction of Alithea and how she drowned trying to escape him. After Gerard reads the narrative, Falkner expects the youth to challenge him to a duel: "His care must be to fall by the young man's hand. There was a sort of poetical justice in this idea, a noble and fitting ending to his disastrous story, that solaced his pride, and filled him . . . with triumph" (199). He is, however, arrested for the murder of Alithea and is forced to undergo a "public ignominious trial" (221).

In prison, Falkner "endure[s] the worst" and experiences "the singular relief which *confession* brings to the human heart. Guilt hidden in the recesses of the conscience assumes gigantic and distorted dimensions. When the secret is shared by another, it falls back at once into its natural proportion" (241, emphasis Shelley's). Convinced that Falkner did not murder his mother, Gerard testifies on his behalf, and "everyone [becomes] prepossessed in his favour" (282). Having been "acquitted before all the world" (298), Falkner remembers "the past with the same remorse" but is "honestly though calmly glad" (287–88). He is not, like Deloraine, doomed to live a fugitive from justice, "the worthy object of universal hate" (*Deloraine*, 285). While the hearing before the magistrate in *Caleb Williams* proves traumatic rather than therapeutic, the judicial proceedings in *Falkner* serve to reconcile the protagonist to himself, Alithea's son, and his fellow citizens. After Gerard forgives him and marries Elizabeth, Falkner experiences "As much happiness as any one can enjoy, whose inner mind bears the unhealing wound of a culpable act" (299). He has not exorcised his guilt, but he has overcome his suicidal impulses and his self-hatred.

As we have seen, Mary Shelley's fictions return repeatedly to the predicament of a suffering human being torn between the impulse to communicate and the urge to retreat into isolation and death. More often than not, the result is psychic paralysis, the opposite of the meliorism championed by Percy Shelley. Ultimately, however, an ephemeral sort of consolation can be found in the act of writing, as Lionel Verney discovers at the end of Mary Shelley's apocalyptic *Last Man.* Because he is the last man on earth, Lionel Verney's compositions seem the most futile of all self-expressions—no one will read them. Yet, in writing his narrative, Verney rejoins, temporarily, all of the people he has loved: "I lingered fondly on my early years, and recorded with sacred zeal the virtues of my companions. They have been with me during the fulfillment of my task. I have brought it to an end—I lift my eyes from my paper—again they are lost to me" (339). Even Mary Shelley's most repressed characters, such as Mathilda and Ellen-Clarice, find themselves compelled to express themselves in writing, just as Shelley herself, mourning the deaths of her husband and two of her children, and facing the prospect of social ostracism and emotional deprivation, was moved to present her state of mind in *The Last Man.*[28]

Moreover, in her 2 October 1822 journal entry, her first journal entry after Percy's death, Mary clearly states her need for the therapy provided by written rather than spoken self-expression: "Now I am alone! . . . The stars may behold my tears, & the winds drink my sighs—but my thoughts are a sealed treasure which I can confide to none. White paper—wilt thou be my confident [*sic*]? I will trust thee fully, for none shall see what I write."[29] While in her bereavement Mary Shelley finds social "intercourse with others extremely disagreable [*sic*]," she feels compelled to record her emotions in her journal: "coming home I write this, so necessary is it for me to express in words the force of my feelings."[30] Although the acts of speaking or writing may not cure psychological problems or bring the dead back to life, these forms of self-expression can provide some comfort, and as Godwin and Shelley suggest in their fiction, that momentary comfort often is the only consolation allowed to suffering humanity.[31]

5
Dreams

IN A FAMOUS PASSAGE FROM HER 1831 INTRODUCTION TO *FRANKENstein*, Mary Shelley claims that her novel was inspired by a peculiar mental state:

> When I placed my head on my pillow, I did not sleep, nor could I be said to think. My imagination, unbidden, possessed and guided me, gifting the successive images that arose in my mind with a vividness far beyond the usual bounds of reverie. I saw—with shut eyes, but acute mental vision,—I saw the pale student of unhallowed arts kneeling beside the thing he had put together.[1]

Shelley describes this state largely in negative terms—it is not a dream, because she is not asleep (although her eyes are closed), nor is it conscious thought, and it is too vivid to be a reverie. Her passive mind is, she asserts, "possessed" by her imagination. While the experience has some of the characteristics of a dream or nightmare, and ends abruptly when she opens her eyes, it also has some of the characteristics of a waking vision. Although, like most dreams, it progresses involuntarily, or in an "unbidden" way, it contains a relatively clear, linear narrative and is exceptionally vivid rather than blurry or confused. The truthfulness of Shelley's account of her "acute mental vision" has been questioned by some critics. However, whether the story is factual or an invention, it suggests that there was a strong connection, in Shelley's mind, between the imagination and dreams, that she conceived of imaginative "possession" as having the frightening, controlling quality of a full-blown nightmare.[2]

In this chapter I will discuss the roles that reveries and dreams play in the works of Godwin and Shelley. *St. Leon* and *Frankenstein* illustrate how reveries can be dangerous in the case of individuals who are prone to neglect practical or personal considerations in their obsessional pursuit "of some interesting train of ideas." However, while Godwin focuses on the negative consequences of reveries, Shelley tends to emphasize their therapeutic effect. Both Godwin and Shelley present dreams that provide valuable insights into the psyche of the dreamer by revealing his or her patterns of mental associations. But as we will see, dreams play a far more important role in Shelley's fiction than in Godwin's. Whereas Godwin's novels characterize dreams as unreliable, Shelley's works explore the relationship between dreams, the imagination, and prophecy.

In her introduction to *Frankenstein* Shelley compares her "possession" to reverie. Erasmus Darwin defines reverie in *Zoonomia*:

> When we are employed with great sensation of pleasure, or with great efforts of volition, in the pursuit of some interesting train of ideas, we cease to be conscious of our existence, are inattentive to time and place, and do not distinguish this train of sensitive and voluntary ideas from the irritative ones excited by the presence of external objects, though our organs of sense are surrounded with their accustomed stimuli, till at length this interesting train of ideas becomes exhausted, or the appulses of external objects are applied with unusual violence, and we return with surprise, or with regret, into the common track of life. This is termed reverie or studium.[3]

Unlike dreams, reveries are volitional, but they resemble dreams in the subject's inattention to external stimuli. They are frequently escapist: after the reverie runs its course or is interrupted, the daydreamer returns "with surprise, or with regret, into the common track of life." Rousseau was fond of reveries because they offered him a respite from the pressures and miseries of external reality.[4] As Shelley writes in her *Cabinet Cyclopaedia* article, Rousseau's "real life was replete with indignity and suffering; in reverie, he was enterprising, noble, and free."[5]

Godwin uses the term reverie inconsistently. In *An Enquiry Concerning Political Justice,* he defines reverie as waking "thoughts untransmitted to the memory," which he contrasts to "our more express and digested thoughts," but in other instances he employs the word to refer to remembered as well as forgotten daydreaming.[6] For example, in his *Autobiography* he describes "long reveries" he had when he was about fourteen years old, which were both "express" and remembered: "I made whole books as I walked, books of fictitious adventures in the mode of Richardson (I had then only read Richardson in an abridgement), and books of imaginary institutions in education and government, where all was to be faultless: there were also books of incident and adventure. . . . It was my disposition to proceed in somewhat of a regular train."[7] In his fiction, he presents this kind of conscious daydreaming as a dangerous activity. For example, after St. Leon's acquisition of the philosopher's stone and the elixir of life, he falls into frequent reveries. His "domestic character [is] wholly destroyed" (168), and "deep reveries" become "among the most frequent habits of [his] mind" (275). This preoccupation with "speculation and fancy" inflicts "severe and unmerited pains on those [he] love[s]" (169). St. Leon's reveries inspire him to perform a series of "experiments," which all end in disaster.

In *Fleetwood* the protagonist believes that reveries are dangerous because they promote delusions of grandeur. As a young "man of feeling," Fleetwood rambles through the Welsh countryside and develops "a habit of being absent in mind from the scene which [is] before [his] senses": "The state thus produced was sometimes that which we perhaps most exactly understand by the term reverie, when the mind has neither action nor distinct ideas, but is swallowed up in a living death, which, at the same time that it is indolent and inert, is not destitute of a certain voluptuousness." He also has, however, "more busy and definite . . . waking dreams." He suggests that these conscious reveries had a negative effect on his development:

> In the dream of the night, our powers are blunted, and we are but half ourselves: the day-dream on the contrary is the triumph of man; our invention is full, our complacency is pure; and, if there is any mixture of imbecility or folly in the fable, it is a mixture to which the dreamer at the moment scarcely adverts. The tendency, therefore, of this species of dreaming, when frequently indulged, is to inspire a certain propensity to despotism, and to render him who admits it impatient of opposition, and prepared to feel every cross accident, as a usurpation upon his rights, and a blot upon his greatness. (19)

As in the case of St. Leon, Fleetwood's daydreaming leads to delusional thinking and social maladjustment. He implies that his later problems with his wife are partly due to the "propensity to despotism" engendered by his boyhood fantasies.

Frankenstein also explores the dangers of speculative and fanciful reveries. The title character describes how his reveries impelled him to create the monster: "Even now I cannot recollect, without passion, my reveries while the work was incomplete. I trod heaven in my thoughts, now exulting in my powers, now burning with the idea of their effects" (156). However, in some of her other writings Shelley suggests that reveries can be beneficial. For example, in her journals she describes how her reveries provided her with insights into "the depths of [her] nature." While living in Genoa, she began taking "solitary walks": "my reveries . . . *were* magnificent, deep, pathetic, wild and exalted—I sounded the depths of my own nature; I appealed to the Nature around me to corroborate the testimony ↑ that ↓ my own heart bore to its purity."[8] Like Rousseau, Shelley believes that reveries are the barometers of the soul.[9]

In *Rambles in Germany and Italy* she explores the therapeutic effect of reveries, writing that reveries of "joy and good" were what enabled her to survive "the poverty and desolation of reality." She describes the daydream she had about Isola Bella, an island in Lago Maggiore in northern Italy:

> Such reveries possessed me, as I fancied life spent here, and pictured English friends arriving down from the mighty Simplon, and Italians taking refuge in my halls from persecution and oppression—a little world of my own—a focus whence would emanate some light for the country around—a school for civilisation, a refuge for the unhappy, a support for merit in adversity: from such a gorgeous dream I was awakened when my foot touched shore, and I was transformed from the Queen of Isola Bella into a poor traveller, humbly pursuing her route in an unpretending *vettura*. Such, for the most part, has been my life. Dreams of joy and good, which have lent me wings to leave the poverty and desolation of reality. How without such dreams I could have past long sad years, I know not. (143)

Godwin seldom alludes to the therapeutic effect of reveries in his novels. In *Deloraine* the protagonist enjoys a "delicious reverie" that gives him a temporary respite from his sufferings, but it does "not last more than a quarter of an hour" (249). Shelley's personal experience as a socially isolated widow taught her, however, that reveries are sometimes a marginalized individual's only emotional outlet. Without them, she believes that she would not have been able to survive the "long sad years" following her husband's death. Thus in *Perkin Warbeck* reveries help Monina to overcome her sorrow after her beloved Richard leaves her: "ceaseless reverie [seems her] only refuge from intolerable wretchedness" (105). In *Lodore* Ethel Villiers gives "herself up to reverie" and is happy in spite of her and her husband's desperate financial situation: she dwells "on many an evanescent idea, and revert[s] delightedly to many scenes, which her memory recalled" (231).

In *Falkner* Shelley goes a step further and indicates that, far from endangering domestic life, reveries can enhance it. The adolescent Elizabeth Raby, who is, paradoxically, "no dreamer," tries to be "useful in all her reveries": "Elizabeth was no dreamer. Though brought up abstracted from common worldly pursuits, there was something singularly practical about her. She aimed at being useful in all her reveries. This desire was rendered still more fervent by her affection for Falkner—by her fears on his account—by her ardent wish to make life dear to him" (56). This idea of a "practical" reverie, intended to rehabilitate a loved one, contrasts sharply with the view in *St. Leon* that reveries undermine the "domestic affections." Although Shelley suggests in *Frankenstein* that reveries tend to promote megalomania in privileged males, she indicates in her later works that they provide a needed "refuge" for women who have no other way to ventilate their emotions.

A number of Romantic-era writers shared certain beliefs regarding dream phenomena, but there was no "dream theory" as such that was widely accepted during the period. In fact, as David Miall has argued, not even a dedicated student of dreams like Samuel Taylor Coleridge could be said to have developed a dream theory.[10] According to Sigmund Freud, a dream theory must have the following characteristics: "Any disquisition upon dreams which seeks to explain as many as possible of their observed characteristics from a particular point of view, and which at the same time defines the position occupied by dreams in a wider sphere of phenomena, deserves to be called a theory of dreams."[11] Miall notes that, although Coleridge seems to have been a careful and accurate "observer of his own dreams," he was profoundly ambivalent about "dream thought," and many of his comments simply confirm commonly held beliefs.[12] Similarly, Godwin's and Shelley's presentations of dreams in their fiction do not appear to follow any recognizable theory of dreams. But while they did not employ a dream theory, neither did they write about dreams in a vacuum: their fictional explorations of oneiric phenomena were informed by eighteenth-century and early nineteenth-century conceptions of dreams.[13]

Shelley's narration of her waking dream in the 1831 Introduction to *Frankenstein* has some similarity to Darwin's general description of dreams in Darwin's *Zoonomia*: "our sensations of pleasure and pain are experienced with great vivacity in our dreams; and hence all that motley group of ideas, which are caused by them, called the ideas of imagination, with their various associated trains, are in a very vivid manner acted over in the sensorium."[14] Likewise, Shelley's waking dream is driven by the imagination, generates a train of "successive images," and is characterized by "vividness." One suspects, however, that Darwin and Shelley may well have differed in their conceptions of the imagination: as M. H. Abrams has observed, eighteenth-century writers such as Darwin tend to apply the term imagination "to all non-mnemonic processions of ideas."[15] Although Shelley sometimes uses the word imagination in its broad eighteenth-century sense, in her fiction she tends to present the dreaming imagination as a powerful, mind-altering faculty, which is capable of possessing the mind and leading the person under its control either to prophetic insight or madness. Darwin's explanation of how nightmares occur has, however, little to do with the imagination in any of its manifestations: "the disease called the incubus, or nightmare, is produced [by the] uneasy sensations [caused by] our continued posture in sleep . . . where the sleep is uncommonly profound."[16] In contrast, Godwin and Shelley do not seem concerned with the "posture" of the sleeper during dreams, although Constance's sleeping position in Shelley's "The Dream," on "a narrow ledge of earth and a moss-grown stone bordering on the very verge of [a] precipice" (*Collected Tales and Stories*, 162), could be seen as a partial cause of her "uneasy" dream.

Many of Darwin's other observations on mental activity during sleep were stock ideas during the Romantic period: "in dreams the power of volition is suspended"; "The rapidity of the succession and transactions in our dreams is almost inconceivable"; "dreams in the morning have greater variety and vivacity"; dreams are inconsistent, but, while dreaming, we are never surprised by their inconsistency.[17] His insistence on the vividness of sleeping visions is reflected in Godwin's and Shelley's treatments of dreams. According to Darwin, "The absence of the stimuli of external bodies, and of volition, in our dreams renders the organs of sense liable to be more strongly affected by the powers of sensation, and of association," and this gives dreams a clarity and intensity that cannot be attained when one is awake.[18] Thus St. Leon's dream in Bethlem Gabor's dungeon appears "particularly luminous and vivid" (425). Moreover, in dreams our visual memory is greatly enhanced: "we recal the figure and the features of a long lost friend, whom we loved, in our dreams with much more accuracy and vivacity than in our waking thoughts."[19] This idea informs a passage in Shelley's *The Last Man*, in which Lionel Verney, after having witnessed the extinction of the human race, dreams of his youth: "I fell asleep and dreamed of all dear inland scenes, of hay-makers, of the shepherd's whistle to his dog, when he demanded his help to drive the flock to fold; of sights and sounds peculiar to my boyhood's mountain life, which I had long forgotten" (325). Although dreamers may not be able to control their dream thoughts, dreams enable them to visualize and remember images with "accuracy and vivacity." This quality of intense vividness can make dreams all the more terrifying when they turn into nightmares.

Darwin's discussion of dreams has some resemblances to David Hartley's earlier remarks in *Observations on Man,* which, in turn, may have contributed to Godwin's and Shelley's understanding of dreams. Like Darwin, Hartley emphasizes somatic factors, asserting that dreams are affected by "Indigestions, Spasms, and Flatulencies," and he declares that dreams are wholly imaginative in nature: "Dreams are nothing but the Imaginations, Fancies, or Reveries of a sleeping Man."[20] Moreover, Hartley also anticipates Darwin's recognition of the vividness of dreams, although he is unsure about the cause of this phenomenon: "The Trains of visible Ideas, which occur in Dreams, are far more vivid than common visible Ideas; and therefore may the more easily be taken for actual impressions."[21]

There are, however, two ideas of Hartley's that Darwin did not adopt. The first idea has to do with recurrent dreams of places:

> It happens in Dreams, that the same fictitious Places are presented again and again at the Distance of Weeks and Months, perhaps during the whole Course of Life. These Places are, I suppose, compounded at first, probably early in Youth, of Fragments of real Places, which we have seen. They afterwards recur in Dreams, because the same State of Brain recurs; and when this has happened for some Successions, they may be expected to recur at Intervals during Life. But they may also admit of Variations, especially before frequent Recurrency has established and fixed them.[22]

As I will show, this type of dream is presented in *Valperga* and is alluded to in one of Percy Shelley's prose fragments. In both of these works, however, the dreamer finds out that the place featured in the recurrent dreams actually exists and is terrified as a result.

The second idea of Hartley's that relates to our discussion has to do with the connection between dreams and prophecies. According to Hartley,

> As the Prophecies were, many of them, communicated in the way of divine Visions, Trances, or Dreams, so they bear many of the . . . Marks of Dreams. Thus they deal chiefly in visible Imagery; they abound with apparent Impossibilities, and Deviations from common Life, of which yet the Prophets take not the least Notice[.] . . . And it seems to me, that these, and such-like [criteria] might establish the Genuineness of Prophecies, exclusively of all other evidences.[23]

Although dreams are presented as unreliable guides to the future in *Deloraine*, St. Leon's dream during his imprisonment correctly prophesies his eventual release. Shelley presents a number of premonitory dreams in her fiction, and in her portrayal of Beatrice in *Valperga* she explores the connection between prophecy and dreams.[24]

In *Enquiry Concerning Political Justice,* Godwin argues that dreams cannot produce original ideas because they result from previously conceived "Ideas [succeeding] each other in our sensorium according to certain necessary laws."[25] Mary Hays, who was one of Godwin's disciples during the 1790s, was also skeptical about the originality of dreams.[26] She denies in *Letters and Essays, Moral and Miscellaneous* (1793) that the "fancy presents us, while we sleep, with any scenes really new":

> That our ideas are differently and whimsically combined, from the absence of external objects, I readily allow; but they are always the result of prior impressions made on the brain, however wildly they may be associated; our consciousness is in a measure interrupted, by that rest to our faculties, which nature has kindly ordained to refresh and renovate us for action, and to relieve us from the dangerous pressure of the same ideas. It is also certain that the sounder and more undisturbed our repose is, the less we dream. . . . [A]greeable, or terrifying visions, depend entirely on the state of health, the position of the body, or temper of mind, in which we laid down to sleep.[27]

Hays's assessment of dreams recalls Locke's pronouncement in *Essay Concerning Human Understanding* that "The dreams of sleeping men are . . . all made up of the waking man's ideas; though for the most part oddly put together."[28] She asserts that dreams reflect the dreamer's physical condition and previous emotional state and are neither imaginative nor prophetic. Dreams in Godwin's novels always reflect, in some way, "prior impressions made on the brain." St. Leon's yearning for freedom, Mandeville's obsessional hatred for Clifford, and Margaret Borradale's fears for her beloved William are vividly expressed in their dreams.

The protagonist of *St. Leon* is imprisoned by a man who hates him and who intends for him to die in confinement. St. Leon has, however, a prophetic dream that convinces him that he will be released "by some striking event":

> I imagined I saw a knight, cased complete in proof [armor], enter my prison. A smile of angelic kindness beamed on his countenance. He embraced me with ardour; he made a sign to me to follow him. I felt that I had seen him somewhere, that he had been my intimate friend. Yet all the efforts I made in sleep, or afterwards when I was awake, were unavailing to remove the mystery that hung upon his features. I rose to obey him; the ground trembled under my feet like an earthquake. Presently, with the incoherency usually attendant on a dream, the figure changed to that of a female of unblemished grace and beauty; it unfolded a pair of radiant wings; we ascended together in the air; I looked down, and saw the castle of Bethlem Gabor a prey to devouring flames.—Here ended my dream.

This dream of an androgynous rescuer helps St. Leon to preserve his sanity. Although he can "reason [him]self out of all confidence in the presages of this wild and incongruous vision," he refuses to do so. Instead, he decides "to ruminate on this vision, not with the sternness of a syllogist, but with the colouring of a painter, and the rapture of a bard" (425). As a result of his aesthetic meditation, the dream recurs night after night and gives him the strength to resist Bethlem Gabor: "Slumbers like these were truly refreshing, and armed and nerved me for the contentions of my tyrant" (426).

St. Leon's vision also proves to be prophetic: Gabor's castle falls "prey to devouring flames," he is rescued by a knight "clothed in complete armour" (431) who provides him with "assurances of kindness" (437), and the knight turns out to be a person who was once his "intimate friend." In fact, his rescuer is his son Charles, whom St. Leon has not seen for fifteen years. Because St. Leon has used the elixir of life to preserve his youthful appearance, Charles does not recognize his "misguided" (439) father, and for a brief period the two are close friends. The transformation of the dream-knight into an angelic "female of unblemished grace and beauty" is not, in a literal sense, prophetic, but it anticipates St. Leon's close association of his son with his dead wife: "there was something of Marguerite in the countenance of Charles" (434). He transfers to Charles "all the affection [he] entertained for [his] peerless, murdered mother," (465) and he decides to become "the unknown benefactor of the son of Marguerite de Damville" (434), paying homage to Charles's "unblemished" mother by rewarding her son.

Resolutions based on dreams invariably lead to disaster in Godwin's fiction. In St. Leon's case, his schemes on his son's behalf nearly destroy Charles's relationship with Pandora. The alchemist anonymously provides her with a dowry and establishes "a friendly intercourse" (455) with Pandora that leads to rumors that he rather than Charles is to marry her. Heartbroken and jealous, the young man breaks off the engagement. Later, Charles learns that his friend was formerly "the infamous Chatillon" (474), "a dealer in the black art" (472) and an ally of the hated Turks. He swears to pursue St. Leon "to the death" (474). The protagonist's plan to become "the benefactor of [his] son [is] terminated by a declaration on [Charles's] part, that nothing could appease the animosity he cherished against [him], short of rioting in the blood of his father's heart" (475). Thus St. Leon's dream, like the nightmares of Mandeville and Margaret Borradale, proves defective as a guide to future action.

In *Mandeville*, the title character finds himself unable to overcome his obsessional hatred for Clifford. He decides, however, that he can avoid the evil consequences of his ruling passion by staying away from his rival. Yearning for tranquillity, he visits "a franklin near Winchester" (175) and adopts his rural lifestyle. For a brief time it seems to him that he has found peace in this "life spent in dulcet idleness, forgetting all, and by all forgotten," but a nightmare persuades him that his ruling passion can never be exorcized:

> I dreamed of Clifford. Long was the scenic controversy in which we were engaged, and various the actors. [My sister] Henrietta was joined in inflicting on me the torture that distracted my sleeping thoughts. Some charge was made upon me, the particulars of which, after I awoke, I could never exactly recollect, but which had fired my blood, and distended every fibre of my frame. Some misconstruction was made of my words, some foul and calumnious accusation started against me, void of the remotest foundation in truth, but which all

> the asserverations I could make were ineffectual to remove. I threw myself upon my knees with impassioned vehemence, and uttered the most dreadful imprecations upon myself, if there were a particle of truth in what was alleged against me. My hair seemed to me, as I slept, to stand erect, and my eyes to have their balls enlarged, as ready to burst from their sockets. Scarcely ever, when I was awake, and engaged in the heart-appalling realities of life, had I experienced an equally tumultuous commotion of soul. (176)

Although Mandeville's nightmare is not as prophetic as St. Leon's dream, it foreshadows Henrietta's eventual decision to marry Clifford and, in so doing, ally herself with those whom he regards as his enemies. The nightmare also reveals to him that, although he has been able to banish his hatred for his rival from his waking mind, it is still his ruling passion, capable of driving him into a frenzy. Moreover, it reminds him of the previous times in his life (at Winchester School and Oxford) in which he failed to disprove a "foul and calumnious accusation" made against him.

It could be argued, however, that Mandeville allows his dream to be prophetic, that he makes the mistake of following the dictates of his dreaming mind rather than his reason. After the dream he rejects "the brutish philosophy" (176) that has taught him to find happiness in rural life. Although Henrietta attempts to be his "physician" after he leaves the farm and to distract him from this obsession, she never regains her "unlimited power" over him (178). His ruling passion grows stronger and stronger in part because he believes that his "sleeping thoughts" have taught him that "Clifford is [his] fate" (176). Rather than providing enlightenment, Mandeville's nightmare has a negative effect on his future behavior. It motivates him to leave the farm where he briefly experienced happy forgetfulness and discourages him from seriously attempting to overcome his paranoid obsession with Clifford.

Unlike Godwin's other dreaming characters, Mandeville describes his physical responses to his nightmare: he writes that his blood was "fired," "every fibre of [his] frame" was "distended," his hair "seemed . . . to stand erect," and his eyeballs were "enlarged, as ready to burst from their sockets." He does not, of course, know what his hair and eyeballs were doing while he was asleep. Yet, he assumes that such a terrifying and infuriating nightmare must have "distended every fibre of [his] frame." Whereas Darwin and Hartley contend that the contents of dreams are frequently determined by the condition of the body, in his description of his nightmare Mandeville reverses this cause-and-effect relationship. He believes that his paranoid dream provoked a number of somatic symptoms and led to a "tumultuous commotion of soul" that he has "Scarcely ever . . . experienced" even while "engaged in the heart-appalling realities of life" (176).

While Mandeville emphasizes the physical and emotive effects of dreams, the narrator of *Deloraine* focuses on their amorality. Deloraine asserts that

> In dreams the reins of the soul are no longer under the guidance of reflection or reason. The power, whatever it is, that presides over that state of existence, hurries us wherever it will. The rudder of the mind is powerless; our sense of morality is reduced to almost nothing. We witness crimes, and we commit them, undogged by that moral sense, of which the disciplined spirit can at no time divest itself, while the sun is in the heavens, or the sun of truth penetrates the inner man with its beams. (69)

In his view dreamers are completely passive. During their dreams, they are possessed by an irrational "power" that "hurries" them to witness or commit crimes. Unlike Freud, he does not draw a connection between this apparently arbitrary power and the dreamer's explicit or repressed desires, even though the power seems intent on guiding the sleeping mind to scenes of transgressive action. Deloraine's description of dreams should, however, be considered within the context of his murder of William and the subsequent death of his traumatized wife: it reflects his preoccupation with the crime that he believes has transformed him into "the most atrocious of offenders" (285). Consumed by endless remorse, he longs to have the dreamer's freedom from "that moral sense, of which the disciplined spirit can at no time divest itself." According to him, dreams represent the fantasy of crime without guilt.

The significant dreams presented in *Deloraine* are not, however, consistent with the protagonist's theory: they are ruled by guilty feelings rather than an amoral power. In spite of Margaret Borradale's love for William, her father compels her to reject him in favor of her wealthy cousin. Her dreams dramatize her emotional conflict: "The image of her William was perpetually before her; she saw him in her dreams, sometimes emphatically and earnestly claiming the performance of that which she had given him cause to expect, and sometimes with a melancholy and wintery countenance, reproaching her for her inconstancy, and assuring her that he could not survive the shock that was given him'' (59). Devastated by her decision to break off their engagement, William decides to seek his fortune in Canada, and Margaret has a nightmare:

> She saw her lover sometimes in a mood of bitter upbraidings, and at other times the wasted, wan and colourless shadow of desolation and despair. She saw her favoured suitor assault him, now that the gallant youth seemed deprived by melancholy and sorrow of his wonted energies of defence, and pierce his manly limbs with a thousand wounds, and scatter his remains to all the winds of heaven. In this situation her imaged William would utter the most piercing screams, and implore her to interfere to save him, while lord Borradale and her father held her back with inexorable effort from making the smallest advance to his rescue. The recollection of his voyage to Canada would then occur to her; she saw him standing in the gallery of the ship; a sudden tempest would assault the vessel; he was washed overboard; he was devoured by a shark; and in the countenance of the shark she all at once discovered the lineaments of her destined husband. Repeatedly did she start out of her sleep with the terror of what she had appeared to behold; and it was often a very long time before she could thoroughly convince herself, that what had so exceedingly terrified her was unbased on reality. (69)

This nightmare, like St. Leon's and Mandeville's dreams, is only partly prophetic, and it proves treacherous as a guide to action. As the nightmare predicts, William falls overboard during a storm at sea, but he is rescued by an English frigate and after a series of misadventures finds himself in St. Domingo in the Carribean. Rather than being devoured by a shark, he saves the life of another young man, Travers, by killing a shark with a sword (175). Far from assaulting William, Margaret's ''destined husband'' conducts himself with ''the most edifying philosophy'' (78) when their engagement is broken off: the murderous shark turns out to be Deloraine, whom she marries after William's apparent drowning.

Margaret's nightmare makes her expect the worst when William's ship capsizes. She quickly assumes that he is dead even though his body is never found:

> He had been reported to be dead. But it is the first dictate of true love, to cling with unalterable tenacity to the object of its adoration . . . even though the evidence of our senses should be called in to induce us to relax our hold. But to yield to rumour! . . . the law has wisely

> provided, that no one shall be condemned and executed for murder, till it has been shewn that the individual supposed to be murdered is actually dead. . . . And was not William entitled to [this] precaution and scruple[?] (114–15)

Under the influence of her nightmare and a "doleful presentiment" (86), she drifts into "melancholy and cheerless resignation" (87) and passively agrees to a loveless marriage with Deloraine. This decision paves the way for William's murder, Margaret's death, and Deloraine's subsequent life as a remorseful fugitive. After she marries Deloraine, Margaret sees William "perpetually in her dreams . . . but . . . as a ghost" (109).

Whereas Margaret's nightmare and subsequent dreams mislead and torment her, Deloraine's dreams chart his changing attitude toward his crime. At first he considers himself a wronged husband who has murdered his wife's lover in defense of his honor: he fears legal retribution but does not believe himself morally culpable. Soon after his crime he has a nightmare:

> I . . . fell into a sort of slumber. This was merely a license, delivering my mind from the laws which govern that of a man awake, and introducing every thing that was most frightful and odious. I passed in imagination through all the scenes of the preceding day. I saw Margaret and William, my victims. I bathed my hands, and besmeared my arms in his blood. He seemed to expire in agonies. The moment after, he appeared to revive, and mock the impotence of my revenge. He and Margaret joined to insult, to gibe at, and torment me. These scenes were acted over and over again, I know not how oft. Then succeeded visions of chains, of dungeons and trial. By some strange combination of inconsistency, Margaret and William appeared to be the principal among the witnesses against me, urging my fate, and invoking an ample retribution. (149)

While earlier in his narrative he stresses the amorality of dreams (see *Deloraine*, 69 and above), here he asserts that slumber gives the mind a "license" to introduce everything that is "most frightful and odious." His nightmare reflects his fears of punishment, impotence, and Margaret's and William's vampiric revenge. Deloraine bathes his hands in and besmears himself with William's blood in a primitive ritual that could represent either exorcism or baptism. However, his revenge, like his love for Margaret, is impotent. His sense of powerlessness is expressed in his vision of William and his dead wife coming from their graves like vampires to insult, mock, and indict him.

As Deloraine flees from his nemesis, Travers, he replays his "persecutions" in his sleep: "My dreams were endless; I wandered among rocks and deserts with failing and wearied steps; yet the actual time consumed by these dreams was but as a moment: I started and awoke with ever-fresh alarm, as if of some terrific certainty" (219). However, as time passes he realizes that William and Margaret are the real victims, and his change in attitude is reflected in his dreams:

> Hitherto, if I thought of William and Margaret in my dreams, amidst the watches of the night, I thought of them as delinquents. I was persuaded that they were criminal towards me . . . and that they cowered before the resistless energy of my justice. Now, if I saw them in my dreams, I viewed in the countenance of each a look of unspeakable reproach, in Margaret that said, I have given up for you every thing that is valuable in life, I have repulsed every whisper of human frailty, and behold my reward!—in William, that reproached me, first for having ravished from him a treasure that he valued more than all the world, and then that with a most dastard and cowardly act I had taken his life. I awoke in agonies. I could not sustain the passive reproachfulness of their looks; I could not sustain the bitterness of my remorse. (246)

Thus Deloraine revises his assessment of dreams: whereas some dreams may consist of scenes of criminal behavior conjured up by an amoral "power," others can sharpen the sleeper's moral vision. In suggesting that the conscience can play a role in dreams, he calls into question his earlier association of dreams with transgressive fantasies. His nightmares following his murder of William present him with courtrooms rather than crimes and feature his reanimated victims, chains, dungeons, a trial, "the resistless energy of [his] justice," and, finally, his remorse. Unfortunately, however, these dreams resolve nothing. They are no substitute for an actual judicial proceeding, such as Caleb's semicathartic confrontation of Falkland before a tribunal. Filled with remorse, Deloraine burns "with a continual fever": "If I eat of animal food, I image the flesh of him I have murdered. If I drink, my cup appears mingled with blood. . . .—This cannot last long" (285). Deloraine's dream of bathing his hands in blood becomes transformed into a waking vision of drinking blood: he, not William or Margaret, is the real vampire. Tormented by guilty dreams, he devotes the remainder of his sterile existence to filling his "cup of remorse to the brim" (284).

Thus in *St. Leon*, *Mandeville*, and *Deloraine*, dreams offer important insights into the sleepers' psyches. Godwin's characters tend, however, to misinterpret or react irrationally to their dreams, which frequently promote delusional or destructive thinking rather than self-knowledge. Mandeville's nightmare serves to legitimate his obsessional hatred for Clifford; Margaret Borradale's dream leads her to consent to an ill-advised marriage; and Deloraine's nightmares paralyze him with feelings of despair. While St. Leon's recurrent dream of being rescued enables him to retain his sanity, it also inspires his mismanagement of his son's life. Although Godwin denies the "originality" of dreams in *Enquiry*, in his fiction they sometimes provide his characters with premonitions that have profound and generally negative effects on their attitudes and actions.

One of Godwin's novelistic treatments of dreams may have influenced Shelley's rendering of Frankenstein's famous nightmare. In *Caleb Williams* the protagonist has a dream in which he is being pursued by an agent of Mr. Falkland, who intends to assassinate him. In the dream, he finds himself paralyzed, with the murderer approaching: "He came up to the corner where I was placed, and then stopped. The idea became too terrible, I started, opened my eyes, and beheld the execrable hag [the caretaker of the house in which Caleb is staying] standing over me with a butcher's cleaver" (231). Frankenstein has the following dream after the creation of the monster:

> I thought I saw Elizabeth, in the bloom of health, walking in the streets of Ingolstadt. Delighted and surprised, I embraced her; but as I imprinted the first kiss on her lips, they became livid with the hue of death; her features appeared to change, and I thought that I held the corpse of my dead mother in my arms; a shroud enveloped her form, and I saw the grave-worms crawling in the folds of the flannel. I started from my sleep with horror; . . . when, by the dim and yellow light of the moon, as it forced its way through the window-shutters, I beheld the wretch—the miserable monster whom I had created. (43)

Like Caleb, Frankenstein awakes from a terrifying nightmare to perhaps an even more horrifying reality—dream and reality seem to reflect each other, as reality itself takes on a surrealistic quality.

The nightmare vision of Frankenstein I have quoted has been examined by a number of critics, who have focused on its thematic significance, or who have used twentieth-century psychological theories to interpret it.[29] It can, however, also be considered in the context of Hartleian psychology. According to Hartley, "the visible Imagery in Dreams is composed, in a considerable Degree, of Fragments of visible Appearances lately impressed. . . . [Because of] the Imperfection and Interruption of the Associations, only Fragments, not whole Images, will generally appear."[30] After seeing the hideous body of the monster, created from corpses, Frankenstein falls asleep, and his dream quickly shifts from his embrace of his fiancée, Elizabeth, to his embrace of "the corpse of [his] dead mother" with "grave-worms crawling in the folds of the flannel" (43). His mother's decaying body is the "fragment" of a recent visible appearance, the creature who has been reanimated from corruption. In his discussion of dreams, Hartley also stresses the relationship between bodily health and "the general Pleasantness or Unpleasantness of . . . dreams."[31] Thus Frankenstein's "unpleasant" dream can at least be partially explained by his ill health, his "slow fever" and "painful" nervousness (42): soon after having fled the monster, he encounters his friend, Clerval, and falls down "in a fit" (46). Moreover, the connection Frankenstein's sleeping mind makes between Elizabeth and Frankenstein's dead mother, Caroline, seems in accordance with Hartley's theory of the association of ideas.[32] Although Hartley recognized that the sleeping mind could not receive sense impressions, he believed that it could still make associations between remembered impressions in dreams, although in an imperfect and interrupted way. According to Frankenstein's account, when Elizabeth was stricken with scarlet fever, Caroline tended her, became infected, and died from the disease. As a result of these events, Elizabeth is associated in Frankenstein's mind with his dead mother, an association that is strengthened by the fact that, after Caroline's death, Elizabeth assumes her place in the Frankenstein household. In the dream, then, this association is rehearsed as the living Elizabeth turns into the rotting corpse of the mother who was infected with her disease and then replaced by her.

Lastly, the dream has a premonitory significance that recalls Hartley's discussion of the dreamlike nature of prophecies: it foreshadows Elizabeth's death on her wedding night, which is represented in the dream by her transformation into a corpse after Frankenstein's kiss. Of course, Mary Shelley also could have been inspired by the prophetic dreams she encountered in literary works, including a nightmare in Percy Shelley's Gothic novel *Zastrozzi* (1810), in which the villainous Matilda dreams that Verezzi, the man she intends to marry, consents to their marriage and offers her his hand. However, the flesh of Verezzi's hand crumbles at her touch, and he is reduced to "a shrieking spectre."[33] Later on in the novel, after marrying Matilda and then discovering that the woman he truly loves is still alive, Verezzi commits suicide, thus fulfilling the dream's prophecy.[34] But while Frankenstein's nightmare has a number of literary antecedents, it is also consistent with Hartleian psychology, which suggests that Shelley was striving to create dreams that would, among other things, be perceived as psychologically realistic by her contemporaries.[35] Inasmuch as Shelley associated dreams with the imagination, Frankenstein's nightmare suggests that the imagination can be both prophetic and terrifying, although in Frankenstein's case the warning is not heeded.

Shelley continues her exploration of dreams in *Mathilda*. Mathilda's prophetic nightmare is foreshadowed when she, recovering from her father's traumatic revelation of his incestuous passion for her, "[awakes] to life as from a dream" (203). Before falling asleep, she realizes that she will "be pursued by dreams, but [does] not dread [or anticipate] the frightful one" that she actually has (205). As in the case of Frankenstein's nightmare, this dream is based on a recent impression (her father's shocking confession), and a reworking of the associations derived from that impression. Like Frankenstein's nightmare, Mathilda's dream has a clear premonitory significance. In her dream, she is searching for her father to tell him that they must part; when she sees him, he is sitting underneath a tree, beckoning to her. There is "something unearthly in his mien that awe[s] and chill[s]" her, and, as she nears him, she sees that he is "dead-lily pale, and clothed in flowing garments of white" (205). Her father's "dead-lily" pallor and the flowing white clothes clearly prefigure his fate: when Mathilda next sees him, he is a drowned corpse covered with a sheet. Yet, the next element of the dream is unexpected, because, in her actual encounter with her father, Mathilda was the one who ran away. In the nightmare, her father flees from her, and she pursues him. This could be read, of course, as an indication that Mathilda has nursed incestuous fantasies as well, that she has, in fact, been struggling between conflicting impulses. The rapid flight of Mathilda and her father covers fields, woods, and riverbanks, and it ends when her father plunges from a cliff into the sea: "I heard the roar of waters: he held his course right on towards the brink and I became breathless with fear lest he should plunge down the dreadful precipice; I tried to augment my speed, but my knees failed beneath me, yet

I had just reached him; just caught a part of his flowing robe, when he leapt down and I awoke with a violent scream" (205).

According to Darwin, dreams are a reshuffling of our waking thoughts: "the trains of ideas, which are carried on in our waking thoughts, are in our dreams dissevered in a thousand places by the suspension of volition, and the absence of irritative ideas, and are hence perpetually falling into new catenations."[36] Mathilda's nightmare certainly is a reordering of her encounter with her father, but given its prophetic nature, it seems hardly random. In fact, it lends itself to a number of Freudian interpretations. For example, Freud would probably argue that her father's death is a fulfillment of Mathilda's wish, and certainly his demise, although traumatic, eliminates the possibility that they will violate the incest taboo.[37] Moreover, the reversal of the pursuer and the pursued is highly suggestive, especially since Mathilda's comparison of herself with Oedipus, and her admiration of Vittorio Alfieri's tragedy *Myrrha*, which focuses on the incestuous love of a daughter for her father (192), has prepared the reader for the possibility that she harbors an incestuous impulse. Mathilda's nightmare also has, however, some of the characteristics outlined by Hartley: it is composed "of Fragments of visible Appearances lately impressed," which are altered and mixed up with other appearances because of the "Imperfection" of the associations. For example, the precipice in the dream might be a visual representation of the metaphorical chasm alluded to by Mathilda's father after he has revealed his secret to his daughter: "Now I have dashed from the top of the rock to the bottom! Now I have precipitated myself down the fearful chasm!" (201). And Mathilda's actual flight from her unconscious father is mixed up in the dream with her aggressive attitude toward him during their conversation. In her interrogation of him, she is, in fact, the pursuer who draws her father "with frantic heedlessness into the abyss" (201). Furthermore, her vision of her father as "dead-lily pale" in her dream is retrospective as well as prophetic: when she leaves him after their last conversation, "his cheeks [are] deathly pale," and she exclaims, "Aye, this is his grave!" (202). Although Mathilda suggests that she did not anticipate this dream, according to the theories of Hartley or Darwin, her nightmare is precisely the kind of dream she should have expected, a vivid reordering of recent waking impressions.

As I have noted, Mathilda's dream is also a prophecy, a warning that she belatedly heeds. Her dreaming imagination foresees not only her father's suicide, but the manner of his death. After reading a letter from him, in which he asks for her forgiveness and tells her that he will never see her again, she immediately concludes that he intends to commit suicide. She then rushes off in pursuit, as she does in her dream, and she ultimately finds out that her father has, indeed, committed suicide by drowning. In fact, when she hears the roaring of the sea, she recognizes that it is the same sound as in her dream, and that her father must be dead: "Almost fainting I slowly approached the fatal waters; when we had quitted the town we heard their roaring. I whispered to myself in a muttering voice—'The sound is the same as that which I heard in my dream. It is the knell of my father which I hear' " (214). Her suspicion of her father's death is also uncannily confirmed when she sees an oak in the midst of a thunderstorm. She declares to her servant that "if the next flash of lightning rend not that oak [her] father will be alive" (213), and, accordingly, lightning immediately strikes down the tree. It is possible that this whim also has a connection to her dream, because at the beginning of her nightmare her father is pictured sitting under a tree.

After her father's suicide, Mathilda becomes a miserable recluse, tortured by remorse, and she wills herself to a premature death. In *Mathilda*, as in *Frankenstein*, the dreaming imagination is given a prescience not possessed by the waking mind, but in neither case can these visions of the future be used to avert disaster. On the contrary, these prophecies only serve to terrify the dreamers, to give them a foretaste of the sufferings they are unable to prevent. Shelley does not, therefore, present dreams and their effects in a very positive light in these novels; in fact, the lack of volition experienced in the nightmares of Frankenstein and Mathilda seems to extend to their lives in general.

In *Valperga* Shelley associates dreams with madness. According to Jane Blumberg, the tragic fate of Beatrice represents "Shelley's own fears about the power of the imagination to overcome the individual."[38] For Beatrice, "dreams [are] realities" (150), and, as we will see, her inability to separate a recurrent dream from reality contributes to her final insanity and death. She devotes herself "to contemplation and solitude, and to . . . the wild dreams of her imagination" (136); "she passes many hours of each day in solitary meditation, or rather in dreams, to which her active imagination gives a reality and life which confirm her in her mistakes" (136–37). She is, in fact, the embodiment of dreams, prophecy, and the imagination, and thus she brings together the themes explored earlier in *Frankenstein* and *Mathilda*.

After Castruccio seduces her, Beatrice continues her intense fantasizing. Her illusions give way, however, to "harsh reality" (155) when Castruccio reveals that he loves Euthanasia, and, "possessed by a spirit of martyrdom" (253), she decides to become a pilgrim and humble herself before her rival. Beatrice's conscious will to forget Castruccio is no match for her dreams, which force her to remember him: "I tried to banish him [from] my thoughts; he recurred in my dreams, which I could not control. I saw him there, beautiful as his real self, and my heart was burnt by my emotion" (253). Unfortunately, Beatrice's pilgrimage to Euthanasia does not help her, and her dreams intrude more and more into her waking thoughts: "miserable dreams haunted my sleep; and their recollected images strayed among my day-thoughts, as thin and grim ghosts, frightening and astounding me" (256). Although Shelley could not have read Coleridge's *Notebooks*, his sense of an evil power controlling his nightmares has much in common with Beatrice's sensations: "a completed Night-mair . . . gave the *idea* and *sensation* of actual grasp or touch contrary to *my* will, & in apparent consequence of the malignant will of the external Form, actually appearing or . . . believed to exist/in which latter case tho' I have two or three times felt a horrid *touch* of Hatred, a *grasp*, or a *weight*, of Hate and Horror."[39] Similarly, Beatrice feels as if she were overshadowed by a malevolent force: "the shadow of some mightier spirit was cast over to darken and depress me. I was haunted as by a prophecy, or rather a sense of evil, which I could neither define nor understand" (256).

Beatrice's evil "genius" or "daemon" is a recurrent dream that comes to her "always on the eve of some great misfortune." She describes the dream to Euthanasia:

> there was a wide plain flooded by the waters of an overflowing river, the road was dry, being on the side of a hill above the level of the plain, and I kept along the path which declined, wondering if I should come to an insurmountable obstacle; at a distance before me they were driving a flock of sheep; on my left, on the side of the hill, there was a ruined circuit of wall, which inclosed [*sic*] the dilapidated houses of a deserted town; at some distance a dreary, large, ruinous house, half like a castle, yet without a tower, dilapidated, and overgrown with moss, was dimly seen, islanded by the flood on which it cast a night-black shade; the scirocco blew, and covered the sky with fleecy clouds; and the mists in the distance hovered low over the plain; a bat above me wheeled around. Then something happened, what I cannot now tell, terrific it most certainly was; Euthanasia,

> there is something in this strange world, that we none of us understand. (256)

In an unfinished essay on dreams, Percy Shelley briefly discusses recurrent dreams of places, in which "Neither the dream could be dissociated from the landscape, [nor] the landscape from the dream, nor feelings, such as neither singly could have awakened, from both."[40] In the same fragmentary essay, Percy describes how he encountered a view at Oxford that conformed exactly with a scene he remembered seeing in a dream, and then he breaks off his discussion with the remark: "*Here I was obliged to leave off, overcome by thrilling horror.*"[41] Likewise, Beatrice is overcome by fear when the landscape of her sinister dream unfolds before her: "my glazed eyes caught a glance of an old, large, dilapidated house islanded in the flood,—the dream flashed across my memory; I uttered a wild shriek, and fell lifeless on the road" (257). The terror experienced by Percy Shelley and Mary Shelley's character seems to be caused by the sense that the dreamworld, and its dreamscapes, is invading waking life, that the lack of control associated with dreams is creeping into reality. Moreover, Beatrice's belief that an evil power directs her recurrent dreams, which are the harbingers "of some great misfortune," intensifies her panic. As Mary Shelley declares in her essay "On Ghosts," "There is something beyond us of which we are ignorant."[42]

After she recovers from her swoon, Beatrice finds herself the prisoner of a fiendish man who appears "for a time . . . only a continuation of [her] dream" (257), and she is tortured by this evil being until "the shadow of a false vision overpower[s]" her (258). This waking nightmare continues for three years, until the death of her tormentor, and she comes to the conclusion that God invented the imagination to torture humankind: "He, the damned and triumphant one, sat meditating many thousand years for the conclusion, the consummation, the final crown, the seal of all misery, which he might set on man's brain and heart to doom him to endless torment; and he created the Imagination" (244). For Beatrice, dreams and the imagination are both instruments designed by a divine sadist to ensure her mental suffering. At the instigation of Fior di Mandragola, Beatrice recalls more of her nightmare:

> There was a vast, black house standing in the midst of the water; . . . and suddenly I was transported into a boat which was to convey me to that mansion. Strange! another boat like to mine moved beside us;

> . . . a woman sate near the stern, aghast and wild as I;—We landed together; I could not walk for fear; I was carried into a large room, and left alone; I leaned against the hangings, and there advanced to meet me another form. It was myself; I knew it; it stood before me, melancholy and silent; the very air about it was still. (274)

Beatrice's dream of her double lends itself to a number of interpretations, and the witch who hears it immediately claims that Beatrice has come into contact with her "other self, which at one time lives within [her], and anon wanders at will over the boundless universe, . . . a pure and immediate emanation of the divinity [which] commands all creatures, be they earthly or ethereal" (275). Of course Mandragola arrives at the interpretation that best suits her mischief-making proclivities—it cannot be taken as a serious attempt at dream analysis. Like the other dreams discussed here, Beatrice's dream has a premonitory significance. As James Rieger notes, Mary Shelley "read and studied for [*Valperga*] at Naples in the winter of 1818–1819 while [Percy] Shelley was completing the First Act of *Prometheus Unbound*."[43] In *Prometheus Unbound*, the Earth tells how Magus Zoroaster encountered his own image:

> The Magus Zoroaster, my dead child,
> Met his own image walking in the garden.
> . . . For know, there are two worlds of life and death:
> One that which thou beholdest, but the other
> Is underneath the grave, where do inhabit
> The shadows of all forms that think and live
> Till death unite them, and they part no more.
>
> (I.i.192–99)

Interpreted according to the myth outlined in this passage, Beatrice's dream indicates that she is about to unite with her shadow-double in death, and, as if to fulfill this prophecy, Beatrice declines into madness and dies. And as we will see, this myth of the Zoroastrian double also figures in Percy Shelley's premonitory nightmare before his drowning at sea.

By drugging her with henbane, Mandragola ensures that Beatrice's dream will "visit [her] waking reveries" (275), and one symptom of Beatrice's final madness is her increasing inability to distinguish between dreams and reality. In *Valperga*, dreams and the imagination lead to madness, especially when the dream takes over reality, and the dreamer can longer order or control her impressions. Moreover, Beatrice's nightmare is not simply the reordering of recent impressions or associations one would expect from Darwin's or Hartley's descriptions of dreams: in having Beatrice encounter her double in a sequence that has little to do with her waking experience, Shelley goes beyond contemporary psychological theories and breaks new ground. As I have noted, the dream can be seen as prophetic if one interprets it in the context of the Magus Zoroaster section of *Prometheus Unbound*, but the medieval Beatrice finds it simply unintelligible, and Mandragola's analysis of it is motivated by her desire to wreak havoc. *Valperga* suggests that there are regions of the mind that are ultimately inexplicable: in her allegorical description of the mind as "a vast cave" (262), Euthanasia envisions a confusing, contradictory "inner cave" (263) in which madness, poetry, and the imagination coexist. This inner cave, dominated by the imagination rather than reason, has little in common with Hartley's mechanistic view of the mind, and it clearly has the potential to engender dreams that could not be explained by his theory of impressions and associations.

In general, dreams predict negative events in Mary Shelley's fiction: we have seen how Frankenstein's dream foretells Elizabeth's death, how Mathilda's nightmare foreshadows the death of her father, and how Beatrice's dream prophesies her own end. In *The Last Man* (1826), moreover, Lionel Verney has a dream that prophesies the end of the world. After unsuccessfully searching for Raymond, Lionel has the following nightmare:

> Methought I had been invited to Timon's last feast; I came with keen appetite, the covers were removed, the hot water sent up its unsatisfying steams, while I fled before the anger of the host, who assumed the form of Raymond; while to my diseased fancy, the vessels hurled by him after me, were surcharged with fetid vapour, and my friend's shape, altered by a thousand distortions, expanded into a gigantic phantom, bearing on its brow the sign of pestilence. The growing shadow rose and rose, filling, and then seeming to endeavour to burst beyond, the adamantine vault that bent over, sustaining and enclosing the world. The night-mare became torture; with a strong effort I threw off sleep, and recalled reason to her wonted functions. (146)

As Lionel later learns, Raymond has been crushed by a "falling ruin" (149) while riding through Constantinople, which forms the epicenter of the plague. In *The Last Man* the premonitory vision does nothing less than predict the end of mankind, which is eventually exterminated (with the exception of Lionel) by pestilence. Lionel's nightmare is perhaps the most grimly prophetic of all of Shelley's fictional dreams.

Shelley's short story "The Dream" (1831) offers, however, an example of a dream that is therapeutic rather than ominous in nature. The protagonist of the tale, Constance, has lost her father and two brothers in the civil wars preceding the accession of Henry IV of France to the throne. She is in love with Gaspar, but she will not marry him because he fought on the side that exterminated the male members of her family. Torn between the conflicting demands of family loyalty and her passion for Gaspar, Constance decides to "sleep on St. Catherine's couch" (*Collected Tales and Stories*, 158), "a narrow ledge of earth and a moss-grown stone" (162) on the edge of a cliff overlooking the Loire river. According to local superstition, the saint guides those who sleep on this "couch" through their dreams. In Constance's case, her dream is beneficial: it allows her to resolve her internal conflicts, to end her increasingly morbid devotion to the dead and begin a new life with Gaspar. Like many of the other dreams presented in Shelley's fiction, it is prophetic, but in this case the prophecy depends on whether or not Constance decides to marry Gaspar. In her dream Constance sees her two possible fates, "now pining in a cloister, now a bride—now grateful to Heaven for the full measure of bliss presented to her, now weeping away her sad days." Her dream also indicates that if Gaspar is spurned by her and ends up fighting in the Holy Land, he will end up a prisoner in a dark dungeon cell: "On the floor lay one with soiled and tattered garments, with unkempt locks and wild matted beard. His cheek was worn and thin; his eyes had lost their fire; his form was a mere skeleton; the chains hung loosely on the fleshless bones" (164).

The dream offers Constance two choices rather than simply indicating one tragic outcome; in contrast, the prophetic nightmares of Frankenstein, Mathilda, and Lionel foretell events that the protagonists seem unable to avoid. Whereas Frankenstein awakes from his nightmare to see a hideous monster, when Constance opens her eyes she beholds her lover, who has "caught her light form ready to fall from the perilous couch" (164). The transition from sleep to waking is positive rather than negative. In "The Dream," Shelley suggests that dreams need not be ominous, sinister, or fatalistic: they can allow one to overcome the inhibitions and conflicts that impede the conscious mind. Thus Constance's dream allows her to choose love over perpetual mourning, life over death.

In Shelley's *Falkner*, Gerard Neville's recurrent dream of his dead mother, which becomes conflated with visions of his beloved Elizabeth Raby, forcibly recalls Frankenstein's nightmare following the creation of the monster. Neville has been traumatized by the mysterious abduction of his mother, Alithea Neville, during his childhood. After conversing with Alithea in a country lane, a stranger pulls her away from Neville and pushes her into a carriage. As she is borne away, she screams: "My child! my son!" (99). Her sudden disappearance gives rise to speculation that she ran away from her husband and children in order to be with a lover, and Neville, who is devoted to her, dedicates himself to clearing her name. He describes his dreams of her to Elizabeth: "Still in his dreams . . . he sometimes felt pressed in her arms, and kissed with all the passionate affection of a maternal heart; in such sweet visions her cry of agony would mingle; it seemed the last shriek of woe and death" (149). Later in the novel, Neville learns that his mother was abducted by Falkner and drowned while trying to escape from him. The man he must seek vengeance against is the adoptive father of the woman he loves. He must choose between his dead mother and Elizabeth, who become increasingly linked together in his mind.

Soon after the discovery of his mother's grave, and the identification of her "small heap of bones, abhorrent to the eye" (220), Neville returns to the beach where she is buried and throws himself down on the sands:

> His mother's decaying form lay beneath the sands on which he was stretched, death was there in its most hideous form; beauty, and even form had deserted that frame-work which once was the dear being, whose caresses, so warm and fond, it yet often thrilled him to remember. He had demanded from Heaven the revelation of his mother's fate . . .—did he thank Heaven? even while he did, he felt with bitterness that the granting of his prayer was inextricably linked with the ruin of a being, as good and fair as she, whose honour he had so earnestly desired to vindicate. (221)

Yearning for his dead mother's embrace, Neville lies over her corpse, contrasting her former beauty with her present hideousness, her past caresses with her current dismemberment. He also associates her with Elizabeth, "as good and fair as she," who will be ruined by his mother's vindication. Alithea Neville, now "hideous," seems to reach from the grave and destroy the other woman he loves.

In his dreams Neville is haunted by both his mother and Elizabeth, whose adoptive father is being tried for the murder of Alithea. He describes his fears and his dreams to Elizabeth: "I saw you writhing beneath the tortures of despair, wasting away under the influence of intense misery. You haunted my dreams, accompanied by every image of horror—sometimes you were bleeding, ghastly, dying—sometimes you took my poor mother's form, . . . snatched cold and pale from the waves—other visions flitted by, still more frightful" (258). Neville's feelings for Elizabeth become intertwined with his nightmare image of his drowned mother—he associates the women he loves with misery, bleeding, coldness, pallor, death, and "still more frightful" visions.

Like Frankenstein, whose beloved is also named Elizabeth, his early and sudden separation from his mother has affected and perhaps retarded his emotional development. Love for him becomes a form of necrophilia, and it is clear that he must put his mother to rest by forgiving Falkner, who is implicated in her death, before he can begin a normal relationship with Elizabeth. Similarly, Frankenstein must come to terms with his monster, the product of his necrophilia, before he can start a life with his Elizabeth. But while Neville befriends Falkner (297), Frankenstein repudiates the monster, and, as a result, loses his bride. Unlike Frankenstein, Neville comes to realize that the being who has caused him so much misery, "though a criminal, [is not] quite a monster" (154). Whereas Frankenstein essentially disregards his prophetic dream, Neville recognizes that if he does not overcome his obsession with his dead mother, reflected in his recurrent nightmares involving both Alithea and Elizabeth, Elizabeth will become the next victim.

For Mary Shelley, prophetic dreams were more than a literary phenomenon. Before his drowning, Percy Shelley had premonitions, recorded in one of Mary Shelley's letters (dated 15 August 1822), which recall the encounters with doubles depicted in both *Prometheus Unbound* and *Valperga*: "he had seen the figure of himself which met him as he walked on the terrace & said to him—'How long do you mean to be content.' "[44] This vision was confirmed, Mary believed, by the unimaginative Jane Williams, who saw a figure resembling Percy pass by on the terrace when he was actually "far off at the time she saw him." Percy also had a nightmare that seemed, in retrospect, to have foretold his and Edward Williams's death:

> He dreamt that lying as he did in bed Edward & Jane [Williams] came into him, they were in the most horrible condition, their bodies lacer-

> ated—their bones starting through their skin, the faces pale yet stained with blood, they could hardly walk, but Edward was the weakest & Jane was supporting him—Edward said—"Get up, Shelley, the sea is flooding the house & it is all coming down." S. got up, he thought, & went to the his [*sic*] window that looked on the terrace & the sea & thought he saw the sea rushing in. Suddenly his vision changed & he saw the figure of himself strangling me, that had made him rush into my room, yet fearful of frightening me he dared not approch [*sic*] the bed, when my jumping out awoke him, or as he phrased it caused his vision to vanish.[45]

Percy's double (or "figure of himself") is seen strangling Mary Shelley in this nightmare, and thus Percy's drowning is foreshadowed in at least two ways: by the "sea rushing in" his window and by the presence of his double from the world of death. In her letter, however, Mary Shelley does not insist on the premonitory nature of the dream. In fact, she asserts that the words of Percy's double are "No[t] very terrific words & certainly not prophetic of what has occurred." Jane Williams's testimony is more significant to her, but even in this case she reports that, after hearing Williams's account, she and the others at Casa Magni "thought {no} more of these things."[46] In her response to the visions and dreams preceding Percy's death, Mary Shelley seems neither superstitious nor dismissive. After all, Percy had a history of visionary experiences, and although Mary takes these phenomena seriously, she also looks for corroborating evidence (such as Williams's testimony), and she does not dwell on these uncanny events until she is reminded of them after Percy's death.

Mary Shelley's attitude toward dreams was, then, ambivalent. After her husband's drowning, she began to question the skeptical assessment of the validity and significance of night visions advanced by Godwin and Hays. In her fiction she is torn between her desire to present dreams "realistically," according to the conceptions of eighteenth-century psychological writers, and her more Romantic, visionary sense of oneiric phenomena. Her treatments of nightmares tend to focus on the dreamer's lack of volition, a helplessness that frequently extends to the dreamer's experience in waking reality. The most frightening aspect of these visions is their controlling quality, their ability to possess the dreamer's mind and predict disasters that the dreamer is powerless to prevent. Moreover, as O'Sullivan observes, after Percy's drowning Mary Shelley began to believe that "she had prophesied his death in her fiction."[47] Euthanasia's drowning in

Valperga and the suicidal drowning of Mathilda's father were seen by her as foreshadowing Percy's tragic fate.[48] Thus she came to believe that the association between the imagination and prophecy presented in her fiction was confirmed in her life: as Beatrice's nightmare becomes reality, Shelley's imagination appeared to foretell her husband's death at sea. Beatrice's indeterminate conclusion, that "there is something in this strange world, that we none of us understand," may have come to express Mary Shelley's own sentiments as she struggled to deal with her literary premonitions and the seemingly unavoidable tragedies of her life.

In general, the mental anatomies of Godwin and Shelley focus on the fragility and vulnerability of the human mind. Their characters typically are unstable, unable to control either the train of associations that drives their thoughts or the obsessional passions that motivate their behavior. They often struggle against madness and despair, and word therapy seldom provides them with any lasting relief. While Godwin's characters tend to be misled by dreams, in Shelley's *Valperga* nightmares threaten Beatrice's grasp of reality. Their works suggest that if free will exists it is extremely limited: in Godwin's words, "much is indisputably to be attributed to the empire of circumstances."

There are, however, differences as well as similarities between Godwin's and Shelley's treatments of psychological themes and phenomena. Unlike Godwin, Shelley writes what I have called victim-confessions, first-person narrations which (with the exception of *The Last Man*) present the plights of female characters. Because of their positions in patriarchal societies, these fictional women have even less freedom than their male counterparts in Godwin's novels. In addition, whereas Godwin's works reflect his Enlightenment horror of madness, Shelley's writings suggest that certain types of madness can be more inspirational than debilitating. While Godwin is consistently skeptical about the significance of dreams, after her husband's death Shelley came to believe that they could be prophetic.

Godwin's belief, confidently expressed in his preface to *Cloudesley*, that the psychological insights provided by "fictitious history" can advance "the science of man" (8), is often belied by his and Shelley's mental anatomies, which are as liable to complicate as they are to clarify the reader's understanding of the mind. The

Rousseauistic ideal of mental transparency is seldom achieved by Godwin's and Shelley's unreliable and frequently unstable narrators. Moreover, Godwin and Shelley regard the boundaries between madness and sanity as shifting and blurry, and they also appear uncertain about the relationship between dreams and waking reality.

According to Godwin, however, we cannot conclude from our inability to understand certain individuals and mental processes that they will always remain mysteries. As he points out in his defense of his necessitarian doctrine in *Enquiry Concerning Political Justice*, "The politician and philosopher" never introduce free will "into their scheme of accounting for events":

> If an incident turn out otherwise than they expected, they take it for granted, that there was some unobserved bias, some habit of thinking, some prejudice of education, some singular association of ideas, that disappointed their prediction; and, if they be of an active and enterprising temper, they return, like the natural philosopher, to search out the secret spring of this unlooked for event.[49]

While Caleb Williams is unable to "account" for his "rapture" following his confirmation of Falkland's guilt (*Caleb Williams*, 129–30), a mental anatomist with "an active and enterprising temper" may be able to discover the "secret spring" of his "unlooked for" ecstasy. Shelley writes in her essay "Madame D'Houtetot" that far from discouraging students of the mind, Rousseau's complexity and contradictions "have given a spur to our researches": "We delight to unravel a knotty point, and we study with the greatest pleasure those characters, whose ruling feeling we do not entirely comprehend. They oblige us to disentangle our ideas with delicate precision, and to make subtle differences, at once exercising our talents and our patience."[50]

The complexity of the human mind should not, therefore, discourage mental anatomists from their "researches." Even if they do not discover an individual's "ruling feeling," their analysis of his or her character will help them become more precise, discriminating, and patient. Thus Godwin's and Shelley's mental anatomies should be regarded as contributions to an ongoing project rather than as attempts to provide definitive presentations of the human psyche and its processes. Each work of fiction that explores the mind makes a contribution to a body of literature that was begun, they assert, in the early modern period.

Notes

Introduction

1. Thomas Reid, *An Inquiry into the Human Mind*, ed. Timothy Duggan (Chicago: Univ. of Chicago Press, 1970), 5. Hunter and Macalpine credit Reid with introducing "the scientific method" to "the study of mind': "Before Reid philosophical studies of the mind were mostly theoretical disputations on the 'soul' as it thinks, feels and moves—which later became the physiology of the senses and motion—, the three faculties imagination, reason and memory, and the origin and combination of passions and ideas. Instead Reid proposed a direct study of mind in action by introspection and 'analysis' applying the method of observation and induction which Bentham (1817) called 'psychological dynamics' and which today is dynamic psychology" (Richard A. Hunter and Ida Macalpine, *Three Hundred Years of Psychiatry, 1535–1860: A History Presented in Selected English Texts* [London: Oxford Univ. Press, 1963], 431). In a 3 June 1812 letter to Godwin, who was then his chief mentor, Percy Bysshe Shelley lists Reid, along with Locke and Hume, as one of the writers of "metaphysics" he had studied before reading *Enquiry Concerning Political Justice* (*The Letters of Percy Bysshe Shelley*, ed. Frederick L. Jones, 2 vols. [Oxford: Oxford Univ. Press, 1964], 1:303).

2. Preface to *Fleetwood*, 10. Godwin also alludes to mental anatomy in his last novel, *Deloraine*, in which the title character observes "the present state of [his daughter's] faculties with something of the same diligence, that an anatomist takes up his dissecting knife" (36).

3. Mary Hays, *Memoirs of Emma Courtney*, ed. Eleanor Ty (1796; Oxford: Oxford Univ. Press, 1996), 3; Joanna Baillie, *A Series of Plays: in which It Is Attempted to Delineate the Stronger Passions of the Mind. Each Passion Being the Subject of a Tragedy and a Comedy* (1798; Oxford: Woodstock Books, 1990), 30–31. Marilyn Gaull suggests that there is a link between Baillie's project of anatomizing the passions in her plays and her brother's landmark medical work, *The Morbid Anatomy of Some of the Most Important Parts of the Human Body* (first edition published in 1793) (*English Romanticism: The Human Context* [New York: Norton, 1988], 409n 20).

4. Godwin and Shelley are, of course, only two of many Romantic-era mental anatomists. I could have focused this study on many other writers, including Mary Wollstonecraft, Mary Hays, Joanna Baillie, William Wordsworth, Mary Brunton, Charlotte Dacre, Lord Byron, Charles Maturin, and Percy Bysshe Shelley.

5. John Gibson Lockhart, "Remarks on Godwin's New Novel, Mandeville," *Blackwood's Edinburgh Magazine* 2 (Dec. 1817): 269, 270–71.

6. J. W. Croker, "Review of Godwin's *Mandeville*," *Quarterly Review* 18 (Oct. 1817): 177. Thomas Love Peacock satirizes *Mandeville* in *Nightmare*

Abbey (1818), renaming it "Devilman." Mr. Flosky assesses it as follows: " 'Devilman, a novel.' Hm. Hatred—revenge—misanthropy—and quotations from the Bible. Hm. This is the morbid anatomy of black bile [melancholy].—" (*Nightmare Abbey*, ed. H. F. B. Brett-Smith and C. E. Jones, *The Works of Thomas Peacock*, vol. 3 [London: Constable, 1924], 39). Later in the novel, Flosky alludes to "that new region of the belles lettres, which I have called the Morbid Anatomy of Black Bile" (53).

7. "[Cloudesley]," ed. Pamela Clemit, *The Novels and Selected Works of Mary Shelley*, vol. 2 (London: Pickering & Chatto, 1996), 2:203.

8. J. W. Croker, "Review of *Frankenstein*," *Quarterly Review* 18 (Jan. 1818): 382.

9. "Review of *Frankenstein*, by Mary Shelley," *The Edinburgh Magazine, and Literary Miscellany* 2 (1818): 249.

10. *The Prose Works of Percy Bysshe Shelley*, ed. E. B. Murray, vol. 1 (Oxford: Clarendon Press, 1993), 177.

11. *The Prose Works of Percy Bysshe Shelley*, 282.

12. Katherine C. Hill-Miller, *"My Hideous Progeny": Mary Shelley, William Godwin, and the Father-Daughter Relationship* (Newark: University of Delaware Press, 1995), 9.

13. Pamela Clemit, *The Godwinian Novel: The Rational Fictions of Godwin, Brockden Brown, Mary Shelley* (Oxford: Clarendon Press, 1993), 2.

14. Clemit, 154–55.

15. Hill-Miller, 12.

16. Hill-Miller, 11. There are several other important studies of the Godwin-Shelley relationship, including an essay by U. C. Knoepflmacher, who argues that "Mary Shelley's deep ambivalence about William Godwin informs most of her works of fiction" ("Thoughts on the Aggression of Daughters," in *The Endurance of Frankenstein: Essays on Mary Shelley's Novel*, ed. George Levine and U. C. Knoepflmacher [Berkeley: Univ. of California Press, 1979], 118); Katherine Richardson Powers's book-length study of Godwin's influence on Shelley's novels, which focuses on the following topics: reason, benevolence, justice, and aesthetic considerations (genre, point of view, setting, plot, character, style, and tone) (*The Influence of William Godwin on the Novels of Mary Shelley* [New York: Arno Press, 1980]); and Gregory Maertz's article on the influence of Godwin's *St. Leon* on Shelley's *Frankenstein* ("Family Resemblances: Intertextual Dialogue between Father and Daughter Novelists in Godwin's *St. Leon* and Shelley's *Frankenstein*," *University of Mississippi Studies in English* 11–12 [1993–1995]: 301–20). Mary Poovey also discusses the Godwin-Shelley relationship in *The Proper Lady and the Woman Writer: Ideology as Style in the Works of Mary Wollstonecraft, Mary Shelley, and Jane Austen* (Chicago: Univ. of Chicago Press, 1984), 160–69.

17. See "Giovanni Villani" (1823), *The Novels and Collected Works of Mary Shelley*, 2:130. For a discussion of what Mary Shelley "might have known of Rousseau," see David Marshall, *The Surprising Effects of Sympathy: Marivaux, Diderot, Rousseau, and Mary Shelley* (Chicago: University of Chicago Press, 1988), 228–33.

18. William Godwin, *Political and Philosophical Writings of William Godwin*, general ed. Mark Philp, 7 vols. (London: Pickering & Chatto, 1993), 6:218.

19. *Political and Philosophical Writings*, 5:298, 5:299. Godwin wrote "Essay of History and Romance" when *The Enquirer* "was in the press" (*Political and Philosophical Writings*, 5:290), which would have been between 28 January and 27 February 1797 (*Political and Philosophical Writings*, 5:73).

20. This passage is quoted approvingly by Shelley in her review of *Cloudesley* (*The Novels and Selected Works of Mary Shelley*, 2:201–9).

21. Godwin's belief that poets and fiction writers can offer insights into the human psyche anticipates the observations of a number of twentieth-century psychologists, including Sigmund Freud. Freud, using the same quotation from *Hamlet* that Godwin cites in his Preface to *Cloudesley*, claims in "Delusions and Dreams in Jensen's *Gradiva*" (1907) that "creative writers are valuable allies and their evidence is to be prized highly, for they are apt to know a whole host of things between heaven and earth of which our philosophy has not yet let us dream. In their knowledge of the mind they are far in advance of us everyday people, for they draw upon sources which we have not yet opened up for science" (trans. James Strachey, *The Standard Edition of the Complete Psychological Works of Sigmund Freud*, vol. 9 [London: Hogarth Press, 1959], 8). In *The Literary Mind* (New York: Oxford University Press, 1996), Mark Turner argues that the human mind is "essentially literary" (5): "We imagine realities and construct meanings. The everyday mind performs these feats by means of mental processes that are literary and that have always been judged to be literary" (11). Like Godwin he believes that in reading a narrative we gain insight into both the narrator's psyche and the way the human mind generally works.

22. David Hume, *A Treatise of Human Nature*, ed. Ernest C. Mossner (London: Penguin, 1969), 44. Both Godwin and Shelley were well-versed in Hume's philosophy. After reading Hume's *Treatise of Human Nature* (1739–40) in 1795, Godwin rethought and revised much of *Political Justice* (see Peter H. Marshall, *William Godwin* [New Haven: Yale University Press, 1984], 160, and Don Locke, *A Fantasy of Reason: The Life and Thought of William Godwin* [London: Routledge & Kegan Paul, 1980], 142). Shelley's readings of Hume included *Essays and Treatises on several subjects* (1753–56) and *Four Dissertations* (1757) (she specifically mentions "A Dissertation on the Passions"; see *The Journals of Mary Shelley: 1814–1844*, ed. Paula R. Feldman and Diana Scott-Kilvert [Baltimore: Johns Hopkins University Press, 1987], 190, 654).

23. William Wordsworth and Dorothy Wordsworth, *The Letters of William and Dorothy Wordsworth: The Early Years 1787–1805*, ed. Ernest de Selincourt, 2d ed. rev. Chester L. Shaver, vol. 1 (Oxford: Clarendon Press, 1967), 1:355.

24. *An Inquiry into the Human Mind*, 5.

25. *The Journals of Mary Shelley*, 400.

26. *The Novels and Selected Works of Mary Shelley*, 2:129–30.

27. *The Prose Works of Percy Bysshe Shelley*, 1:141.

28. *Political and Philosophical Writings*, 4:19.

29. Hume, *Treatise of Human Nature*, 308–9.

30. According to Gary Kelly, the word "mind," as used by a late eighteenth-century novelist like Godwin's friend Thomas Holcroft, refers to "an Enlightenment version of the inward self as moral-intellectual authenticity" (*English Fiction of the Romantic Period, 1789–1830* [London: Longman, 1989], 31).

31. *Political and Philosophical Writings*, 6:42. In *Essay Concerning Human Understanding*, Locke also avoids speculating about the physical aspects of the mind: "I shall not . . . meddle with the physical consideration of the mind; or trouble myself to examine wherein its essence consists; or by what motions of our spirits or alterations of our bodies we come to have any *sensation* by our organs, or any *ideas* in our understandings; and whether those ideas do in their formation . . . depend on matter or not" (ed. Alexander Campbell Fraser, 2 vols. [New York: Dover Publications, 1959], 1:26). As J. Allan Hobson points out,

however, the brain had been identified as the site of the mind by Galen in ancient times, and "In 1614, the British anatomist Thomas Willis (1621–75) localized consciousness to the tissue of the brain and . . . emphasized the cerebral ventricles" (*The Dreaming Brain* [New York: Basic Books, 1988], 86).

32. Michel Foucault, *Madness and Civilization: A History of Insanity in the Age of Reason*, trans. Richard Howard (New York: Random House, 1965), 197. Foucault's classical study has been critiqued by a number of historians: see, for example, H. C. Erik Midelfort, "Madness and Civilization in Early Modern Europe: A Reappraisal of Michel Foucault," in *After the Reformation: Essays in Honor of J. H. Hexter*, ed. Barbara C. Malament (Philadelphia: University of Pennsylvania Press, 1980), 247–65. Regarding Foucault's assessment of Samuel Tuke's Retreat, see Anne Digby, "Moral Treatment at the Retreat, 1796–1846," in *The Anatomy of Madness: Essays in the History of Psychiatry*, ed. W. F. Bynum, Roy Porter, and Michael Shepherd, vol. 2 (London: Tavistock, 1985), 53–54, 68.

33. William Battie, *A Treatise on Madness* (1758; New York: Brunner/Mazel, 1969), 94. Battie lists the treatments his contemporaries used to cure insanity, treatments which he regards as worse than useless.

34. "Montaigne," in *Lives of Eminent Literary and Scientific Men of France, The Cabinet Cyclopedia*, conducted by Rev. Dionysius Lardner, vol. 2 (London: Longman, Orme, Brown, Green & Longmans, 1839), 22.

35. *Political and Philosophical Writings*, 6:86. Also see Godwin's comments on Shakespeare in the Preface to *Cloudesley*: "[Shakespeare's] conceptions are drawn from the profoundest abysses of thought; . . . he had therefore comparatively little need, like inferior artists, to proceed step by step in unfolding the seeds of character, and to watch with timid and cautious observation the modes in which they expand themselves, and the peculiarities by which they are divided" (8).

36. Robert Burton, *The Anatomy of Melancholy*, ed. Floyd Dell and Paul Jordan-Smith (New York: Farrar & Rinehart, 1927), 101.

37. *The Novels and Selected Works of Mary Shelley*, 2:130.

38. *The Novels and Selected Works of Mary Shelley*, 2:130.

39. *Political and Philosophical Writings*, 3:15.

40. John Locke, 1:529.

41. David Hartley, *Observations on Man, His Frame, His Duty, and His Expectations*, 2 vols. (1749; New York: Garland, 1971), 1:5. As M. H. Abrams notes, the associationist psychology described by both Hume and Hartley owes something to "the elementary concepts of matter, motion, and force composing Newton's science of mechanics" (*The Mirror and the Lamp: Romantic Theory and the Critical Tradition* [London: Oxford Univ. Press, 1953], 163). See Hume's "A Dissertation on the Passions," in *The Philosophical Works*, ed. Thomas Hill Green and Thomas Hodge Grose, 4 vols. (London: Longmans, Green, and Co., 1874–75), 166, and Hartley, 1:5.

42. Hartley, 1:82.

43. The influence of Hartley on Mary Shelley is somewhat problematic because she does not mention *Observations on Man* in her letters or journals. Sue Weaver Schopf notes, however, that Mary Shelley had access to copies of *Observations on Man* owned by Godwin (whose *Enquiry Concerning Political Justice* is heavily influenced by Hartley) and Percy Shelley (who annotated the 1810 edition). She further argues that the monster's development in *Frankenstein* "is couched in explicitly Hartleian terms and accords precisely with the seven-

step system of mental and spiritual development outlined in Hartley's *Observations*" (" 'Of what a strange nature is knowledge!': Hartleian Psychology and the Creature's Arrested Moral Sense in Mary Shelley's *Frankenstein*," *Romanticism: Past and Present*, 5.1 [1981]: 35). Anne Mellor discusses the influence of both Locke and Hartley on *Frankenstein* (*Mary Shelley: Her Life, Her Fiction, Her Monsters* [New York: Methuen, 1988], 48).

44. Jean-Jacques Rousseau, *The Confessions*, trans. J. M. Cohen (Harmondsworth, Eng.: Penguin, 1953), 169; *Les Confessions*, *Oeuvres Complètes*, vol. 1, ed. Bernard Gagnebin and Marcel Raymond (Paris: Gallimard, 1959), 175.

45. Mary Shelley, *The Letters of Mary Wollstonecraft Shelley*, ed. Betty T. Bennett, 3 vols. (Baltimore: Johns Hopkins University Press, 1980–88), 1:401.

46. *Political and Philosophical Writings*, 5:91.

47. José Barchelon, Introduction, *Madness and Civilization: A History of Insanity in the Age of Reason*, by Michel Foucault, v.

48. *Political and Philosophical Writings*, 5:324, emphasis mine. Similarly, Erasmus Darwin refers to authors who study "idea, perception, sensation, recollection, suggestion, and association" as "writers of metaphysic" (*Zoonomia; or, The Laws of Organic Life*, 2 vols. [1794–96; New York: AMS Press, 1974], 1:2). Raymond Williams provides the following history of the word "psychological": "**Psychological** is recorded from 1794: the 'psychological unity which we call the mind.' It was also used by D'Israeli, with a German reference, in 1812. Yet in 1818, distinguishing between Shakespeare's 'two methods . . . the Psychological . . . the Poetical,' Coleridge begged 'pardon for the use of this *insolens verbum*: but it is one of which our language stands in great need. We have no single term to express the Philosophy of the Human Mind' " (*Keywords: A Vocabulary of Culture and Society* [New York: Oxford University Press, 1976], 246).

49. Thomas Medwin, *The Life of Percy Bysshe Shelley*, New ed. (London: Oxford University Press, 1913), 279.

50. Alan Gauld, *A History of Hypnotism* (Cambridge: Cambridge University Press, 1992), 44.

51. Morton F. Reiser, a noted neurobiologist, describes dream content as follows: "dream content can be related to current life problems that have been of sufficient concern to be on—at times in the front of—the dreamer's mind. Frequently the dreamer can recall having been preoccupied with them at times during the day of the dream. . . . [M]nemic images in the mind are stored in nodal networks, arranged and held in place by affective associational connections—so called because the images are grouped by (and perhaps even arranged according to the strength of) their capacity to evoke, or potentially to evoke, the same feelings. In this way dream imagery is prepackaged during the day, not randomly but according to its affective associations" (*Memory in Mind and Brain: What Dream Imagery Reveals* [New York: Basic Books, 1990], 177). This description forcibly recalls Hartley's description of mental processes in *Observations on Man*.

52. Peter Melville Logan, "Narrating Hysteria: *Caleb Williams* and the Cultural History of Nerves," *Novel: A Forum of Fiction* 29.2 (Winter 1996): 209.

53. Jerome J. McGann, *The Beauty of Inflections: Literary Investigations in Historical Method and Theory* (Oxford: Clarendon Press, 1985), 12–13.

54. Paul Youngquist, *Madness and Blake's Myth* (University Park: Pennsylvania State University Press, 1989), ix–x. Frederick Burwick takes a similar approach in *Poetic Madness and the Romantic Imagination*. He writes: "Rather

than impose the theories of Freud, or Jung, or Lacan, I have emphasized the prevailing social and medical attitudes toward madness and the so-called poetic rapture" ([University Park: Pennsylvania State University Press, 1996], 7–8).

55. Kenneth Neill Cameron, ed., *Shelley and His Circle, 1773–1822*, vol. 3 (Cambridge: Harvard University Press, 1970), 102.

56. *Political and Philosophical Writings*, 3:27.

Chapter 1. The Transparent Mind

1. See, for example, David Marshall's discussion of Rousseau's influence on *Frankenstein* (*The Surprising Effects of Sympathy*, 181–95). Gary Kelly discusses Rousseau's influence on Godwin briefly in *The English Jacobin Novel, 1780–1805* (Oxford: Clarendon Press, 1976), 243–45.

2. *Autobiographical Fragments and Reflections*, ed. Mark Philp, *Collected Novels and Memoirs of William Godwin*, vol. 1 (London: Pickering & Chatto, 1992), 55.

3. Introduction, *Collected Novels and Memoirs of William Godwin*, 1:26.

4. *Political and Philosophical Writings*, 3:273 n.

5. C. Kegan Paul, *William Godwin: His Friends and Contemporaries*, 2 vols. (1876; New York: AMS Press, 1970), 1:13.

6. See *Collected Novels and Memoirs of William Godwin*, 1:58.

7. *Autobiography*, *Collected Novels and Memoirs of William Godwin*, 1:37.

8. Peter Marshall, *William Godwin*, 20. Marshall also suggests that Hilkiah Bradford, Mandeville's tutor, is an unflattering portrait of Newton. Maurice Hindle has affirmed Marshall's biographical reading of the Caleb-Falkland relationship (Introduction, *Caleb Williams*, by William Godwin [London: Penguin, 1987], xxx).

9. Edward Duffy, *Rousseau in England: The Context for Shelley's Critique of the Enlightenment* (Berkeley: University of California Press, 1979), 51.

10. *Mary* and *The Wrongs of Woman*, ed. Gary Kelly (Oxford: Oxford University Press, 1976), 89.

11. *The Prose Works of Percy Bysshe Shelley*, 1:217.

12. *The Journals of Mary Shelley*, 121, 182–83.

13. Paul A. Cantor, *Creature and Creator: Myth-making and English Romanticism* (Cambridge: Cambridge Univ. Press, 1984), 120, David Marshall, 183–95. Other critics who discuss the influence of Rousseau on *Frankenstein* include Lawrence Lipking, "*Frankenstein*, the True Story; or, Rousseau Judges Jean-Jacques," in *Frankenstein*, ed. J. Paul Hunter (New York: W.W. Norton, 1996), 321–30; Alan Richardson, "From *Emile* to *Frankenstein*: The Education of Monsters," *European Romantic Review* 1.2 (Winter 1991): 147–162; and James O'Rourke, " 'Nothing More Unnatural': Mary Shelley's Revision of Rousseau," *ELH* 56 (1989): 543–69.

14. *The Novels and Selected Works of Mary Shelley*, 2:117.

15. *The Novels and Selected Works of Mary Shelley*, 2:130.

16. "Rousseau," *Lives of Eminent Literary and Scientific Men of France*, *The Cabinet Cyclopedia*, 2:125.

17. "Rousseau," 2:126.

18. "Rousseau," 2:174. Shelley is particularly enthralled with *Rêveries*: " 'Promenades d'un Solitaire' [is], with the exception of some of the letters of the 'Nouvelle Heloise,' and a few passages in the 'Confessions,' . . . the most

finished, the most interesting, and eloquent of his works: the peculiar charm of Rousseau reigns throughout; a mixture of lofty enthusiasm, of calm repose, and of the most delicate taste" ("Rousseau," 2:169).

19. "Rousseau," 2:165, 171.

20. *The Confessions*, 46; *Les Confessions*, 38–39.

21. *The Confessions*, 126; *Les Confessions*, 128.

22. *The Confessions*, 380; *Les Confessions*, 408.

23. *The Confessions*, 144; *Les Confessions*, 148.

24. *The Confessions*, 169–170; *Les Confessions*, 175.

25. Jean Starobinski, *Jean-Jacques Rousseau: Transparency and Obstruction*, trans. Arthur Goldhammer (Chicago: Univ. of Chicago Press, 1988), 189.

26. 10 December 1812, *Godwin/Shelley Correspondence*, ed. Mark Philp, *Collected Novels and Memoirs of William Godwin*, 1:81.

27. In *Political Justice*, Godwin argues that sincerity, or "the habit of telling every man the truth, regardless of the dictates of worldly prudence and custom," has important ramifications in terms of moral and social improvement: "Did every man . . . regard himself as not authorised to conceal any part of his character and conduct, this circumstance alone would prevent millions of actions from being perpetrated, in which we are now induced to engage by the prospect of secrecy and impunity. . . . It has been justly observed that the popish practice of auricular confession is attended with some salutary effects" (*Political and Philosophical Writings*, 4:161). Also see *Political and Philosophical Writings*, 3:136.

28. *The Confessions*, 381; *Les Confessions*, 409.

29. *Political and Philosophical Writings*, 3:160–61.

30. *Collected Novels and Memoirs of William Godwin*, 1:58.

31. *Political and Philosophical Writings*, 5:234.

32. *Life of Geoffrey Chaucer, the Early English Poet: Including Memoirs of His Near Friend and Kinsman, John of Gaunt, Duke of Lancaster: with Sketches of the Manners, Opinions, Arts and Literature of England in the Fourteenth Century*, 4 vols., 2nd ed. (London: Richard Phillips, 1804), I:vi.

33. It is likely that Walter Scott, whose novels Shelley read voraciously from 1815 to 1822, also influenced her decision to write historical fiction (see *The Journals of Mary Shelley*, 671–72, and Jean de Palacio, *Mary Shelley dans son oeuvre* [Paris: Editions Klincksieck, 1969], 143–44).

34. Betty T. Bennett, "The Political Philosophy of Mary Shelley's Historical Novels: *Valperga* and *Perkin Warbeck*," in *The Evidence of the Imagination: Studies of Interactions between Life and Art in English Romantic Literature*, ed. Donald H. Reiman, Michael C. Jaye, and Betty T. Bennett (New York: New York Univ. Press, 1978), 368.

35. In Shelley's recently rediscovered story, *Maurice, or the Fisher's Cot* (written August 1820), the title character seems impervious to the forces of environmental conditioning. Maurice (whose real name is Henry) is kidnapped at the age of two and experiences abuse at the hands of his foster father. However, he never becomes bitter, forgives those who wronged him, and (after his real parents reclaim him) distinguishes himself by "doing all the good a little boy could do" (ed. Claire Tomalin [New York: Alfred A. Knopf, 1998], 113). One cannot place too much weight on this story, written to entertain the young daughter of Shelley's friend Countess Mountcashell, but it provides an interesting contrast to much of Shelley's other fiction in which "nurture" plays a dominant role in the formation of character (see Tomalin's introduction to *Maurice*, 14).

36. Mathilda in particular has inspired autobiographical readings: see Hill-Miller (101–27) and Terence Harpold, " 'Did you get Mathilda from Papa?': Seduction Fantasy and the Circulation of Mary Shelley's *Mathilda*," *Studies in Romanticism* 28 (Spring 1989): 49–67. Ranita Chatterjee asserts that "As the daughter of William Godwin, Shelley's representation of a father-daughter incestuous passion [in *Mathilda*] becomes a trope for the apprenticeship of the literary daughter to her father's patriarchal, hierarchical profession" ("*Mathilda*: Mary Shelley, William Godwin, and the Ideologies of Incest," in *Iconoclastic Departures: Mary Shelley after Frankenstein: essays in honor of the bicentenary of Mary Shelley's birth*, ed. Syndy Conger, Frederick S. Frank, and Gregory O'Dea [Madison, N.J.: Fairleigh Dickinson Univ. Press, 1997], 146). Charlene E. Bunnell warns, however, that Shelley's sensibility should be separated from her fictional narrator's: "The novella . . . reveals Mary Shelley's careful craftsmanship in creating a character who constructs her life as a dramatic text, thereby depicting the dangers of a debilitating confusion of life with art and reality with illusion" ("*Mathilda*: Mary Shelley's Romantic Tragedy," *Keats-Shelley Journal* 46 [1997]: 76).

37. *The Confessions*, 262; *Les Confessions*, 278.

38. *The Confessions*, 65; Les *Confessions*, 59.

39. *Political and Philosophical Writings*, 4:161.

40. *Political and Philosophical Writings*, 6:201. In *The Enquirer* Godwin asserts: "Without the habits of entire, unqualified sincerity, the human character can never be raised to its true eminence" (*Political and Philosophical Writings*, 5:230).

41. *English Fiction of the Romantic Period*, 36.

42. *The Confessions*, 373; *Les Confessions*, 400.

43. Eric Daffron, " 'Magnetical Sympathy': Strategies of Power and Resistance in Godwin's *Caleb Williams*," *Criticism* 37.2 (Spring 1995): 218.

44. Peter Melville Logan, "Narrating Hysteria: *Caleb Williams* and the Cultural History of Nerves," *Novel: A Forum of Fiction* 29.2 (Winter 1996): 207, 211.

45. *Political and Philosophical Writings*, 4:72

46. "*Caleb Williams* and *Frankenstein*: First-Person Narratives and 'Things as They Are,' " *Genre* 10 (Winter 1997): 617. According to Clifford, "Rousseau's *Confessions* are perhaps the extreme example of the kind of writing that is referred inward to sentiment and conscience, spontaneity of feeling as shown in the act of writing becoming the authentication of the narrative. What is so powerful, and ultimately so oppressive, about the *Confessions* is the sense that this maneuver attempts rhetorically to allow the present 'I' exclusive responsibility over the past 'I,' an exclusiveness that ultimately becomes a denial of the past. Both Godwin and Mary Shelley intuited the solipsist consequences of such maneuvers and presented heroes who pretend to history when they ought properly to have the courage to use autobiography" (616–17).

47. *Collected Novels and Memoirs*, 5:10.

48. "Pursuing Conversations: *Caleb Williams* and the Romantic Construction of the Reader," *Studies in Romanticism* 33 (Winter 1994): 609, 607.

49. Clemit discusses St. Leon's unreliability as a narrator, arguing that "His emphasis on unspoken knowledge is . . . written into the tale, subverting all claims to frank communication between equals" (94).

50. Clemit, 93.

51. *Reveries of the Solitary Walker*, trans. Peter France (London: Penguin

Books, 1979), 34; *Les Rêveries du Promeneur Solitaire, Oeuvres Complètes*, vol. 1, ed. Marcel Raymond (Paris: Gallimard, 1959), 1001.

52. *The Confessions*, 42, 261; *Les Confessions*, 34, 277.

53. Kelly briefly discusses the influence of *Confessions* and *La Nouvelle Héloïse* on *Fleetwood* (*The English Jacobin Novel*, 243–45).

54. *Political and Philosophical Writings*, 4:24.

55. In a canceled passage in the manuscript of *Fleetwood*, Godwin has his protagonist explain that his later marital problems, specifically his anger over his wife's appropriation of one of his closets, were "engendered . . . in early life": "[My resentment] fell in . . . with the misanthropy & misogyny, which had been engendered in me in early life, & caused that, which would otherwise have been a fleeting impression, to become rooted as a sentiment" (Cameron, ed., *Shelley and His Circle, 1773–1822*, 1:371).

56. *Political and Philosophical Writings*, 4:44.

57. Adam Smith, *The Theory of Moral Sentiments*, ed. D. D. Raphael and A. L. Mactie (Oxford: Clarendon Press, 1976), 9.

58. *The Confessions*, 300; *Les Confessions*, 320.

59. Steven Bruhm, *Gothic Bodies: The Politics of Pain in Romantic Fiction* (Philadelphia: University of Pennsylvania Press, 1994), 117.

60. *The Enquirer, Political and Philosophical Writings*, 5:206. In a manuscript variant draft of *Political Justice*, Godwin writes that mental differences can be attributed to the imperfect nature of society: "Mind will appear from every definition that can possibly be given to be independent and individual. From the moment of my birth I have had a series of perceptions peculiarly my own, and which it is impossible should altogether coincide with those of any other man. I have my own method of viewing every subject that comes before me, and from the premises that are presented to me shall draw my own conclusions. The more imperfection there is in the world, the more will this appear to be the case; the greater shall be the progress of mind, in the greater variety of particulars will human sentiments agree" (*Political and Philosophical Writings*, 4:224).

61. Significantly, Godwin claims to write his preface to *Mandeville* in the "style of confession and unreserve" (8).

62. According to Godwin, just as historians reveal "secrets of [their] own heart[s]" in their narratives, "the portraits made by any artist, exhibit, as strikingly, and as much beyond question, certain qualities of his own mind, as of the persons they pretend to represent" (*Life of Chaucer*, 4:210–11).

63. See *The Confessions*, 50; *Les Confessions*, 43–44.

64. *Emile, or On Education*, trans. Allan Bloom (New York: Basic Books, 1979), 90; *Émile on de l'éducation,* ed. François and Pierre Richard (Paris: Éditions Garnier Frères, 1961), 78.

65. See *Emile*, 90–91; *Émile*, 78–79.

66. Baillie, *A Series of Plays*, 42.

67. Clemit, 99–100.

68. *The Confessions*, 574; *Les Confessions*, 622.

69. *The Confessions*, 456; *Les Confessions*, 492.

70. *The Confessions*, 17; *Les Confessions*, 5.

71. Thomas McFarland, *Romanticism and the Heritage of Rousseau* (Oxford: Clarendon Press, 1995), 55.

72. Butler and Philp describe Deloraine "as a man who, contrary to his own theoretical principles and self-estimation, has behaved like an old-fashioned pa-

triarch and a domestic tyrant, wanting to possess women as chattels, not allow them autonomy" (42).

73. Barbara Johnson, "My Monster/My Self," *Diacritics* 12 (Summer 1982): 3. Similarly, Beth Newman has noted that the purpose of both the monster's and Frankenstein's tales is to bind their listeners to a promise ("Narratives of Seduction and the Seductions of Narrative: The Frame Structure of *Frankenstein*," *ELH* 53.1 [Spring 1986]: 153).

74. David Marshall, 195.

75. See Godwin's *Political and Philosophical Writings*, 3:273n, and Shelley's "Rousseau," 2:169, 174.

76. Mellor, 171–74; also see Poovey, 133–35.

77. *The Confessions*, 327–28; Les *Confessions*, 351.

78. Peter Brooks, " 'Godlike Science/Unhallowed Arts': Language, Nature, and Monstrosity," in *The Endurance of* Frankenstein: *Essays on Mary Shelley's Novel*, 209; Schopf, 49.

79. *The Prose Works of Percy Bysshe Shelley*, 1:283.

80. *The Confessions*, 88–89; *Les Confessions*, 86–87.

81. Cantor contends that the monster and Frankenstein evade responsibility for their actions by blaming each other (132).

82. Janet Todd, Introduction, *Mary Wollstonecraft* Mary *and* Maria, *Mary Shelley* Matilda, ed. Janet Todd (London: Penguin, 1991), vii.

83. Mary Wollstonecraft, *Mary and the Wrongs of Woman*, ed. Gary Kelly (Oxford: Oxford University Press, 1976), 4.

84. Wollstonecraft, *Mary* and *The Wrongs of Woman*, 138.

85. Wollstonecraft, *Mary* and *The Wrongs of Woman*, 46.

86. See Wollstonecraft, *Mary* and *The Wrongs of Woman*, 116, 137.

87. Theodore Roszak, *The Memoirs of Elizabeth Frankenstein* (New York: Random House, 1995), 419.

88. In *Thoughts on Man*, written near the end of his career, Godwin qualifies some of his earlier views on sincerity: "we ought ever to be on the alert, that we may not induce our friend into evil. We should be upon our guard, that we may not from over-weening arrogance and self-conceit dictate to another, overpower his more sober judgment, and assume a rashness for him, in which perhaps we would not dare to indulge for ourselves. We should be modest in our suggestions, and rather supply him with materials for decision, than with a decision absolutely made " (*Political and Philosophical Writings*, 6:204).

89. "Rousseau," 2:164. See *The Confessions*, 605; *Les Confessions*, 656.

90. Barbara Jane O'Sullivan, "Beatrice in *Valperga*: A New Cassandra," in *The Other Mary Shelley: Beyond* Frankenstein, ed. Audrey A. Fisch, Anne K. Mellor, and Esther H. Schor (New York: Oxford Univ. Press, 1993), 145.

91. O'Sullivan, 144.

92. Hill-Miller, 101–27; Harpold, 49–67, Burton R. Pollin, "Mary Shelley as the Parvenue," *A Review of English Literature* 8.3 (July 1967): 10. Charles E. Robinson disagrees with some of Pollins's claims (*Collected Tales and Stories*, 392).

93. Mellor, 157–59.

94. *The Journals of Mary Shelley*, 476–77.

95. *The Journals of Mary Shelley*, 478.

96. "Rousseau," 2:173, 172.

97. *The Confessions*, 39; *Les Confessions*, 30–31.

98. Of course, in a suttee a widow is burned on the funeral pyre of her dead

husband. Although Falkner's suicide attempt may be inspired by this custom, it also departs from it in a number of ways, because he is male and is not married to Alithea. Godwin's reference to suttee in *St. Leon* suggests, however, that either the husband or wife ("the survivor") may "perish upon the funeral pyre of the deceased."

99. *Political and Philosophical Writings*, 3:19.

100. For a fuller discussion of Falkner's Indian acculturation, see my article "Unnationalized Englishmen in Mary Shelley's Fiction," *Romanticism on the Net* 11 (August 1998): n.p., On-line, Internet (August 1998) http://users.ox.ac.uk/~scat0385/mwsfiction.html.

101. "Rousseau," 2:119.

102. *Political and Philosophical Writings*, 4:72–73.

103. Deloraine's situation, is, however, quite different from Falkner's: unlike Shelley's protagonist, he has benefited from a privileged upbringing and an excellent education. Thus his tyrannical conscience can be seen as the product of his social conditioning.

104. John Locke, 1:72.

105. As Don Locke notes, in the second and third editions of *Political Justice*, Godwin concedes that some aspects of a children's character may be present at birth (141). See *Political and Philosophical Writings*, 4.238: "It is difficult accurately to decide, how much of the characters of men is produced, by causes that operated upon them in the period preceding their birth, and how much is the moral effect of education, in its extensive sense. Children certainly bring into the world with them a part of the characters of their parents, nay, it is probable that the human race is meliorated, somewhat in the same way as the races of brutes, and that every generation, in a civilised state, is further removed, in its physical structure, from the savage and uncultivated man." Even in these later editions, however, Godwin still asserts that "the characters and dispositions of mankind are the offspring of circumstances and events, and not of any original determination that they bring into the world" (*Political and Philosophical Writings*, 4.16–17).

106. *Political and Philosophical Writings*, 3.136.

107. *Political and Philosophical Writings*, 3.158.

108. *Political and Philosophical Writings*, 5.299.

Chapter 2. The Ruling Passions

1. *William Wordsworth*, ed. Stephen Gill Oxford Authors (New York: Oxford Univ. Press, 1984), 597.

2. *The Prose Works of Percy Bysshe Shelley*, 1:177.

3. *A Treatise of Human Nature*, 465, 462. For an illuminating discussion of Hume's theory of passions, see Adela Pinch, *Strange Fits of Passion: Epistemologies of Emotion, Hume to Austen* (Stanford, Calif.: Stanford University Press, 1996), 17–50.

4. Reid, *Essays on the Active Powers of the Human Mind*, 179.

5. Reid, 178.

6. William St. Clair, *The Godwins and the Shelleys* (New York: Norton, 1989), 15.

7. Claude Arien Helvétius, *De L'Esprit; or, Essays on the Mind and Its Several Faculties*, trans. anonymous (1758; New York: Burt Franklin, 1970), 229.

8. Helvétius, 230.
9. Helvétius, 233.
10. Helvétius, 235.
11. *Political and Philosophical Writings*, 5:20.
12. *Political and Philosophical Writings*, 5:234.
13. *Political and Philosophical Writings*, 4:39. In the 1793 ed. of *Political Justice*, Godwin also refers to the vagueness of the term passion: "This word passion, which has produced such extensive mischief in the philosophy of mind, and has no real archetype, is perpetually shifting its meaning" (*Political and Philosophical Writings*, 3:446).
14. *Political and Philosophical Writings*, 4:39.
15. See the 1802 preface to *Lyrical Ballads*, *William Wordsworth*, Oxford Authors, 599.
16. Ann Radcliffe, *The Mysteries of Udolpho: A Romance*, ed. Bonamy Dobrée (Oxford: Oxford University Press, 1970), 646.
17. Joanna Baillie, *A Series of Plays, 1798* (Oxford: Woodstock Books, 1990), 38.
18. *The Poetical Works of Pope*, ed. Herbert Davis (Oxford: Oxford University Press, 1966), lines 2:128–40.
19. Rebecca Ferguson, *The Unbalanced Mind: Pope and the Rule of Passion* (Philadelphia: University of Pennsylvania Press, 2986), xii.
20. In *Political Justice*, Godwin summarizes Hartley's psychological theory as "a system of associations to be carried on by traces to be made upon the medullary substance of the brain, by means of which past and present impressions are connected according to certain laws, as the traces happen to approach or run into each other; and we have then a complete scheme for accounting in a certain way for all the phenomena of human action" (*Political and Philosophical Writings*, 3:176).
21. Hartley, 1:398–99.
22. Mary Hays, *Memoirs of Emma Courtney*, ed. Eleanor Ty (1796; Oxford: Oxford University Press, 1996), 131.
23. Hartley, 1:81.
24. Hays, *Memoirs of Emma Courtney*, 93. Eleanor Ty notes that Hays's treatment of passion in *Memoirs of Emma Courtney* is heavily influenced by Hélvetius (Introduction, *Memoirs of Emma Courtney*, xix–xxi).
25. Baillie, *A Series of Plays*, 43. In light of Baillie's views on drama's potential to provide psychological guidance, it is interesting to note that in Alan Bennett's recent play, *The Madness of George III* (subsequently made into a film entitled *The Madness of King George*), he has the mentally disturbed monarch read *King Lear* with some of his attendants, Lear's part being performed by the king. After this reading, King George appears to have regained his sanity (of course, King George's "madness" was caused by porphyria, and, as Bennett knows, was in no way "cured" by reading *King Lear*. See Bennett, *The Madness of George III* [London: Faber and Faber, 1992], 80–82).
26. Mary Brunton, *Self-Control: A Novel* (Edinburgh: Manners and Miller, 1811), vi.
27. Brunton, vi–vii.
28. It should be noted, however, that Smith's notion of sympathy is not identical to Hume's: whereas Hume (in *A Treatise of Human Nature*) holds that sympathy allows an individual to feel another's passion fully, Smith (in *The Theory of Moral Sentiments*) asserts that sympathy only enables a spectator to

imagine (sometimes inaccurately) the passions of those he or she observes. See John Mullan, *Sentiment and Sociability: The Language of Feeling in the Eighteenth Century* (Oxford: Clarendon Press, 1988), 43–56, for a comparison of Hume's and Smith's conceptions of sympathy.

29. Smith, 317.

30. Hume, 628.

31. William Wordsworth, *The Borderers*, ed. Robert Osborn (Ithaca, N.Y.: Cornell Univ. Press, 1982), 62.

32. *The Borderers*, 65.

33. Smith, 153.

34. George Gordon Byron, Baron, *Byron*, ed. Jerome J. McGann, The Oxford Authors (Oxford: Oxford Univ. Press, 1986), *Manfred*, II.i.64–65; II.i.72–73.

35. *A Series of Plays*, 39.

36. *Collected Novels and Memoirs*, 1:36, 1:58.

37. *Collected Novels and Memoirs*, 1:59, 1:60.

38. *Collected Novels and Memoirs*, 1:117.

39. *Collected Novels and Memoirs*, 1:92.

40. *Collected Novels and Memoirs*, 1:48.

41. Hays has Emma Courtney quote this passage from *Caleb Williams*: see *Memoirs of Emma Courtney*, 141.

42. *Political and Philosophical Writings*, 4:40.

43. *Political and Philosophical Writings*, 6:187.

44. Hume, 474.

45. See Darwin, 2:363–65.

46. Hume, 467.

47. Hume, 468.

48. Darwin, 2:386.

49. Hume, 468.

50. *Mandeville*, 91 n.

51. Mandeville's ambivalence toward Clifford could be considered an instance of "male homosexual panic" (see Eve Kosofsky Sedgwick, *Epistemology of the Closet* [Berkeley: University of California Press, 1990], 182–212).

52. Laurence Sterne, *A Sentimental Journey through France and Italy with The Journal to Eliza and A Political Romance*, ed. Ian Jack (London: Oxford Univ. Press), 28.

53. Hays, 104; *Shelley's Poetry and Prose*, 474.

54. *The Mary Shelley Reader*, 183–84. Shelley also alludes to Sterne's apostrophe to love in her journals: "as Sterne ↑ says ↓ that in solitude he would worship a tree—so in the world I should attach myself to those who bore the semblance of those qualities which I ~~had~~ admire" (*The Journals of Mary Shelley*, 399).

55. Wollstonecraft, 86.

56. Jean-Jacques Rousseau, *Emile, or On Education*, trans. Allan Bloom (New York: Basic Books, 1979), 415; *Émile ou de l'éducation*, ed. François and Pierre Richard (Paris: Éditions Garnier Frères, 1961), 528. This passage is quoted (in a different translation) by the protagonist of *Memoirs of Emma Courtney* in her assessment of the importance of her first love on her emotional development (Hays, 60–61).

57. *Political and Philosophical Writings*, 5:20.

58. Smith, 317, 38. Smith discusses Hutcheson's philosophy in *The Theory of Moral Sentiments* (301, 321–22). Hutcheson was Smith's teacher at the University of Glasgow (*The Theory of Moral Sentiments*, 301 n. 3).

59. *The Novels and Selected Works of Mary Shelley*, 2:255.

60. *The Fields of Fancy*, *Mathilda*, ed. Elizabeth Nitchie (Chapel Hill: University of North Carolina Press, 1959), 94, 96.

61. *The Fields of Fancy*, 98.

62. *The Letters of Mary Wollstonecraft Shelley*, 2:185.

63. Poovey contends that Elizabeth unintentionally punishes Falkner: "Through Elizabeth . . . Falkner is doubly punished: he is called to personal and public account for his passionate behavior, and he is forced to seek forgiveness from the very person whose vengeance occasions his public humiliation" (165). Elizabeth's influence on her foster father is, however, therapeutic as well as punitive: it allows him to experience the "singular relief which *confession* brings to the human heart" (see *Falkner*, 241, and my discussion of language therapy in chapter 4).

64. *The Fields of Fancy*, 98.

65. *The Journals of Mary Shelley*, 399.

66. *Political and Philosophical Writings*, 4:40.

67. The concept of an involuntary crime is also alluded to in Shelley's *Perkin Warbeck*, in which the protagonist vows to establish a church in order to atone "for his involuntary crime in the death of Meiler Trangmar" (115), an assassin who also happens to be a monk.

68. See *The Journals of Mary Shelley*, 24, 55. The manuscript of *Hate* has never been found.

69. Joanna Baillie, *The Dramatic and Poetical Works (1851)* (Hildesheim: Georg Olms Verlag, 1976), 169.

70. *The Dramatic and Poetical Works*, 188.

71. For a brief discussion of the role of the "imposter-prophet," see Audrey A. Fisch, "Plaguing Politics: AIDS, Deconstruction, and *The Last Man*," in *The Other Mary Shelley: Beyond* Frankenstein," 276–77.

72. Mary Shelley quotes from lines 25–36 of " 'Tis Said, that Some Have Died for Love."

73. Mary Wollstonecraft, *A Vindication of the Rights of Woman*, ed. Carol H. Poston, 2nd ed. (New York: Norton, 1988), 114. Mary Shelley read *A Vindication of the Rights of Woman* in December 1816 and May 1820. See *The Journals of Mary Shelley*, 149, 318.

74. Mary Shelley's own education was considered masculine by her contemporary, the poet and journalist Leigh Hunt. Hunt, in an article in his journal *Examiner*, wrote that Mary Shelley possessed "what is called a masculine understanding, that is to say, . . . great natural abilities not obstructed by a *bad* education" (*The Letters of Mary Wollstonecraft Shelley*, 1:54 n. 2).

75. Wollstonecraft, *A Vindication of the Rights of Woman*, 22.

76. Wollstonecraft, *Vindication*, 61.

77. In *Vindication* Mary Wollstonecraft criticizes superstitious women like Beatrice who, in their "thoughtlessness, and irrational devotion" (180), follow the advice of astrologers, mesmerizers, and other quacks.

78. Mellor, 210.

79. Wollstonecraft, *Vindication*, 192

80. *Vindication*, 194.

81. See *The Letters of Mary Wollstonecraft Shelley*, 1:566, and *The Journals of Mary Shelley*, 478.

82. Lord Byron, *Byron's Letters and Journals*, ed. Leslie A. Marchand, 12 vols. (Cambridge: Harvard Univ. Press, 1973–82), 4:221–22.

83. Betty T. Bennett, 365.

84. Hill-Miller persuasively argues that *Falkner* was written in response to *Deloraine* (166–201). Her emphasis is, however, quite different from mine.

85. Also see *St. Leon*: "The human mind insatiably thirsts for a confident [*sic*] and a friend" (161–62).

Chapter 3. Episodes of Madness

1. See Hunter and Macalpine, *Three Hundred Years of Psychiatry*, 509, and Allan Ingram, *The Madhouse of Language: Writing and Reading Madness in the Eighteenth Century* (London: Routledge, 1991), 1–5.

2. Michael V. DePorte, *Nightmares and Hobbyhorses: Swift, Sterne, and Augustan Ideas of Madness* (San Marino, Calif.: The Huntington Library, 1974), 3.

3. Henry Mackenzie, *The Man of Feeling* (New York: Norton, 1958), 19.

4. St. Clair, 503.

5. John Locke, 1:528–29.

6. Foucault, 211–12.

7. Samuel Johnson, *Rasselas and Other Tales*, ed. Gwin J. Kolb, *The Yale Edition of the Works of Samuel Johnson*, vol. XVI (New Haven: Yale University Press, 1990), 149.

8. Wollstonecraft, *The Wrongs of Woman*, 84.

9. Samuel Warren, "The Spectre-Smitten," *Tales of Terror from* Blackwood's Magazine, ed. Robert Morrison and Chris Baldick (Oxford: Oxford University Press, 1995), 235.

10. John Locke, 1:209. The "glass delusion," which "was widespread from the beginning of the seventeenth century up to 1850," is described in an article by Antonie Luyendijk-Elshout, "Of Masks and Mills: The Enlightened Doctor and His Frightened Patient," *The Languages of the Psyche: Mind and Body in Enlightenment Thought*, ed. G. S. Rousseau (Berkeley: University of California Press, 1990), 196–97.

11. Hartley, 1:400.

12. Hartley, 1:400–401.

13. Hartley, 1:403.

14. Hartley 1:401.

15. Hunter and Macalpine, *Three Hundred Years of Psychiatry*, 405.

16. William Battie, *A Treatise on Madness* (New York: Brunner/Mazel, 1969), 5–6.

17. Battie, 43–44.

18. Battie, 71–72.

19. Battie, 98–99.

20. Battie, 68, 69.

21. Hunter and Macalpine, *Three Hundred Years of Psychiatry*, 405.

22. *The Journals of Mary Shelley*, 180.

23. See Battie, 17. Smollett's allusion to Battie was first noted by Hunter and Macalpine ("Smollett's Reading in Psychiatry," *Modern Language Review*, 51 [1956], 409–10). For a discussion of "mad language" in *Sir Launcelot Greaves*, see Ingram, 98–101.

24. Tobias Smollett, *The Life and Adventures of Sir Launcelot Greaves*, ed. David Evans (London: Oxford Univ. Press, 1973), 187.

25. Hunter and Macalpine, *Three Hundred Years of Psychiatry*, 463–64.

26. Darwin, 2:351.

27. Darwin, 1:436–37.
28. Darwin, 2:360.
29. Darwin, 2:352.
30. Darwin, 2:361–62.
31. Darwin, 2:362.
32. Darwin, 2:358.
33. The theory employed in *Fleetwood* that madness, like a fever, climaxes in a "crisis," after which the patient either recovers or completely succumbs to the disease, also informs Warren's "The Spectre-Smitten": "The roaring flame of insanity sinks suddenly into the sullen smouldering embers of complete fatuity, and remains so for months; when . . . it will instantaneously gather up and concentrate its expiring energies into one terrific blaze—one final paroxysm of outrageous mania—and lo! it has consumed itself utterly—burnt itself out—and the patient is unexpectedly restored to reason" (*Tales of Terror from* Blackwood's Magazine, 236).
34. *Political and Philosophical Writings*, 6:98.
35. John Locke, 1:209.
36. Hartley, 1:401.
37. I use the term psychoneurosis rather than neurosis because in the late eighteenth century the word neurosis, coined by William Cullen in *First Lines in the Practice of Physic* (1784), referred to a "disordered nerve function without structural pathology." In the nineteenth century the term psychoneurosis was introduced to designate "nervous disorders caused psychologically" (Hunter and Macalpine, *Three Hundred Years of Psychiatry*, 474).
38. Darwin, 2:353.
39. *Dr. Willis's Practice of Physick* (1684), 206; qtd. in DePorte, 6.
40. Hartley, 1:401.
41. Hartley, 1:402.
42. As Allan Young observes, the definition of memory has changed significantly since the eighteenth century: "In eighteenth-century Europe, the prevailing conception was that a memory consists of mental images and verbal content: a person sees, says, or otherwise apprehends the things that he remembers. During the next century, the boundaries of memory were expanded to include contents located in acts and bodily conditions (e.g., automatisms, hysterical contractures) as well as words and images. Further, the very fact that these acts and conditions were 'memory' was unknown to the person who owned the memory" (*The Harmony of Illusions: Inventing Post-Traumatic Stress Disorder* [Princeton, N.J.: Princeton Univ. Press, 1995], 4).
43. Quoted in St. Clair, 460–61.
44. For a brief discussion of this scene in *Rambles*, see Esther H. Schor, "Mary Shelley in Transit," *The Other Mary Shelley: Beyond* Frankenstein, 243.
45. Helvétius, 242. For the influence of Helvétius's *De l'Esprit* on Godwin, see St. Clair, 15. Percy Shelley read *De l'Esprit* in 1811 (*The Letters of Percy Bysshe Shelley*, l:82); I have not been able to determine whether Mary Shelley read this influential volume.
46. The link between madness and genius is, of course, a commonplace in literature. John Dryden famously asserts in *Absalom and Achitophel* (1681) that "Great wits are sure to madness near allied, / And thin partitions do their bounds divide" (l. 163–64). Burwick has described how "the century-old notion of the *furor poeticus* was reinterpreted as a revolutionary and liberating madness that could free the imagination from the 'restraint of conformity' . . . [d]uring the romantic period" (2).

47. *Shelley's Poetry and Prose*, 125.
48. Battie, 68.
49. Battie, 68–69.
50. *Byron* (Oxford Authors), 1050 n.
51. Hartley, 1:402.
52. Marion Kingston Stocking, ed., *The Clairmont Correspondence: Letters of Claire Clairmont, Charles Clairmont, and Fanny Imlay Godwin*, 2 vols. (Baltimore: Johns Hopkins Univ. Press, 1995), 2:362–63.
53. Stocking, 2:406.
54. Stocking, 2:418–19.
55. Stocking, 2:441.
56. *The Letters of Mary Wollstonecraft Shelley*, 3:172.
57. Godwin read Brown's *Wieland*, *Edgar Huntly*, *Ormond*, *Philip Stanley*, and *Jane Talbot* in 1816 (St. Clair, 380); Shelley read Brown's *Clara Howard*, *Edgar Huntly*, and *Jane Talbot* in 1814, *Ormond* and *Wieland* in 1815, and *Arthur Mervyn* in 1817 (*The Journals of Mary Shelley*, 638).
58. Charles Brockden Brown, *Wieland; or The Transformation. An American Tale*, ed. Sydney J. Krause and S. W. Reid (Kent, Ohio: Kent State University Press, 1977), 230.
59. Brown, *Wieland*, 188–89.
60. Charles Brockden Brown, *Edgar Huntly; or, Memoirs of a Sleep-Walker*, ed. Sydney J. Krause and S. W. Reid (Kent, Ohio: Kent State University Press, 1984), 278–79.

Chapter 4. The Therapeutic Value of Language

1. Jacques Lacan, *Écrits: A Selection*, trans. Alan Sheridan (New York: Norton, 1977), 46.
2. Sigmund Freud, *Introductory Lectures on Psycho-Analysis*, trans. and ed. James Strachey (New York: Norton, 1966), 19.
3. Smith, 153–54.
4. St. Clair, 544 n. 10.
5. *Life of Geoffrey Chaucer*, 1:78. In *Enquiry Concerning Political Justice*, Godwin asserts that "It has been justly observed that the popish practice of auricular confession has been attended with some salutary effects" (*Political and Philosophical Works*, 3:136).
6. *Life of Geoffrey Chaucer*, 1:76.
7. *Life of Geoffrey Chaucer*, 1:78.
8. Smith, 154.
9. *The Prose Works of Percy Bysshe Shelley*, 279.
10. Both O'Sullivan and Joseph W. Lew ("God's Sister: History and Ideology in *Valperga*," in *The Other Mary Shelley: Beyond* Frankenstein, 167) focus on Beatrice in their recent articles on *Valperga*.
11. Marc A. Rubenstein, "*Frankenstein*: Search for the Mother," *Studies in Romanticism*, 15 (Spring 1976), 168.
12. Rubenstein, 168.
13. For a more extensive presentation of Percy Shelley's attitudes toward language, see William Keach, *Shelley's Style* (New York: Methuen, 1984), 1–41.
14. *Shelley's Poetry and Prose*, 475, 477.
15. *Shelley's Poetry and Prose*, 474.

16. *Shelley's Poetry and Prose*, 482.

17. *Political and Philosophical Writings*, 5:101.

18. *Political and Philosophical Writings*, 5:102.

19. For an analysis of the monster's acquisition of language, see Peter Brooks, " 'Godlike Science/Unhallowed Arts': Language, Nature, and Monstrosity," in *The Endurance of* Frankenstein: *Essays on Mary Shelley's Novel*, 208–13.

20. Emily W. Sunstein, *Mary Shelley: Romance and Reality* (Baltimore: Johns Hopkins Univ. Press, 1989), 40.

21. In "The Parvenue," Shelley has a character begin the tale by asking: "Why do I write my melancholy story?" (*Collected Tales and Stories*, 266).

22. Anne McWhir, "The Light and the Knife: Ab/Using Language in *The Cenci*," *Keats-Shelley Journal* XXXVIII (1989): 148. Michael Worton argues that "Beatrice's inability to speak coherently of her sufferings indicates that language cannot codify extreme emotion" ("Speech and Silence in *The Cenci*," in *Essays on Shelley*, ed. Miriam Allott [Totowa, N.J.: Barnes & Noble, 1982], 110).

23. Elizabeth Nitchie, ed., *Mathilda*, by Mary Wollstonecraft Shelley, *Studies in Philology* extra ser. 3 (Chapel Hill: Univ. of North Carolina Press, 1959), 100. In *The Fields of Fancy* draft edited by E. B. Murray, Mathilda's faith in the therapeutic value of relating her story is even more evident. Mathilda says: "Never on earth was that fearful tale unfolded—here among the shadows of the dead It may be—And I feel that the bonds that in this existence as well as in that past weigh heavily on me, will be broken" (*A Facsimile of Bodleian MS. Shelley d.1*, vol. 4 of *The Bodleian Shelley Manuscripts* in 2 parts [New York: Garland, 1988], 1:271).

24. *The Complete Works of Percy Bysshe Shelley*, ed. Roger Ingpen and Walter E. Peck, 10 vols. (New York: Gordian Press, 1965), 1:145, and McWhir, 148–49. Locke asserts that a "great abuse of words is, the *taking them for things*" (*Essay Concerning Human Understanding*, 2:132).

25. Mary Shelley's Beatrice is specifically compared to the historical Beatrice Cenci: see *Valperga*, 127.

26. *An Inquiry into the Human Mind*, 5.

27. One wonders if the failures of the Percy Shelley surrogates as psychological counselors in *Mathilda* and "The Mourner" reflect Percy's own failures during Mary's periods of emotional crisis.

28. See *The Journals of Mary Shelley*, 476–77.

29. *The Journals of Mary Shelley*, 429.

30. *The Journals of Mary Shelley*, 440.

31. It should be noted that as Mary Shelley's sense of isolation following her husband's death deepened, even writing failed her as a form of therapy: "I can speak to none—writing this is useless—it does not even soothe me—on the contrary it irritates me by shewing the pityful [*sic*] expedient to which I am reduced" (*Mary Shelley's Journal*, 485).

Chapter 5. Dreams

1. *The Mary Shelley Reader*, 170.

2. James Rieger is skeptical about the truthfulness of Shelley's 1831 Introduction (*The Mutiny Within: The Heresies of Percy Bysshe Shelley* [New York:

George Braziller, 1967], 240–45), as is Jonathan C. Glance ("Gates of Horn: The Function of Dreams in Nineteenth-Century British Prose Fiction" [Diss., University of North Carolina at Chapel Hill, 1991], 169–70).

3. Darwin, 1:220.
4. See, for example, the Fifth Walk in *Reveries of the Solitary Walker*.
5. "Rousseau," 115.
6. *Political and Philosophical Writings*, 3:182.
7. "Autobiography," *Collected Novels and Memoirs*, 1:37–38.
8. *The Journals of Mary Shelley*, 471.
9. Rousseau writes that in recording his "rêveries" he applies "la barometre à [son] ame [*sic*]" (*Les Rêveries*, 1000–1001).
10. David S. Miall, "The Meaning of Dreams: Coleridge's Ambivalence," *Studies in Romanticism* 21 (Spring 1982), 58–59.
11. Sigmund Freud, *The Interpretation of Dreams*, trans. James Strachey (New York: Avon Books, 1965), 106.
12. Miall, 64, 59.
13. Douglas B. Wilson provides a brief discussion of eighteenth-century dream theories, focusing on John Locke, Dugald Stewart, and David Hartley (*The Romantic Dream: Wordsworth and the Poetics of the Unconscious* [Lincoln: Univ. of Nebraska Press, 1993], 12–15).
14. Darwin, 1:199.
15. Abrams, 161.
16. Darwin, 1:200–201.
17. Darwin, 1:204, 1:205, 1:210, 1:215.
18. Darwin, 1:205.
19. Darwin, 1:205.
20. Hartley, 1:384.
21. Hartley, 1:385.
22. Hartley, 1:387–88.
23. Hartley, 1:389.
24. Wilson argues that Wordsworth also associated dreams with prophecy: "Dream for Wordsworth merges with imagination and, hence, shares the act of prophecy" (139).
25. *Political and Philosophical Writings*, 3:185.
26. For an account of Godwin's relationship to Hays, see St. Clair, 145–46.
27. Mary Hays, *Letters and Essays, Moral and Miscellaneous* (New York: Garland, 1974), 171–72.
28. Locke, 1:136.
29. See for example, Fred Botting, *Making Monstrous:* Frankenstein, *Criticism, Theory* (Manchester, Eng.: Manchester Univ. Press, 1991), 118–38; Andrew Griffin, "Fire and Ice in *Frankenstein*," *The Endurance of Frankenstein: Essays on Mary Shelley's Novel*, 62–64; Mellor, 115; and David Collings, "The Monster and the Imaginary Mother: A Lacanian Reading of *Frankenstein*," *Case Studies in Contemporary Criticism:* Frankenstein, by Mary Shelley, ed. Johanna M. Smith (Boston: Bedford Books, 1992), 248–50.
30. Hartley, 1:387.
31. Hartley, 1:389.
32. Glance also discusses Frankenstein's dream within the context of associationist psychology (see 166–67).
33. Percy Bysshe Shelley, *Zastrozzi and St. Irvyne*, ed. Stephen C. Behrendt (Oxford: Oxford University Press, 1986), 71.

34. See Glance's comparison of Frankenstein's premonitory dream to the one presented in *Zastrozzi* (166).

35. In fact, in her 1824 essay "On Ghosts," Shelley describes a dream that is not unlike Frankenstein's: "I never saw a ghost except once in a dream. I feared it in my sleep; I awoke trembling, and lights and the speech of others could hardly dissipate my fear" (*The Novels and Selected Works of Mary Shelley*, 2:142). Because this dream is not dated, we cannot know whether or not Shelley had it in mind when she wrote *Frankenstein*, but it is perhaps significant that Shelley claims to have had an actual dream that was roughly similar to Frankenstein's nightmare: in both cases, the dreamer has a fearful vision of a dead person and awakes in terror.

36. Darwin, 1:205.

37. Freud, *The Interpretation of Dreams*, 282.

38. Jane Blumberg, *Mary Shelley's Early Novels: "This Child of Imagination and Misery"* (Iowa City: University of Iowa Press, 1993), 100. In the same vein, O'Sullivan considers *Valperga* as, in part, "a cautionary tale of Beatrice's uncritical indulgence in fantasy" (146).

39. Samuel Taylor Coleridge, *The Notebooks of Samuel Taylor Coleridge*, ed. Kathleen Coburn, 3 vols. (New York: Pantheon, 1957–61; Princeton, N.J.: Princeton University Press, 1973), 2:2468. Because Coleridge was a frequent visitor at the Godwin household when Mary Shelley was a child, one is tempted to speculate that she overheard some of his ideas regarding dreams. She was, of course, familiar with his poetic treatments of dreams.

40. *Shelley's Prose; or, The Trumpet of a Prophecy*, ed. David Lee Clark (Albuquerque: University of Mexico Press, 1954), 193–94.

41. *Shelley's Prose*, 194n.

42. *The Novels and Selected Works of Mary Shelley*, 2:143.

43. Rieger, 122.

44. *The Mary Shelley Reader*, 397; *The Letters of Mary Wollstonecraft Shelley*, 1:245. Shelley also alludes to Percy's vision in *Lodore*. Shortly before his death, the title character is startled by a "warning voice" that asks: "How long will you be at peace?" (21). In this case, however, Lodore does not see a "figure of himself": the "spirit" is "invisible to sight."

45. *Mary Shelley Reader*, 396–97; *Letters of Mary Wollstonecraft Shelley*, 1:245.

46. *The Mary Shelley Reader*, 397; *Letters*, 1:245–46.

47. O'Sullivan, 151.

48. See *Letters of Mary Wollstonecraft Shelley*, 1:307 and 1:336.

49. *Political and Philosophical Writings*, 3:162.

50. *Novels and Selected Works of Mary Shelley*, 2:117.

Bibliography

Abrams, M. H. *The Mirror and the Lamp: Romantic Theory and the Critical Tradition*. London: Oxford University Press, 1953.

Baillie, Joanna. *A Series of Plays: in which It Is Attempted to Delineate the Stronger Passions of the Mind. Each Passion Being the Subject of a Tragedy and a Comedy*. 1798; Oxford: Woodstock Books, 1990.

———. *The Dramatic and Poetical Works (1851)*. Hildesheim, Germany: Georg Olms Verlag, 1976.

Barchelon, José. Introduction to *Madness and Civilization: A History of Insanity in the Age of Reason*, by Michel Foucault. New York: Random House, 1965. v–viii.

Battie, William. *A Treatise on Madness*. 1758; New York: Brunner/Mazel, 1969.

Bennett, Alan. *The Madness of George III*. London: Faber and Faber, 1992.

Bennett, Betty T. "The Political Philosophy of Mary Shelley's Historical Novels: *Valperga* and *Perkin Warbeck*." In *The Evidence of the Imagination: Studies of Interactions between Life and Art in English Romantic Literature*. Edited by Donald H. Reiman, Michael C. Jaye, and Betty T. Bennett. New York: New York University Press, 1978. 354–71.

Blumberg, Jane. *Mary Shelley's Early Novels: "This Child of Imagination and Misery"*. Iowa City: Univ. of Iowa Press, 1993.

Botting, Fred. *Making Monstrous:* Frankenstein, *Criticism, Theory*. Manchester, Eng.: Manchester University Press, 1991.

Brooks, Peter. " 'Godlike Science/Unhallowed Arts': Language, Nature, and Monstrosity." In *The Endurance of* Frankenstein: *Essays on Mary Shelley's Novel*. Edited by George Levine and U. C. Knoepflmacher. Berkeley: University of California Press, 1979. 205–20.

Brown, Charles Brockden. *Edgar Huntly; or, Memoirs of a Sleep-Walker*. Edited by Sydney J. Krause and S. W. Reid. Kent, Ohio: Kent State University Press, 1984.

———. *Wieland; or The Transformation. An American Tale*. Edited by Sydney J. Krause and S. W. Reid. Kent, Ohio: Kent State University Press, 1977.

Bruhm, Steven. *Gothic Bodies: The Politics of Pain in Romantic Fiction*. Philadelphia: University of Pennsylvania Press, 1994.

Brunton, Mary. *Self-Control: A Novel*. Edinburgh: Manners and Miller, 1811.

Bunnell, Charlene E. "*Mathilda*: Mary Shelley's Romantic Tragedy." *Keats-Shelley Journal* 46 (1997): 75–96.

Burton, Robert. *The Anatomy of Melancholy*. Edited by Floyd Dell and Paul Jordan-Smith. New York: Farrar & Rinehart, 1927.

Burwick, Frederick. *Poetic Madness and the Romantic Imagination*. University Park: Pennsylvania State University Press, 1996.

Butler, Marilyn, and Mark Philp. Introduction to *Collected Novels and Memoirs of William Godwin*. Vol. 1. London: Pickering & Chatto, 1992. 7–46.

Byron, George Gordon, Baron. *Byron*. Edited by Jerome J. McGann. The Oxford Authors. Oxford: Oxford University Press, 1986.

———. *Byron's Letters and Journals*. Edited by Leslie A. Marchand. 12 vols. Cambridge: Harvard University Press, 1973–1982.

Cameron, Kenneth Neill, ed. *Shelley and His Circle, 1773–1822*. Vol. 1. Cambridge: Harvard University Press, 1961.

———. ed. *Shelley and his Circle, 1773–1822*. Vol. 3. Cambridge: Harvard University Press, 1970.

Cantor, Paul A. *Creature and Creator: Myth-making and English Romanticism*. Cambridge: Cambridge University Press, 1984.

Chatterjee, Ranita. "*Mathilda*: Mary Shelley, William Godwin, and the Ideologies of Incest." In *Iconoclastic Departures: Mary Shelley after Frankenstein: essays in honor of the bicentenary of Mary Shelley's birth*. Edited by Syndy M. Conger, Frederick S. Frank, and Gregory O'Dea. Madison, N.J.: Fairleigh Dickinson University Press, 1997. 130–49.

Clemit, Pamela. *The Godwinian Novel: The Rational Fictions of Godwin, Brockden Brown, Mary Shelley*. Oxford: Clarendon Press, 1993.

Clifford, Gay. "*Caleb Williams* and *Frankenstein*: First-Person Narratives and 'Things as They Are.' " *Genre* 10 (Winter 1977): 601–17.

Coleridge, Samuel Taylor. *The Notebooks of Samuel Taylor Coleridge*. Edited by Kathleen Coburn. 3 vols. New York: Pantheon, 1957–61; Princeton, N.J.: Princeton University Press, 1973.

Collings, David. "The Monster and the Imaginary Mother: A Lacanian Reading of *Frankenstein*." In *Case Studies in Contemporary Criticism*: Frankenstein, *by Mary Shelley*. Edited by Johanna M. Smith. Boston: Bedford Books, 1992. 245–58.

Conger, Syndy McMillen. "Multivocality in Mary Shelley's Unfinished Memoirs of Her Father." *European Romantic Review* 9.3 (Summer 1998): 303–22.

Croker, J. W. "Review of *Frankenstein*." *Quarterly Review* 18 (Jan. 1818): 379–85.

———. "Review of Godwin's *Mandeville*." *Quarterly Review* 18 (Oct. 1817): 176–77.

Daffron, Eric. " 'Magnetical Sympathy': Strategies of Power and Resistance in Godwin's *Caleb Williams*." *Criticism* 37.2 (Spring 1995): 213–32.

Darwin, Erasmus. *Zoonomia; or, The Laws of Organic Life*. 2 vols. 1794–1796; New York: AMS Press, 1974.

DePorte, Michael V. *Nightmares and Hobbyhorses: Swift, Sterne, and Augustan Ideas of Madness*. San Marino, Calif.: Huntington Library, 1974.

Digby, Anne. "Moral Treatment at the Retreat, 1796–1846." In *The Anatomy of Madness: Essays in the History of Psychiatry*. Edited by W. F. Bynum, Roy Porter, and Michael Shepherd. Vol. 2. London: Tavistock, 1985: 52–72.

Duffy, Edward. *Rousseau in England: The Context for Shelley's Critique of the Enlightenment*. Berkeley: University of California Press, 1979.

Ferguson, Rebecca. *The Unbalanced Mind: Pope and the Rule of Passion*. Philadelphia: Univ. of Pennsylvania Press, 1986.

Fisch, Audrey A. "Plaguing Politics: AIDS, Deconstruction, and *The Last Man*." In *The Other Mary Shelley: Beyond* Frankenstein. Edited by Audrey A. Fisch, Anne K. Mellor, and Esther H. Schor. New York: Oxford University Press, 1993. 267–86.

Foucault, Michel. *Madness and Civilization: A History of Insanity in the Age of Reason*. Translated by Richard Howard. New York: Random House, 1965.

Freud, Sigmund. "Delusions and Dreams in Jensen's *Gradiva*." Translated by James Strachey. *The Standard Edition of the Complete Psychological Works of Sigmund Freud*. Vol. 9. London: Hogarth Press, 1959. 7–93.

———. *The Interpretation of Dreams*. Translated by James Strachey. New York: Avon Books, 1965.

———. *Introductory Lectures on Psycho-Analysis*. Translated and edited by James Strachey. New York: Norton, 1966.

Gauld, Alan. *A History of Hypnotism*. Cambridge: Cambridge University Press, 1992.

Gaull, Marilyn. *English Romanticism: The Human Context*. New York: Norton, 1988.

Glance, Jonathan C. "Gates of Horn: The Function of Dreams in Nineteenth-Century British Prose Fiction." Diss., University of North Carolina at Chapel Hill, 1991.

Godwin, William. *Autobiographical Fragments and Reflections*. Edited by Mark Philp. *Collected Novels and Memoirs of William Godwin*. Vol. 1. London: Pickering & Chatto, 1992. 41–65.

———. *Autobiography*. *Collected Novels and Memoirs of William Godwin*. Vol. 1. 3–38.

———. *Caleb Williams*. Edited by David McCracken. New York: Norton, 1977.

———. *Cloudesley*. Edited by Maurice Hindle. In *Collected Novels and Memoirs of William Godwin*. Vol. 7.

———. *Deloraine*. Edited by Maurice Hindle. In *Collected Novels and Memoirs of William Godwin*. Vol. 8.

———. *Fleetwood*. Edited by Pamela Clemit. In *Collected Novels and Memoirs of William Godwin*. Vol. 5.

———. *Godwin/Shelley Correspondence*. Edited by Mark Philp. In *Collected Novels and Memoirs of William Godwin*. Vol. 1. 69–82.

———. *Life of Geoffrey Chaucer, the Early English Poet: Including Memoirs of His Near Friend and Kinsman, John of Gaunt, Duke of Lancaster: with Sketches of the Manners, Opinions, Arts and Literature of England in the Fourteenth Century*. 4 vols. 2nd ed. London: Richard Phillips, 1804.

———. *Mandeville*. Edited by Pamela Clemit. In *Collected Novels and Memoirs of William Godwin*. Vol. 6.

———. *Political and Philosophical Writings of William Godwin*. General editor Mark Philp. 7 vols. London: Pickering & Chatto, 1993.

———. *St. Leon*. Edited by Pamela Clemit. Oxford: Oxford Univ. Press, 1994.

Griffin, Andrew. "Fire and Ice in *Frankenstein*." In *The Endurance of Frankenstein: Essays on Mary Shelley's Novel*. Edited by George Levine and U. C. Knoepflmacher. Berkeley: University of California Press, 1979. 49–73.

Harpold, Terence. " 'Did you get Mathilda from Papa?': Seduction Fantasy and the Circulation of Mary Shelley's *Mathilda*." *Studies in Romanticism* 28 (Spring 1989): 49–67.

Hartley, David. *Observations on Man, His Frame, His Duty, and His Expectations*. 2 vols. 1749; New York: Garland, 1971.

Hays, Mary. *Letters and Essays, Moral and Miscellaneous*. 1793; New York, Garland, 1974.

———. *Memoirs of Emma Courtney*. Edited by Eleanor Ty. 1796; Oxford: Oxford University Press, 1996.

Helvétius, Claude Arien. *De l'Esprit: or, Essays on the Mind and Its Several Faculties*. Translator anonymous. 1758; New York: Burt Franklin, 1970.

Hill-Miller, Katherine C. *"My Hideous Progeny": Mary Shelley, William Godwin, and the Father-Daughter Relationship*. Newark: University of Delaware Press, 1995.

Hindle, Maurice. Introduction to *Caleb Williams*, by William Godwin. London: Penguin, 1987. ix–xlv.

Hobson, J. Allan. *The Dreaming Brain*. New York: Basic Books, 1988.

Hume, David. "A Dissertation on the Passions." In *The Philosophical Works*. Edited by Thomas Hill Green and Thomas Hodge Grose. 4 vols. London: Longmans, Green, and Co., 1874–75. 139–66.

———. *A Treatise of Human Nature*. Edited by Ernest C. Mossner. London: Penguin, 1969.

Hunter, Richard A., and Ida Macalpine. "Smollett's Reading in Psychiatry." *Modern Language Review* 51 (1956): 409–11.

———. *Three Hundred Years of Psychiatry, 1535–1860: A History Presented in Selected English Texts*. London: Oxford University Press, 1963.

Ingram, Allan. *The Madhouse of Language: Writing and Reading Madness in the Eighteenth Century*. London: Routledge, 1991.

Johnson, Barbara. "My Monster/My Self." *Diacritics* 12 (Summer 1982): 2–10.

Johnson, Samuel. *Rasselas and Other Tales*. Edited by Gwin J. Kolb. In *The Yale Edition of the Works of Samuel Johnson*. Vol. XVI. New Haven: Yale University Press, 1990.

Keach, William. *Shelley's Style*. New York: Methuen, 1984.

Kelly, Gary. *English Fiction of the Romantic Period, 1789–1830*. London: Longman, 1989.

———. *The English Jacobin Novel, 1780–1805*. Oxford: Clarendon Press, 1976.

Knoepflmacher, U. C. "Thoughts on the Aggression of Daughters." In *The Endurance of Frankenstein: Essays on Mary Shelley's Novel*. Edited by George Levine and U. C. Knoepflmacher. Berkeley: University of California Press, 1979.

Lacan, Jacques. *Écrits: A Selection*. Translated by Alan Sheridan. New York: Norton, 1977.

Leaver, Kristen. "Pursuing Conversations: *Caleb Williams* and the Romantic Construction of the Reader." *Studies in Romanticism* 33 (Winter 1994): 589–610.

Lew, Joseph W. "God's Sister: History and Ideology in *Valperga*." In *The Other*

Mary Shelley: Beyond Frankenstein. Edited by Audrey A. Fisch, Anne K. Mellor, and Esther H. Schor. New York: Oxford University Press, 1993. 159–81.

Lipking, Lawrence. "*Frankenstein*, the True Story; or, Rousseau Judges Jean-Jacques." In *Frankenstein*, by Mary Shelley. Edited by J. Paul Hunter. New York: W. W. Norton, 1996. 313–31.

Locke, Don. *A Fantasy of Reason: The Life and Thought of William Godwin*. London: Routledge & Kegan Paul, 1980.

Locke, John. *An Essay Concerning Human Understanding*. Edited by Alexander Campbell Fraser. 2 vols. New York: Dover Publications, 1959.

Lockhart, John Gibson. "Remarks on Godwin's New Novel, Mandeville." *Blackwood's Edinburgh Magazine* 2 (Dec. 1817): 268–79.

Logan, Peter Melville. "Narrating Hysteria: *Caleb Williams* and the Cultural History of Nerves." *Novel: A Forum of Fiction* 29.2 (Winter 1996): 206–22.

Luyendijk-Elshout, Antonie. "Of Masks and Mills: The Enlightened Doctor and His Frightened Patient." In *The Languages of the Psyche: Mind and Body in Enlightenment Thought*. Edited by G. S. Rousseau. Berkeley: University of California Press, 1990. 186–230.

Mackenzie, Henry. *The Man of Feeling*. New York: Norton, 1958.

Maertz, Gregory. "Family Resemblances: Intertextual Dialogue between Father and Daughter Novelists in Godwin's *St. Leon* and Shelley's *Frankenstein*." *University of Mississippi Studies in English* 11–12 (1993–1995): 301–20.

Marshall, David. *The Surprising Effects of Sympathy: Marivaux, Diderot, Rousseau, and Mary Shelley*. Chicago: Univ. of Chicago Press, 1988.

Marshall, Peter H. *William Godwin*. New Haven: Yale Univ. Press, 1984.

McFarland, Thomas. *Romanticism and the Heritage of Rousseau*. Oxford: Clarendon Press, 1995.

McGann, Jerome J. *The Beauty of Inflections: Literary Investigations in Historical Method and Theory*. Oxford: Clarendon Press, 1985.

McWhir, Anne. "The Light and the Knife: Ab/Using Language in *The Cenci*." *Keats-Shelley Journal* 38 (1989): 145–61.

Medwin, Thomas. *The Life of Percy Bysshe Shelley*. New ed. London: Oxford University Press, 1913.

Mellor, Anne K. *Mary Shelley: Her Life, Her Fiction, Her Monsters*. New York: Methuen, 1988.

Miall, David S. "The Meaning of Dreams: Coleridge's Ambivalence." *Studies in Romanticism* 21 (Spring 1982): 57–71.

Midelfort, H. C. Erik. "Madness and Civilization in Early Modern Europe: A Reappraisal of Michel Foucault." In *After the Reformation: Essays in Honor of J. H. Hexter*. Edited by Barbara C. Malament. Philadelphia: University of Pennsylvania Press, 1980: 247–65.

Mullan, John. *Sentiment and Sociability: The Language of Feeling in the Eighteenth Century*. Oxford: Clarendon Press, 1988.

Murray, E. B., ed. *A Facsimile of Bodleian MS. Shelley d. 1*. Vol. 4 of *The Bodleian Shelley Manuscripts* in 2 parts. New York: Garland, 1988.

Newman, Beth. "Narratives of Seduction and the Seductions of Narrative: The Frame Structure of *Frankenstein*." *ELH* 53.1 (Spring 1986): 141–63.

Nitchie, Elizabeth, ed. *Mathilda*, by Mary Wollstonecraft Shelley. Studies in Philology, extra ser. 3. Chapel Hill: University of North Carolina Press, 1959.

O'Rourke, James. " 'Nothing More Unnatural': Mary Shelley's Revision of Rousseau." *ELH* 56 (1989): 543–69.

O'Sullivan, Barbara Jane. "Beatrice in *Valperga*: A New Cassandra." In *The Other Mary Shelley: Beyond* Frankenstein. Edited by Audrey A. Fisch, Anne K. Mellor, and Esther H. Schor. New York: Oxford University Press, 1993: 140–58.

Palacio, Jean de. *Mary Shelley dans son oeuvre*. Paris: Editions Klincksieck, 1969.

Paul, C. Kegan. *William Godwin: His Friends and Contemporaries*. 2 vols. 1876; New York: AMS Press, 1970.

Peacock, Thomas Love. *Nightmare Abbey*. Edited by H. F. B. Brett-Smith and C. E. Jones. In *The Works of Thomas Love Peacock*. Vol. 3. London: Constable, 1924. 1–149.

Pinch, Adela. *Strange Fits of Passion: Epistemologies of Emotion, Hume to Austen*. Stanford, Calif.: Stanford Univ. Press, 1996.

Pollin, Burton R. "Mary Shelley as the Parvenue." *Review of English Literature* 8.3 (July 1967): 9–21.

Poovey, Mary. *The Proper Lady and the Woman Writer: Ideology as Style in the Works of Mary Wollstonecraft, Mary Shelley, and Jane Austen*. Chicago: Univ. of Chicago Press, 1984.

Pope, Alexander. *The Poetical Works of Pope*. Edited by Herbert Davis. Oxford: Oxford University Press, 1966.

Powers, Katherine Richardson. *The Influence of William Godwin on the Novels of Mary Shelley*. New York: Arno Press, 1980.

Radcliffe, Ann. *The Mysteries of Udolpho: A Romance*. Edited by Bonamy Dobrée. Oxford: Oxford University Press, 1970.

Reid, Thomas. *An Inquiry into the Human Mind*. Edited by Timothy Duggan. Chicago: University of Chicago Press, 1970.

———. *Essays on the Active Powers of the Human Mind*. Cambridge: M.I.T. Press, 1969.

Reiser, Morton F. *Memory in Mind and Brain: What Dream Imagery Reveals*. New York: Basic Books, 1990.

"Review of *Frankenstein*, by Mary Shelley." *Edinburgh Magazine, and Literary Miscellany* 2 (1818): 249–53.

Richardson, Alan. "From *Emile* to *Frankenstein*: The Education of Monsters." *European Romantic Review* 1.2 (Winter 1991): 147–62.

Rieger, James. *The Mutiny Within: The Heresies of Percy Bysshe Shelley*. New York: George Braziller, 1967.

Roszak, Theodore. *The Memoirs of Elizabeth Frankenstein*. New York: Random House, 1995.

Rousseau, Jean-Jacques. *Émile ou de l'éducation*. Edited by François and Pierre Richard. Paris: Éditions Garnier Frères, 1961.

———. *Emile, or On Education*. Translated by Allan Bloom. New York: Basic Books, 1979.

———. *La Nouvelle Héloïse: Julie, or the New Eloise*. Transited and abridged by

Judith H. McDowell. University Park: Pennsylvania State University Press, 1968.

———. *Les Confessions*. In *Oeuvres Complètes*. Vol. 1. Edited by Bernard Gagnebin and Marcel Raymond. Paris: Gallimard, 1959. 5–656.

———. *Les Rêveries du Promeneur Solitaire*. In *Oeuvres Complètes*. Vol. 1. Edited by Marcel Raymond. Paris: Gallimard, 995–1099.

———. *Reveries of the Solitary Walker*. Translated by Peter France. London: Penguin Books, 1979.

———. *The Confessions*. Translated by J. M. Cohen. Harmondsworth, Eng.: Penguin, 1953.

Rubenstein, Marc A. "*Frankenstein*: Search for the Mother." *Studies in Romanticism* 15 (Spring 1976): 165–94.

Schopf, Sue Weaver. " 'Of what a strange nature is knowledge!': Hartleian Psychology and the Creature's Arrested Moral Sense in Mary Shelley's *Frankenstein*." *Romanticism: Past and Present* 5.1 (1981): 33–52.

Schor, Esther H. "Mary Shelley in Transit." In *The Other Mary Shelley: Beyond* Frankenstein. 235–57.

Sedgwick, Eve Kosofsky. *Epistemology of the Closet*. Berkeley: University of California Press, 1990.

Shelley, Mary. "[Cloudesley]." Edited by Pamela Clemit. In *The Novels and Selected Works of Mary Shelley*. Vol. 2. London: Pickering & Chatto, 1996. 201–9.

———. *Collected Tales and Stories, with Original Engravings*. Edited by Charles E. Robinson. Baltimore: Johns Hopkins University Press, 1976.

———. *Falkner, a Novel*. Edited by Pamela Clemit. In *The Novels and Selected Works of Mary Shelley*. Vol. 7.

———. *The Fields of Fancy*. *Mathilda*. Ed. Elizabeth Nitchie. Chapel Hill: University of North Carolina Press, 1959. 90–102.

———. *The Fortunes of Perkin Warbeck: A Romance*. Edited by Doucet Devin Fischer. In *The Novels and Selected Works of Mary Shelley*. Vol. 5.

———. *Frankenstein* (1818 ed.). In *The Mary Shelley Reader*. Edited by Betty T. Bennett and Charles E. Robinson. New York: Oxford University Press, 1990. 11–165.

———. *Frankenstein*.(1831 ed.). Edited by Johanna M. Smith. Boston: St. Martin's Press, 1992.

———. "Giovanni Villani." Edited by Pamela Clemit. In *The Novels and Selected Works of Mary Shelley*. Vol. 2. 128–39.

———. *The Journals of Mary Shelley: 1814–1844*. Edited by Paula R. Feldman and Diana Scott-Kilvert. Baltimore: Johns Hopkins University Press, 1987.

———. *The Last Man*. Edited by Hugh J. Luke, Jr. Lincoln: University of Nebraska Press, 1965.

———. *The Letters of Mary Wollstonecraft Shelley*. Edited by Betty T. Bennett. 3 vols. Baltimore: Johns Hopkins University Press, 1980–1988.

———. *Lodore*. Edited by Fiona Stafford. In *The Novels and Selected Works of Mary Shelley*. Vol. 6.

———. "Madame D'Houtetot." Edited by Pamela Clemit. In *The Novels and Selected Works of Mary Shelley*. Vol. 2. 117–27.

———. *Mathilda*. In *The Mary Shelley Reader*. 175–246.

———. *Maurice, or the Fisher's Cot. A Tale*. Edited by Claire Tomalin. New York: Alfred A. Knopf, 1998.

———. "Montaigne." In *Lives of Eminent Literary and Scientific Men of France*. Vol. 1. *The Cabinet Cyclopaedia*. Conducted by Rev. Dionysius Lardner. Vol. 2. London: Longman, Orme, Brown, Green & Longmans, 1839. 1–22.

———. *Rambles in Germany and Italy, in 1840, 1842, and 1843*. In *Travel Writing*. Edited by Jeanne Moskal. *The Novels and Selected Works of Mary Shelley*. Vol. 8.

———. "Rousseau." In *Lives of Eminent Literary and Scientific Men of France*. Vol. 1. *The Cabinet Cyclopaedia*. Conducted by Rev. Dionysius Lardner. Vol. 2. London: Longman, Orme, Brown, Green & Longmans, 1839. 111–74.

———. *Valperga: or, the Life and Adventures of Castruccio, Prince of Lucca*. Edited by Nora Crook. In *The Novels and Selected Works of Mary Shelley*. Vol. 3.

Shelley, Percy Bysshe. *The Complete Works of Percy Bysshe Shelley*. Edited by Roger Ingpen and Walter E. Peck. 10 vols. New York: Gordian Press, 1965.

———. *The Letters of Percy Bysshe Shelley*. Edited by Frederick L. Jones. 2 vols. Oxford: Oxford University Press, 1964.

———. *The Prose Works of Percy Bysshe Shelley*. Edited by E. B. Murray. Vol. 1. Oxford: Clarendon Press, 1993.

———. *Shelley's Poetry and Prose*. Edited by Donald H. Reiman and Sharon B. Powers. New York: Norton, 1977.

———. *Shelley's Prose; or, The Trumpet of a Prophecy*. Edited by David Lee Clark. Albuquerque: University of Mexico Press, 1954.

———. *Zastrozzi and St. Irvyne*. Edited by Stephen C. Behrendt. Oxford: Oxford University Press, 1986.

Smith, Adam. *The Theory of Moral Sentiments*. Edited by D. D. Raphael and A. L. Macfie. Oxford: Clarendon Press, 1976.

Smollett, Tobias. *The Life and Adventures of Sir Launcelot Greaves*. Edited by David Evans. London: Oxford University Press, 1973.

Starobinski, Jean. *Jean-Jacques Rousseau: Transparency and Obstruction*. Translated by Arthur Goldhammer. Chicago: University of Chicago Press, 1988.

St. Clair, William. *The Godwins and the Shelleys: The Biography of a Family*. New York: Norton, 1989.

Sterne, Laurence. *A Sentimental Journey through France and Italy with The Journal to Eliza and A Political Romance*. Edited by Ian Jack. London: Oxford University Press, 1972.

Stocking, Marion Kingston, ed. *The Clairmont Correspondence: Letters of Claire Clairmont, Charles Clairmont, and Fanny Imlay Godwin*. 2 vols. Baltimore: Johns Hopkins University Press, 1995.

Sunstein, Emily W. *Mary Shelley: Romance and Reality*. Baltimore: Johns Hopkins Univ. Press, 1989.

Todd, Janet. Introduction to *Mary Wollstonecraft* Mary *and* Maria, *Mary Shelley* Matilda. Edited by Janet Todd. London: Penguin, 1991. vii–xxviii.

Turner, Mark. *The Literary Mind*. New York: Oxford University Press, 1996.

Ty, Eleanor. Introduction to *Memoirs of Emma Courtney*, by Mary Hays. Oxford: Oxford University Press, 1996. vii–xxxvii.

Warren, Samuel. "The Spectre-Smitten." In *Tales of Terror from* Blackwood's Magazine. Edited by Robert Morrison and Chris Baldick. Oxford: Oxford University Press, 1995. 215–41.

Williams, Raymond. *Keywords: A Vocabulary of Culture and Society*. New York: Oxford University Press, 1976.

Willis, Thomas. *Dr. Willis's Practice of Physick*. Translated by Samuel Pordage. London: T. Dring, C. Harper, and J. Leigh, 1684.

Wilson, Douglas B. *The Romantic Dream: Wordsworth and the Poetics of the Unconscious*. Lincoln: University of Nebraska Press, 1993.

Wollstonecraft, Mary. *A Vindication of the Rights of Woman*. Edited by Carol H. Poston. 2d ed. New York: Norton, 1988.

———. *Mary* and *The Wrongs of Woman*. Edited by Gary Kelly. Oxford: Oxford University Press, 1976.

Wordsworth, William. *The Borderers*. Edited by Robert Osborn. Ithaca, N.Y.: Cornell Univ. Press, 1982.

———. *William Wordsworth*. Edited by Stephen Gill. The Oxford Authors. New York: Oxford University Press, 1984.

Wordsworth, William, and Dorothy Wordsworth. *The Letters of William and Dorothy Wordsworth: The Early Years, 1787–1805*. Edited by Ernest de Selincourt. 2d ed. rev. Chester L. Shaver. Vol. I. Oxford: Clarendon Press, 1967.

Worton, Michael. "Speech and Silence in *The Cenci*." In *Essays on Shelley*. Edited by Miriam Allott. Totowa, N.J.: Barnes & Noble, 1982. 105–24.

Young, Allan. *The Harmony of Illusions: Inventing Post-Traumatic Stress Disorder*. Princeton, N.J.: Princeton University Press, 1995.

Youngquist, Paul. *Madness and Blake's Myth*. University Park: Pennsylvania State University Press, 1989.

Index